GAMES AS A SERVICE

GAMES AS A SERVICE

How Free2Play Design Can Make Better Games

OSCAR CLARK

Focal Press
Taylor & Francis Group

NEW YORK AND LONDON

First published 2014
by Focal Press
70 Blanchard Road, Suite 402, Burlington, MA 01803

and by Focal Press
2 Park Square, Milton Park, Abingdon, Oxon OX14 4RN

Focal Press is an imprint of the Taylor & Francis Group, an informa business

© 2014 Taylor & Francis

Notices

Knowledge and best practice in this field are constantly changing. As new
research and experience broaden our understanding, changes in research
methods, professional practices, or medical treatment may become necessary.

Practitioners and researchers must always rely on their own experience and
knowledge in evaluating and using any information, methods, compounds,
or experiments described herein. In using such information or methods they
should be mindful of their own safety and the safety of others, including parties
for whom they have a professional responsibility.

Product or corporate names may be trademarks or registered trademarks, and
are used only for identification and explanation without intent to infringe.

Library of Congress Cataloging-in-Publication Data

Clark, Oscar.
 Games as a service : how free to play design can make better games / Oscar
Clark. — First edition.
  pages cm
1. Video games—Authorship. 2. Video games—Design. I. Title.
 GV1469.34.A97C53 2014
 794.8'1536—dc23   2013039832

ISBN: 978-0-415-73250-5 (pbk)
ISBN: 978-1-315-84910-2 (ebk)

Typeset in Minion Pro
by Apex CoVantage, LLC

A book like this has too many influences to properly thank everyone. I wouldn't have started down this road without the support of Si Shen from Papaya Mobile and Jussi Laakkonen from Applifier. However, games is not just a job for me and my playing buddies Andrew Robertson, Ian Goolding, David Hankins, John Gathercole and Glyn West undoubtedly helped inform my creative approach, despite having nothing to do with the industry. Then there is the fabulous feedback I got during the process of writing from Eric Seufert, Evelyn Stiller, Brian Tinsman, Jacob Naasz and Berni Good.

However, in the end this book has to be dedicated to my wife and illustrator, Melanie, and in particular our amazing daughter Tizzie who continues to teach me about both games and writing.

Bound to Create

You are a creator.

Whatever your form of expression — photography, filmmaking, animation, games, audio, media communication, web design, or theatre — you simply want to create without limitation. Bound by nothing except your own creativity and determination.

Focal Press can help.

For over 75 years Focal has published books that support your creative goals. Our founder, Andor Kraszna-Krausz, established Focal in 1938 so you could have access to leading-edge expert knowledge, techniques, and tools that allow you to create without constraint. We strive to create exceptional, engaging, and practical content that helps you master your passion.

Focal Press and you.

Bound to create.

> We'd love to hear how we've helped
> you create. Share your experience:
> www.focalpress.com/boundtocreate

Contents

Chapter 1
Introduction

First Principles

Whatever you think about mobile or console games, I'm hoping that if you have picked up this book that there is something about the game design process that delights you. It's more than just the pleasure of playing a well-crafted game (regardless of the platform). Game design combines an intellectual and creative challenge to manifest your ideas into something others can play through and want to pay you for the privilege of playing. We want players to be charmed, empowered, surprised, even scared. But unlike other art forms we want players to resolve the experience for themselves; to make their own game. People have been creating and playing games for centuries before the introduction of personal computers, consoles and mobile devices. However, since the 1980s, computer games have largely driven innovation and creative design for games, although arguably not always in the gameplay design itself.

Making a Stand

In this book I'm going to assume you have some idea about what makes a good game, and ideally that you have a little experience making games. Don't worry if you don't. I also plan to provide notes to suggest good sources of inspiration and insight. The purpose of this book is to provide a framework to make it easier for you to make games as services. This will take us back to some of the basics of game design to find lessons that lie at the core of every online, console, or mobile game; perhaps even elements that date back to old-school tabletop board games, card games, and maybe even role-playing games. I also want to show how these lessons can help us rethink the way we approach both the artistic and commercial elements to help you make the best possible games suitable for this era of always connected devices. The technical power and ability to leverage online services has so rapidly filtered into every home and every pocket with laptops, tablets, consoles, and—of course—the cell phone almost all of us now carry. The trouble is that we are still in the midst of this massive change and at the time of writing some of the biggest changes seem to be just over the horizon. So to avoid this book becoming out of date before it's released, I have tried to focus on the deeper, lasting principles that matter to making games as services, rather than the particular trends currently popular. My plan is to then continue to add to this material using the companion website www.GamesAsAService.net; a site that I hope will become a place for designers to share ideas and learn from each other.

Service with a Smile

We are seeing the way we consume and experience games change faster than ever before and at the same time we are seeing this great entertainment medium at last reaching true mass-market audiences, something thought nearly impossible only ten years ago. In particular we are seeing a dramatic rise of 'games as a service' and of course the "freemium" business model, both of which I will argue go hand-in-hand. I believe this will be a driver for greater creativity, allowing us to make better games, not just more profitable ones. I will try to show why we can no longer afford to simply build a game, throw it over to the marketing team or publisher, and then hope that someone buys it. Hope is not a strategy.

In particular the old approach of creating retail 'box-products' is not just inefficient but dangerous, perhaps even suicidal, for game developers—and not just for mobile and tablet games. We need to rethink our approach to development and instead look at the way players now consume their content and use that to build games as services instead.

First Bite of the Apple

The tipping point that brought us this change, for me, was the arrival of the iPhone. However, unlike many people, I believe that it is wrong to think of this first iOS device as an extraordinary technical achievement. At the time it was released, most handset manufacturers had devices that were—at least in part—technically superior to the first iPhone. Let's not forget that the most basic phone-call features of the first iPhone were pretty terrible. However, Apple's little device showed us what was possible when you make the user experience seamless.

Many will argue that it was the simplicity. I'm not convinced by this argument, but this isn't a book about user interface design so I won't bore you with the details of that discussion. However, what I do think is relevant to this book is that, unlike all other handset devices at the time, the iPhone experience was both internally consistent and joyful to use. For me the genius of Apple at this time was making the mental shift towards delighting the end-user not just pushing the technical aspirations of the manufacturers. But even with this, the first iPhone doesn't count in my mind. The really important stuff came in with the iPhone 3G and an almost incidental release Apple made the same day. On June 9, 2008, Apple launched the iPhone 3G and with it the new App Store,[1] which it described as:

providing iPhone users with native applications in a variety of
categories including games, business, news, sports, health, reference
and travel. The App Store on iPhone works over cellular networks
and Wi-Fi, which means it is accessible from just about anywhere,
so you can purchase and download applications wirelessly and start
using them instantly. Some applications are even free and the App
Store notifies you when application updates are available. The App
Store will be available in 62 countries at launch.

That's it. That's how the biggest innovation in application retail was
introduced. In hindsight this might seem an inauspicious start, but we
must remember that the original iPhone release didn't even mention
downloadable apps[2] in fact instead they talked about using Web 2.0
techniques to support third-party apps.[3]

There is no doubting that the Apple team did something amazing,
even if I don't believe it was deliberate. They opened access to everyone
to release any app. It was (and largely still is) possible to get through the
approval cycle within just a couple of weeks. You don't have to convince
anyone of the merits of the app you want to release. You just have to
meet Apple's documented rules. This has removed nearly all of the barriers to entry for developers of any size. It turned out to be a completely
disruptive act and continues to have a profound impact on everything
we do in games. They opened up the floodgates for new content and had
immediately leveled the playing field so anyone could publish a game
and access an audience of millions of users.

Supply and Demand Matters

Of course that has now led to an unprecedented volume of games and
apps, and because the pricing was set by the developers themselves there
was an inevitable consequence. The average price for a game went down.

This is a normal economics principle. The price we are willing to
pay for any good, especially a luxury like a game, is determined by the
supply of that item and its demand. If supply increases and demand
remains unchanged then the price will inevitably fall. On June 10, 2013,
Tim Cook announced that the App Store was now hosting more than
900,000 apps;[4] but by the time of publication, I suspect we will be close
to the 1 million mark. There are now more good games on the store
that I could possibly play in my lifetime. This effectively infinite supply
of content inevitably means that the "natural" price for a game will be
nothing; free.

Not the only Game in Town

The emergence of Apple's little device was not the first or only place where innovation for games pricing has happened. In 2003 we pioneered an early form of mobile in-App purchases at 3UK with the introduction of a "rent" game. It was too early and flawed, but the technical innovation was to allow a user to make a purchase within an app. Also in 2008 Sony introduced PlayStation Home as a Free2Play (F2P) experience for owners of the console. However, the first steps for F2P largely came out of the Massively Multiplayer Online (MMO) world, especially those wanting to target a younger audience—in particular online services such as *Neopets* (1999). Other MMOs followed suit, such as UK-based *RuneScape* (2001)[5]—still recognized as the world's largest MMO[6]—and Korean-based *Maple Story* (2003). *Maple Story* and *Neopets* both involved the purchase of virtual goods within the game, but *RuneScape* initially only offered a subscription service for paying players.

Online browser-based games continued to innovate including notably Big Point's *Dark Orbit* and the sale of their Droid X. This was a virtual good that, on paper, costs $1,000 of their virtual currency; however, when you look under the surface this tenth droid required that the player had all of the previous nine and only cost the full amount if you decided to buy it outright and hadn't earned enough virtual currency already.[7] How much money was actually spend on them is unclear, but the value was clearly set in the minds of the players who owned them.

The Only Certainty is Change

More change and more innovation is coming. The arrival in 2013 of the microconsole heralds another era of change and new device opportunities for developers but, at the time of writing, it seems unlikely that many of the first wave of these smaller, cheaper, open access options are quite right to take over the imagination of all players just yet.

Then of course in the same year we have seen the arrival of the next-generation Xbox One and PS4, both of which had a few missteps in their initial launch PR. However these are both likely to embrace greater flexibility in pricing and retail models and, hopefully, a deeper engagement by the prestige side of the industry with the world of indie development.

Change continues to come at us in many forms and on many devices. I may occasionally focus on the iOS platform as an example, but only as the place where the Darwinian forces are perhaps strongest, where competition is fiercest, and only the fittest will survive.

Whether or not you agree that iPhone's arrival has, as promised, changed everything, the fact remains that everything has changed and the iOS market provides useful information to allow us to gauge that change. Further than that, I believe that change is only really starting. I believe that increasingly, rather than focusing on one device, we need to consider the opportunities and consequences of gameplay on all the available devices of all kinds of color, flavor, shapes, and capabilities. What they will have in common is that we will want to play games on all of them at different times and they will all be connected to the internet. What an amazing time to be in our industry.

No Such Thing as a Free Lunch

Looking at the iOS and Android markets its clear that F2P has become the dominant business model in the mobile market, displacing all but a small number of premium games from the top grossing charts. This transition had happened by June 2011,[8] and has continued to increase its hold over revenue.

In this book we will consider why this is and why, from a psychology perspective and a market perspective, there is a tremendous natural advantage in not charging for your game upfront. Indeed I will argue that we can create more anticipation of value inside our games by doing what games are best at—building engagement. There is then no surprise that when we show our players what they love and offer them different ways to invest in our games, they will spend more.

Free is Only Part of the Story

Going "free" is not just about removing the barriers to players trying out our service. With a freemium game we are no longer selling the gameplay itself, or even the reasons to return to the game. We have to focus on selling things that players want to help improve their playing experience. It doesn't matter whether that is an avatar outfit, a companion in the game, an energy crystal, or a farm building. If a player loves your game and you offer them something that helps them enjoy it more, then they will be willing to pay. But, this only really works if you think of the game you build as a service and continue to invest in the experience, showing you love your game too.

I believe that this requires a complete change in the way we look at game design, playing mechanics, and even production processes. It requires a commitment long after the release of the game to sustain it with new content, events and features. It is a commitment between the developer and the player that shouldn't be started lightly. Indeed typically you should expect 80 percent of the development costs to happen after your initial release.

But There is a Problem . . .

Of course there is a problem here.

A lot of people, especially game designers, don't like the way many freemium games work. Indeed they don't even like the words we use to describe them. How can a game be F2P if you are being constantly asked to spend money? Does "premium" mean you pay for it or just that it is of a higher quality? There have even been investigations, such as by the UK Office of Fair Trade, into the practices of selling in-game assets to children.

Then on the freemium side you have similarly daft people saying that "developers who make Premium games are Zombies. The living dead. Dead, but they just don't know it yet."[9] There have been devastating predictions about the end of premium games as we know it or at least a reduction to "No more than 12 games a year."[10]

So I started to wonder. Was there a way we could find some common ground, a way to look at the market objectively?

Games Market Research Company Newzoo showed the status of the games industry in 2013 by comparing the different platforms;[11] which largely reflects an ongoing position following the past couple of years. Console remain (for now) the largest sector in terms of revenue. However, this has been in decline for some time as we have waited for the next generation to arrive. This decline has been particularly damaging for the console-based studios, which have seen dreadful losses as large, historic studios have gone under. Sony Liverpool Studio and Real-Time Worlds were both notable examples of large scale losses in the UK. However, many of these redundancies have sparked the creation of new independent studios usually focused on mobile games. Studios like Hutch Games exemplify the transfer of talent from the console space into the independent mobile and tablet sector; a sector growing at 35 percent year on year.

This growth is expected to continue with Mobile and Tablet leading the charge.[12]

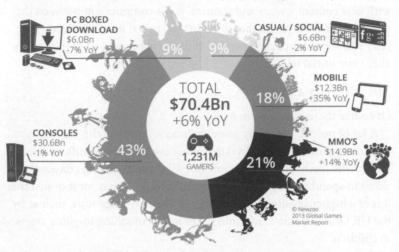

Figure 1.1 The global games market, per segment, 2013. © Newzoo 2013.

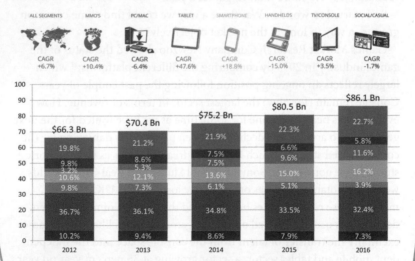

Figure 1.2 Global games market 2012–2016. © Newzoo 2013.

However, what's most interesting is the rapid change in the use of multiple devices. We have been using different devices for quite some time but until relatively recently few players would transition from a game on their phone and pick it up on their laptop, usually preferring one device for specific activities. That appears to have gone and we are increasingly regarding applications as things that should work everywhere, choosing the device that best supports our current circumstances, a "mode of use" if you like.

Figure 1.3 shows the overlapping use of devices and how that changed between March and September 2012, a trend which has continued ever since.

There is clearly a change that has happened. Mobile has manifested this change in the most profound way with games delivering 33 percent of the downloads and 66 percent of the revenue on iOS App Store in 2012. However, we have also seen various experiments for downloadable content (DLC) being made by the traditional console game

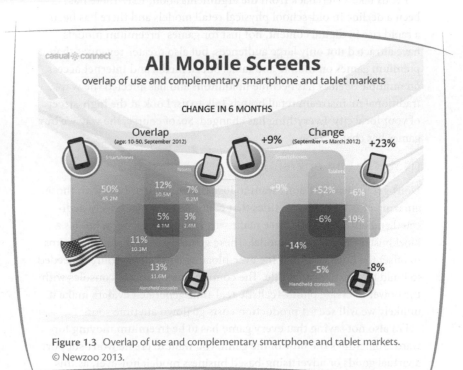

Figure 1.3 Overlap of use and complementary smartphone and tablet markets.
© Newzoo 2013.

publishers to augment their retail box-product sales; even with "Season Passes" being sold to mitigate against the rising secondary market of pre-owned games. However, the more profound impact on console has been the introduction of Xbox LiveArcade and PlayStation Home; both surprisingly successful in their ways. There is no reason to expect consoles will be immune to the F2P model.

A Religious War

Of course even with objective data I won't stop people arguing the relative merits of premium and freemium as the debate has polarized into an unhelpful, almost religious, bickering.

Perhaps there is something more fundamental at work? Perhaps we are looking at the symptom rather than its cause? If I am right then we have used the wrong emphasis by focusing on the money. I think this preoccupation with revenue has hidden a more important change—the move to games as services.

Let us take a step back from the arguments about F2P. There has been a decline in old-school physical retail models and there has been a rapid rise in digital content, not just for games. Freemium models have attracted not only large audiences, but also greater revenues than premium games on mobile and table. Social media and internet access on multiple devices has become ubiquitous and has affected the way traditional mainstream retail brands talk to us. Look at the high-street of your local city. Everything has changed. So, of course, the way we buy games has changed too.

(Not) the End of Premium

Don't get me wrong I don't want to lose the excitement I get with those amazing of AAA[13] console titles that continue to attract hugely dedicated audiences and of course make vast amounts of money, but it's a blockbuster, "hit or miss" model. These games have to make huge sums to offset the huge risks and the ever-bloating costs and resources needed to build the next seminal title. The coming generations of consoles with the power to create photo-realistic real-time generated avatars make it unlikely we will see art production costs go down anytime soon.

I'm also not saying that every game has to be freemium moving forward. Sometimes the flow of the game you want to create won't support a virtual goods or advertising-based business model; however, as this book will explain, that will be the exception rather than the rule and will always compromise the potential audience size and revenue.

These AAA projects typically require multimillion dollar budgets and teams of more than 100 people engaged for three to four years. That's a lot of risk to manage and inevitably creative freedom will be inhibited to some extent, so is it any surprise that we see increasingly fewer AAA games released with an increasingly smaller range of game formulas? Indeed I believe that it is no surprise that many otherwise promising projects are getting cancelled in increasing numbers before we see so much as a trailer.

It All Started With the MMO

The MMO market has faced similar problems. The subscription model has been an amazing ongoing revenue source for these games, but in the last few years, that model has started to break down with many closing down or migrating to a F2P model. Too often this has been a poorly implemented change as well. At their peak, these games showed us just how committed a small niche audience could be and wooed them into buying ongoing subscriptions on top of the original purchase price. *World Of Warcraft* reportedly had over 12 million monthly subscribers at its peak in 2010, but by July 2013 this had dropped to 7.7 million, a loss of 600,000 in just three months and the lowest point since the first expansion, leading to announcements that they were considering a F2P in future. Lots of MMOs launched in recent years have fallen foul of this transition, games such as *Star Wars: The Old Republic*, *Star Trek Online*, *Dungeons & Dragons*, and *Lord of the Rings Online* all launching as subscription games, but having to rapidly transition to a freemium model of some kind despite enormous initial expectations.

Where Did the MMO Fail?

So what has happened? *World of Warcraft*'s initial success came from not just creating a better MMO than had previously existed but by innovating with guilds and raids, to sustain an extremely loyal engagement over time. This leveraged social bonds as well as regular events and updates—something that wasn't being done anywhere else at the time. They backed this up with blockbuster updates, building up the anticipation long before they were released. The trouble is even these great techniques can't sustain games forever. In the end audiences tastes change, as do their lifestyle choices and, despite lots of attempts, none of the more recent released MMOs have captured the same level of audience as *World of Warcraft*. More than that, the competition for the time and attention of that player also change and the alternatives made it easy for many players to move on to something new. Not always another MMO, sometimes a game as simple as *Candy Crush Saga* or *Clash of Clans* can fill the void. These kind of social and mobile games not only satisfy different social playing needs but inevitably make us question the ongoing expenditure of a game subscription.

Social Games Invited Everyone to Play

Games such as *Pet Society*[14] and *FarmVille*, which launched in 2008 and 2009 respectively, went further than that. They didn't just target the already converted players, they unlocked a new, more mass market, audience through their integration with Facebook. What I still find remarkable is the way these games delivered the experiences in an ongoing way. They were constantly updated, even if only to make a tiny tweak to gameplay, remove bugs, or add minor content changes. The innovation was not in the gameplay, after all these new gaming players didn't have the time or inclination to get into complex game mechanics. It was in the way they responded to real player behavior by collecting data and measuring whether each change made improved the game or not. Of course they also brought with them the freemium model. Anyone and everyone could play the game as long as they wanted without paying, but to make progress or to access unique experiences you would want to spend money. Usually to speed up the gameplay.

Now it is Mobile's Turn

Of course, a number of mobile developers such as King and Supercell have followed suit, bringing the service approach and freemium business model to their mobile and tablet games. With the success of *Simpsons Tapped Out* and *Real Racing 3*, even EA's Nick Earl announced that he was "pivoting sharply toward free-to-play models instead of the pay-once 'premium' business model."[15]

Building games as a service means almost inevitably we end up adopting the freemium model. But what about the tarnished image of F2P we have talked about? What does it mean to our ability to be creative?

Players are learning about the nastier tricks and techniques used in different games and unless we change our focus from monetization to delivering better service we may just lose them. But on a more positive note the transition to a service mindset means we can launch the smallest, least risky build of our game (minimum viable product) and get it into the hands of players to test and show us how they like it.

Moving to a service approach changes not only the way you think about the game, but also about how it will be managed and updated. There are technical and cost consequences as well as the need to change to a new business model. We have to have the infrastructure to sustain and support our community over time and the tools to help them communicate with us and each other with all the appropriate moderation that dictates.

Free is Not Cheap

This is costly and resource hungry. It also requires different planning, maintenance, and development skills. Fortunately there are lots of "off-the-shelf" technologies out there that mean it is possible, if you plan it in advance. However, even with the simplest service you have to assume that the need to continually keep your game "alive" with content, events, and functional updates will mean that as a rule of thumb you should plan for at least 80 percent of your total development costs to arise after your initial launch.

But How Does This Lead Us Into Greater Creativity?

Let's take three cliché looks at how people become video game designers. The first is the "old school" designer who learnt their trade by making games for studios, which in turn supplied their talents to publishers. They worked on games that had fixed released dates, planned months (if not years) ahead because they had to compete for precious space on the shelves of the game shops on the high street of your local town. Next we have the "indie-ism" designer, the multitalented self-contained artist/coder savants who start out having something they want to create and then learnt through their own mistakes. Many of these couldn't care less about the money or arguably about what their audience wants to play, but they have an attention to detail about the perfection of their game concept that takes them forward. The last type is the "reborn vets," often a highly experienced coder or artist who has moved away from the big projects, wanting to make the game their former employers were too blind to see, and who admits that they had to learn the hard way in order to fully appreciate the design process and in particular the impact of unintended consequences.

All of these introductions to games design are perfectly valid but the trouble is that they all focus on the game experience rather than the player experience. The move to a service means we have to consider the journey not only of our game character over time, but also the journey of our player.

What Has This Chapter Been About?

This introductory chapter has been about looking at where the games industry has been and the impact that the changing business model has had on that industry over the past few years. I've tried to demonstrate how much change there has been and the impact that this has on almost every aspect of design. F2P is often, wrongly, thought of as only something that affects the way we sell our game. What I hope this book will do is allow you to see that it has a much more profound impact than that.

Free2Play is a Symptom, Not the Cause

This is because F2P is a symptom not the underlying cause in my view. The more profound change has been the change from a retail box-product to an online service industry. When we sell a game upfront, all we have to do is to create enough anticipation to encourage the player to get past the purchase point. Is the idea exciting enough? Does it make me anticipate the joy of playing so much that I have no question about the price tag? Is the gameplay good enough to mean that the game reviews support the marketing story? Sure we want to get better reviews. Sure we want players to rate the experience highly. But none of these reflect the longevity of the player's experience or their lifetime enjoyment. If we are paid upfront we don't have any incentive to really think deeply about each their evolving engagement with our game.

Game services on the other hand only work if, first, enough players play the game regularly and, second, enough of them are willing to continue to spend some money regularly. Those players still have to anticipate the joy of playing, not just at the start of their experience, but every day. They still have to find and choose our game over almost infinite number of other titles available to them.

Free Requires Different Skills

Going free isn't enough to attract an audience anymore. Designing games with the freemium model has unique challenges. Not least of this is that because players have spent nothing, they have nothing invested in the game they have just downloaded. If I have paid upfront, I have no choice but to put up with the layers of tutorial, quicktime videos and partner logo images if I want to make the most of the money I have already spent. If I haven't spent any money I have nothing to lose and I can just switch off if I don't want to put up with all of that clutter. If we don't get our freemium players started playing straight away, it's our fault if they get bored and play another game instead.

The Designer's Job Just Got Tougher

Your job as a game designer, no matter which type you are, just got tougher and more interesting at the same time. We need to look at design differently and constantly consider new techniques, tools, and data if we are going to rise to this challenge. I believe this will have a Darwinian influence on the industry—we have to make better games or we will replaced by others who do.

This book aims to give you the skills and tools to make better games, not just more profitable ones.

Notes

1   www.apple.com/uk/pr/library/2008/06/09Apple-Introduces-the-New-iPhone-3G.html.
2   www.apple.com/uk/pr/library/2007/01/09Apple-Reinvents-the-Phone-with-iPhone.html.
3   www.apple.com/pr/library/2007/06/11iPhone-to-Support-Third-Party-Web-2-0-Applica tions.html.
4   http://news.cnet.com/8301-13579_3-57588534-37/apple-now-hosts-900000-apps-in-app-store.
5   Marketing to children has always been problematic and *RuneScape* denied that it was doing this and had an age requirement of 13. This has now been removed but players under 13 only have access to a limited version of chat (Quick Chat), which restricts players to predefined sentences.
6   The Guinness World Records site records *RuneScape* as the most popular free MMO with 175,365,991 users in November 2010, www.guinnessworldrecords.com/records-7000/most-popular-free-mmorpg.
7   More details of how the BigPoint DroidX works can be found on GamesBrief, www.gamesbrief.com/2011/11/bigpoint-does-sell-the-tenth-drone-for-1000-eur-but-may-not-have-made-eur-2-million-from-it/.
8   The transition from paid to Freemium was complete by June 2011 according to Flurry, http://blog.flurry.com/bid/65656/Free-to-play-Revenue-Overtakes-Premium-Revenue-in-the-App-Store.
9   This quote comes from me by the way. Check out my slideshare presentation "A Developers' Guide To Surviving the Zombie Apocalypse" given at a number of locations, but most notably Game Horizon 2012, Casual Connect Hamburg 2012, and GDC Europe 2012.
10 Again me I'm afraid. In my defense there is logic in this and it's based on the continuous decline in the number of console studios over the past three to four years alongside the increasing costs of development and marketing against the persistent decline in the retail trade. Given these trends, an average of one game per month seemed appropriate at the time.

11   NewZoo's Global Games Market Report infographics can be found at www.newzoo.com/
     infographics/global-games-market-report-infographics.
12   This data was presented by Peter Warman of NewZoo at the Casual Connect In Hamburg
     (February 2012), www.newzoo.com/keynotes/casual-connect-europe-2013-single-screen-
     metrics-in-a-multi-screen-world.
13   As I am often reminded by UK consultant Gina Jackson, AAA is about marketing budget,
     not about the quality of the game. However, for the purposes of convenience I am delib-
     erately confusing the two.
14   Pet Society was shut down in June 2013 by EA who had acquired Playfish in 2009 for $400m
15   www.gamesindustry.biz/articles/2013-04-02-ea-mobile-boss-freemium-haters-a-vocal-
     minority.

Exercise 1: Concept Creation

Throughout this book we will have exercises[1] aimed at helping designers new to Free2Play design to test out their ideas. This can be for your own use or perhaps you will want to visit our website www.GamesAsAService.net to share your thoughts with other designers who are working through the exercises and compare and rate each other's concepts.

There are lots of game design techniques you can use to create a starting concept. We will explore some of them in this exercise and at the end you should select one idea to use for all of the later chapters of the book. Try answering the following questions as quickly as possible, don't worry about being accurate, just put in the first concept you think of for each answer, but you can't duplicate any answer.

QUESTION	YOUR ANSWER
1. What is your favorite long running TV series?	
2. What is your favorite "popcorn" movie?[2]	
3. What is your all-time favorite computer game?	
4. What the last fiction book/comic you read?	
5. In the last week, what game did you play the most?[3]	
6. What was the last traditional or "casual" game you played?	

Pick any one of your answers above and describe, in just one sentence, the basic concept of the story; the objective of usually the lead character, but if there isn't one explain the goal described and finally describe the essential challenge that has to be overcome in the concept, what causes the story arc to be interrupted and difficult.

Feature	One-sentence summary
1. Story	
2. Objective	
3. Challenge faced	

Now pick a second answer from your selection of 1–6 above and describe in just one sentence, the leading character of that concept or, if there isn't a character, what the central mechanic or premise is; then describe the genre or type of story and within that answer try to describe the mood or flavor of the concept; finally, describe what the concept presents as victory conditions or, if that's not obvious, how the concept reaches a conclusion.

Feature	One-sentence summary
4. Leading character, mechanic or premise	
5. Story genre or type and the mood or flavor	
6. Victory conditions or conclusions	

We are going to take these selected concepts and merge them together with the story, objective and challenge of the first concept and the character/premise, challenge and victory conditions of the other. This should form what is essentially a brand new concept, but sometimes we have to throw in something else new, just to be on the safe side to avoid falling into cliché or becoming too derivative. So in order to mix it up a bit, let's use a six-sided die (yes there is a reason why I wanted six concepts and two sets of three features). First roll to determine which feature of your new game concept you need to revise; where 1 = story and 6 = victory conditions. Then roll again and look at the original six answers you gave, where 1 = TV series and 6 = traditional game.

Rewrite the feature you have randomly selected using the concept answer you have randomly selected as a guide. If the randomly selected concept is the same as you used originally, then leave it unchanged.

One-sentence summary	
Feature to change	
Alternative concept	
Rewritten feature	

Next we have to throw in something of our own; you could just decide which one to change, but if you need inspiration why not roll

Permission to photocopy for personal use

that dice again where 1 = story and 6 = victory conditions and add something unique to you. It mustn't come from the six concepts we described in our answers. It needs to be different, ideally inspired from the other features of our concept; perhaps even something a little weird.[4]

One-sentence summary	
Feature to change	
"Weird" feature	

Finally, we need to give this a name. Don't be limited by the source concepts we used to create our descriptions, instead think about the resulting six features of the new concept and reimagine what this game might be called. We can always come back later if we want to change it. While we are at it, let's create a final summary putting everything in one place.

Game name	
1. Story	
2. Objective	
3. Challenge faced	
4. Leading character, mechanic or premise	
5. Story genre or type and the mood or flavor	
6. Victory conditions or conclusions	

That should be enough for us to get started. We aren't actually looking for an earth-shattering idea right now, just something unique to you we can use to work on through the different exercises in the book. It is not even particularly important whether you think this could be a good game, but you should at least find it an entertaining idea. You can always repeat the process until you are happy to use your idea to practice on as you learn the design strategies for games as a service. Through the later sections of this book we will look at the different elements of the game design from the compulsion loops, game mechanic, context and metagames, allowing you to find ways to realize the best possible gameplay from this idea. If you end up wanting to change the concept; just try working through these steps again and try being playful with each concept you explore.

Feel free to check out www.GamesAsAService.net, where you will be able to upload your results onto a webform that will allow you to create a PDF of the eventual game design and, if you like, share it with others for a comments and comparisons.

WORKED EXAMPLE:

QUESTION	YOUR ANSWER
1. What is your favorite long running TV series?[5]	The Sopranos
2. What is your favorite 'popcorn' movie?	Casino Royal (original with David Niven/Peter Sellers/Woody Allen)
3. What is your all-time favorite computer game?	Space Invaders
4. What the last fiction book/comic you read?	Harlen Coban, Six Years
5. In the last week what game did you play the most?	Scrabble
6. What was the last traditional or "casual" game you played?	Sudoko

Feature	One-sentence summary
1. Story	Mafia boss seeks psychiatric help to help him cope with his family life, relationship with his mother and the violence of his "business" interests
2. Objective	Looking after his family day-to-day
3. Challenge faced	The politics of the wider family

Feature	One-sentence summary
4. Leading character, mechanic or premise	You have to keep the b***ards out
5. Story genre or type and the mood or flavor	Science fiction and tension, with inevitable doom
6. Victory conditions or conclusions	Survive as long as possible (get the highest scores)

One-sentence summary	
Feature to change	Leading character or premise
Alternative concept	Harlen Coban, Six Years
Rewritten feature	The leading character is a Professor at an American Midwest university who is looking for his girlfriend who told him not to follow her

One-sentence summary	
Feature to change	Challenge faced
"Weird" feature	The main character loses his memory

FINAL SUMMARY:

Game name	Finding Anthony
1. Story	Mafia boss seeks psychiatric help to help him cope with his family life, relationship with his mother and the violence of his "business" interests
2. Objective	Looking after his family day-to-day
3. Challenge faced	The main character loses his memory
4. Leading character, mechanic or premise	Looking for his girlfriend who told him not to follow her
5. Story genre or type and the mood or flavor	Science fiction and tension, with inevitable doom: Anthony is a cyborg with failing memory circuits and damaged "brain slots"
6. Victory conditions or conclusions	Survive as long as possible (get the highest scores)

Notes

1 Please note that these exercises and the "worked examples" are intended to help you think like a "games as a service" designer. The results won't provide a complete or fully fleshed-out game design document. However, it should provide a good start to that process with this specific approach to design. The worked examples are simply intended to provide a comparison with the kind of answers you might want to think about. This is not a real game (deliberately), just a sample concept intended to show that it is possible to come up with non-standard games with this design process. We will post more fully fleshed examples onto the website.

2   By "popcorn" movie, we are looking for the movie you will watch time and again, rather than the movies you rate as being representative of the highest calibre of the artform.

3   The current game need not be a computer game, or even a traditional game. If you played a game of "dare" or even play around with how accurately you park your car, that could still count.

4   Remember Scott Roger's Triangle of Weirdness, we need some structure around what is new and what is weird, which is why we are picking two familiar concepts and putting them together, then adding one weird/new item to ensure we are introducing originality http://mrbossdesign.blogspot.co.uk/2008/09/triangle-of-weirdness.html.

5   In order to make this example I took the answers to the concept creation questions given to me by my Mum. Hopefully this shows that anyone can do it. I also hope it demonstrates that we can have fun with the process rather always having to try to make best possible creative concept. However, I am surprisingly pleased by the results.

Chapter 2
What is a Game?

What is Fun Anyway?

It is impractical to start off a book on games design without spending
at least some time trying to define what we mean by a "game," and how
that relates to "fun." It would be easy to spend the majority of this
book exploring the different concepts and ideas behind game theory.
However, rather than doing that, I'd like to point you in the right direction to find out for yourself. In this chapter I'll refer to other writers
and provide references in the endnotes for people who have looked into
the theory of gameplay from traditional games all the way to modern
computer games and if you feel you need to know more, please check
out their work. Whether you are familiar with the concepts here or not
it's well worth taking time to step back and to consider these questions.
But where should we start? The very act of definition seems to suck out
the life of what it means to "play."

Can You Define Fun?

Saying that Fun is "enjoyment, amusement, or lighthearted pleasure"
doesn't help us understand how it feels to laugh or what triggers within
a game can delight us.

The easy answer might be to quote some inspirational game design
guru like Rafe Koster.[1] In his *A Theory of Fun* he tries to get us to go
back to basics and to consider the way our brains reward us for success
in pattern-matching. Pattern-matching is a cool way to start. We see
two blue gems alongside a green gem, we know that if we can get a line
of three blue gems we will get a reward, and as long as the grid of gems
changes, we continue to get pleasure from the process of finding such
matches where we can.

It can be hard to accept this fairly reductionist way of thinking about
games. For example playing poker isn't the same thing as playing chess
or a classic match-three style game like *Bejeweled*. There are nuances of
social interaction and decision-making based on predictions of probability in poker, but even these are in themselves forms of pattern-matching.
Texas hold 'em players talk about the board texture based on the "suited-
ness" and "connectedness" of the flop.[2] Chess, as it has evolved, involves
no random influence except the strategies of your opponent, but again
the patterns of the play of the finest players has been detailed and clas-
sified over hundreds of years and many players will instantly recognize
shapes of moves made in the opening, mid and end game sections of play.

At What Price Victory?

Patterns in games are extremely powerful. When trying to create games as a service they are fundamental. We need a game to have something at its heart with a highly repeatable pattern. It's almost like the heartbeat of our game or the meter of a song.

The trouble is (as Koster goes on to state) pattern-matching can become boring.

Writers like Johan Huizinga[3] and Robert Caillois[4] proposed that "rules" form a key factor in helping us to turn the pleasure of pattern-matching into something we could term "play." They create structure and ways to validate our behaviors, whether that applies to sports or games. Rules have to be something that are agreed by the participants and that help us make sense of the experience, allowing us to differentiate what is play from what is not.

Key to these rules is the creation of "victory conditions," something Scott Rogers[5] includes in his definition of what makes a game.

Then, of course, if we accept that there are victory conditions, then it's probable that we also have to accept that there are failure conditions too. Jesper Juul[6] writes about the paradox inherent in knowing that we will experience failure and that we still seek to overcome it is what drives our interest in games. Greg Costikyan[7] uses the example of *Space Invaders* to show that, even where the final outcome is inevitable defeat, players can delight in the playing, not to win but to better their previous score or that of another player. He further argues that a game's outcome can be more than just a binary "win" or "lose."

Many writers also talk about the psychology of games, and as much as I want to be scientific about this, I don't know enough about brain chemistry to be sure whether fun is a chemical response with a dopamine or serotonin release following the successful overcoming of a challenge. But clearly it can be valuable to consider how normal brain responses are triggered from the way a player engages with our game.

Play is Utterly Absorbing

In the end I personally find, despite being written in 1938, Huizinga's definition of play to be extremely useful and I think we can learn a lot about what makes for good game design by analyzing it further. He talks about "play" as "a freestanding activity quite outside ordinary life . . . absorbing the player intensely and utterly."

Think about that for a minute. When we suspend our disbelief and allow ourselves to dwell in the world created by a game experience we gain an amazing release. We free our imagination and creativity to explore and focus on the patterns of whatever it is we are doing. It's almost like we are giving ourselves permission to play. We experience this kind of release when we read a great book, or watch our favorite soap opera. This works whether that is just for a few brief delightful moments of casual play or for the hours we set aside for our favorite hardcore console game. This suspension of disbelief comes from a mutual agreement between the designer and the player. We, as designers, have to create the conditions where the player feels comfortable to accept the rules of that world and we have to keep consistent with those rules to avoid breaking the immersion, or at least limiting those breaks to predictable patterns.

No Material Interest

Huizinga's definition continues by saying that play is an activity with "no material interest or profit gained." That's a bit more challenging, especially where we want to sell virtual goods to the player. But perhaps this helps us gets to the bottom of the negative feelings that we talked about with the Free2Play (F2P) model in the introduction. When players feel that we are only interested in the money we can gain, then is there any wonder that this will feel like a breach of trust; perhaps even feel like we have "broken the rules?" If you can buy your way to success then we remove the challenge and essentially create a method to cheat the victory conditions. I have found this myself in several games where the purchase of virtual goods essentially undermined the purpose of the game mechanic. Why would I want to spend money on in-game grind currency when that very currency was the only meaningful measure of how successful I had been in playing the game?

Crass Commercialization

It is also the case that constant reminders to buy things can stop us from "absorbing the player intensely and utterly." However, when we look at the raw data of how players respond to in-game reminders, this shows that instead of causing players to leave or "churn" from our game, instead we see that "push promotions" can be really effective. Does that mean Huizinga was wrong? I don't think so. The problem is often that there are multiple motivations at play. Players understand that games are commercial properties and often accept that we want to sell to them, but this will still annoy a number of them. Looking at data from some social mobile games it seems that promotions that are in-line with the flow of the game generally perform better. Where possible we should try to find the balance between the need to inform players that it's worth investing their money in the game without breaking the illusion of the game experience.

Farming for Gold

On the other hand this idea of "material interest" is also about what the player themselves might gain. Removing the idea of profit from the definition of "play" helps us consider the phenomenon of gold-farming in MMO games. We can clearly argue that this breaks the fun of the experience, at least for the people gold-farming. However, for the people paying for the extra gold or to eliminate the grind in order to gain access to the higher level playing experiences, this can be an absolute delight. Many games, such as *RuneScape*[8] spend a lot of time trying to minimize the impact of gold-farming, but the question in my mind is whether this activity is essential to preserve the game or a symptom of an untapped demand. What if instead you provided a system to encourage players to gold-farm inside the game and take a small percentage on each transaction? Similar questions apply when you start thinking about the creation of user-generated content. When does this cross the line between creative entertainment and work? Should creators have the opportunity to be paid with grind-money or in-game virtual goods for taking the time to make things in the game? Should they be paid with real-money?

This seems tempting to me, but it does seem at odds with the concept of "material interest." Then there are other complications, such as the legal requirement to prevent money-laundering involved with any real-money transactions.

Gambling With Players?

What is clear to me is that when "profit" or "material interests" impact play, our motivations change. The more personal gain affects our play, the harder it becomes to suspend disbelief.

This question will have a profound impact on the way game companies embrace real-money gambling in their games. As the USA opens up to gambling services, like the UK before it, we will see a "gold rush" for gambling games, but at the risk of blurring two very different playing motivations.[9]

Counting on Uncertainty

In 1958 Roger Caillois, in his *Definition of Play*, expanded on Huizinga's description of play and suggested that doubt itself was a vital part of the process of play. If there is no uncertainty then play simply stops. This applies to games of skill as well as luck, because if the players aren't sufficiently balanced there is no pleasure in the game, as much as if there is no chance of failure or success. Although it is possible that some fun can be achieved through the process of play if there is room for personal impact on the outcome. For example, the fun of playing *FarmVille* is not found in the creation of your farm, but in the journey of making it your own. Juul in his 2013 *The Art of Failure* expands on this by asking us to consider the "Paradox of Painful Art." We wouldn't seek out situations that arouse painful emotions, but we recognize that some art will evoke a painful emotional response and yet we still seek out that art. Similarly, we don't seek to experience the humiliation of failure, but we know that playing some games will result in such a failure and yet we seek out those games as long as we perceive that we have to potential to overcome those goals with practice. Indeed it's the fine balance of challenge and perception of the potential for success that makes a great game impossible to put down. It's worth checking out Greg Costikyan's *Uncertainty in Games* if you want to see how these concepts apply to different classical games from *Super Mario Bros* to *The Curse of Monkey Island*.

Playing Together Alone

There is a public perception of games playing in isolation with a computer is very new and reading Huizinga's work further we see that in his definition of play is the idea that this "promotes the formation of social grouping which tend to surround themselves with secrecy and to stress their differences from the common world by disguise or other means." I find this perspective fascinating not least because this predates Facebook and computer games in general, but it even predates games like *Dungeons & Dragons* by 36 years.

The Cake is a Lie

Think about the way hardcore computer gamers have their own shared memories and affinity to specific platforms and characters. For example if I say "the cake is a lie," most of you reading this will know exactly what I'm talking about and may even have strong memories of a particular song. There are of course a lot of people who won't have a clue what this refers to and indeed who are effectively excluded because of this. Inside knowledge is an important aspect of belonging to a group and becomes a shortcut to sharing the fun when we play. It's also a factor that I believe has largely been overlooked in social game design in recent years.

We Want to Play with Others

Social interactions are vital to playing games. Indeed the idea of playing with others is a key survival trait exhibited by countless social mammals. It allows us to be able to test and trial experiences as well as working out your place in the pecking order without the risk of being harmed in the process.

Since 2008 the idea of a social game has changed dramatically with the arrival of Facebook-based games and the way this innovation dramatically shifted the size and nature of the games playing audience. Zynga and Playfish essentially made it possible for games to reach mainstream users and for the first time made playing games something that almost everyone did. Key to this change was the nature of the platform. It only needed a browser, it didn't require an upfront fee and, because it allowed us to share playing moments everyday with people who matter to us, this unlocked supersized audiences. Of course most of these players had never learnt the "rules" of game-playing and indeed arguably had rejected the very idea of play. At the heart these games had to be simple, repetitive, playful moments; they couldn't get a new audience who had previously rejected computer games to adopt the often complex and obscure mechanics many experienced gamers take for granted.

But are These Games? Are They Social?

We will talk about degrees of sociability in a later chapter, but I would argue that what makes Facebook games work, indeed the genius part of Facebook itself, is its power to deliver asynchronous communication with people who matter to us. We don't have to be at the same place or the same time to be able to share meaningful moments. It is like we are leaving footprints in the sands of time for our friends to discover whenever they are in the mood to find out.

There have been lots of issues since the golden age of *FarmVille* and *Restaurant City*, not least the decision by EA in April 2013 to close *SimCity Social*, *Sim Social* and *Pet Society*. But I don't want to turn this chapter into an analysis of why I think we have seen decline in this area. Instead, I want us to focus on what this concept of social interaction means for game design and the way asynchronous play can vastly broaden our horizons—provided the interactions are meaningful and personal enough.

One of the areas that has regularly been brought into question when considering the Facebook game is where there might be room for failure and challenge. Something I would argue was largely absent from this generation of social gaming and that I expect will come back in the next generation of Facebook-powered online games.

People Are People No Matter What They Play

Of course when we introduce social play we have to consider the way we interact with other people. Richard Bartle[10] has spent a lot of time looking at how people react with each other and how these behaviors impact on how they play games. He looked at the ways people played the first virtual world, the original online text-based *Multi User Dungeon* (*MUD*), and used this to isolate four essential player types. These types were defined to help answer the question of what players wanted from *MUD*s, but has a remarkable relevance to online worlds and to games as a service in general. Looking at this crudely you could say that "achievers" are looking to resolve in-game goals and are essentially motivated by success. "Explorers" gain enjoyment intrinsically from the act of moving through the world and collecting items and information about the world, the completion of the game's goals are less relevant that the knowledge of where those goals occur. "Socializers" are often less motivated by the inherent mechanics of the game and often use the game as an excuse to meet and interact with others. The last category were named "killers" but you could easily call them by the name used on internet forums, "trolls." They actively enjoy the ability to disrupt the play of others and to exploit methods in the game to create unexpected results (even to bring down the servers).

Understanding Motivations

What I believe Bartle is showing us is that players exhibit different reward motivations and it becomes vital to us to understand these different motivations as we try build and maintain a community. We have to anticipate and manage (ideally redirect) the latent frustrations of the killers to avoid them becoming disruptive. We have to have goals and variety for the achievers and explorers respectively to complete that don't simply come to an end after just a few hours of play. We have to create the context for socializers to be able to communicate and create the social glue that sustains your community.

Understanding the range of emotions that we create through play is essential but we still have to simplify these into terms we can communicate easily to others, the press, our investors, our team, and—importantly—to potential players too. That means we also need to consolidate all these ideas down into two deceptively difficult questions. What is our unique player proposition (the core reason why players should care about our game from a purely gameplay perspective) and what is our unique sales proposition (the reason why our players should convert to being regular payers)?

Fun isn't Limited by Technology

I guess my point in all of this is that fun is a basic human emotional response to play and the principles of our behavior have only super-ficially changed over time. We may have handheld devices and cloud computing, but in the end we still play as a free activity, with no care for material profit. Fun is not something that can be forced. It requires a separation from our normal world to exist, usually framed in some commonly agreed rules with some level of uncertainty to its outcome and it's something we want to share with other players. Understanding this and allowing us to consider the implications this raises as well as the harder questions of business models and marketing is what makes our job as designers so much fun.

Notes

1 Game designer Rafe Koster's *A Theory of Fun* is a great inspirational text for budding game designers. Check out www.theoryoffun.com/index.shtml.
2 If you are interested in poker theory, check out this post from "Pokey," which talks about poker strategy in detail, http://archives1.twoplustwo.com/showflat.php?Cat=0&Board=microplnl&Number=8629256.
3 Dutch historian and cultural theorist Johan Huizinga wrote about "play theory" in in 1938 with his title *Homo Ludens*, http://en.wikipedia.org/wiki/Homo_Ludens_(book).
4 In 1961, French sociologist, Robert Caillois published a critique on Huizinga's work in *Man, Play and Games*, http://en.wikipedia.org/wiki/Man,_Play_and_Games.
5 Scott Rogers talks about game design in his book *Level Up: The Guide to Great Video Game Design*. Check out his blog at http://mrbossdesign.blogspot.co.uk.
6 Jesper Juul talks about games as the "Art of Failure" and the paradox of tragedy in relation to video games. His blog can be found at www.jesperjuul.net/ludologist.

7   Greg Costikyan has worked on traditional and computer games as well as Uncertainty in Games http://mitpress.mit.edu/books/uncertainty-games.
8   The *RuneScape* team spends a lot of time trying to reduce the impact of gold-farming on their service, despite being a F2P game, http://services.runescape.com/m=news/anti-gold-farming-measures.
9   I believe that gambling has a very different set of motivations and rewards based on the tension between the result being in and the player knowing whether they have won or lost. This anxiety seems to be heightened by the importance of the stake. Success is generally attributed to personal choice, whereas failure is generally attributed to "bad luck." Unlike non-gambling games, this sense of reward doesn't diminish with repetition and hence, I suspect, players will be more vulnerable to addictive behaviors (of course addiction is a massive topic itself on which few experts agree).
10 Richard Bartle, Professor at the University of Essex, co-creator of *MUD* and author of *Designing Virtual Worlds*, www.mud.co.uk/richard/hcds.htm.

Exercise 2: Who Are Your Players?

In this second exercise we want to consider our audience. We need to identify a selection of different personalities to help us ask questions about our ideas in a useful way. Ideally, these personalities would be based on real segments of our playing audience, but for the purposes of this exercise I will assume that we don't have access to that data yet, not least as we have yet to make our game. When we can use real data we should. This approach is a thought exercise designed to make it easier to question our own ideas as much as to consider the perspectives of other players. With games as a service you are not just making a game for yourself.

For this exercise to be useful we need to be able to put ourselves into the shoes of other players. This mean we need to understand something of what motivates them, who they are, how much experience they have, and, above all, what motivates them to play at all, let alone to play our game. To help with this we will create a stereotype personality based on their age, gender, and background. We want you to build up a picture of them and try to think of people you know, ideally people who have different interests and needs to your own. Then we will add to that by considering their playing experience and motivations to play.

Richard Bartle's player types form a great model for this, but are not the only way to categorize the reward motivations of players and we should feel free to expand on this kind of thinking. We should also consider the principle mode of use (on-the-go; in their front room; on the toilet, etc.) for each player as well as their mood or current objective in playing (escapism, distraction, collection).

It's really important to give them a name. This is a tool that helps you isolate their needs in your own mind and indeed to give yourself per-mission to question your own ideas safely; because it's about what that "person" would feel. This may sound trivial, but it's quite a profound thing in allowing your own inner questions about the game to come through.

Let's start with your principle player, the one who is your ideal target and who will probably be the most typical player of your game.

Who is your principle target player in terms of:	
Name:	
Gender:	
Age:	
Location:	
Principle mode of use:	
Motivation to play:	
Reward they seek:	
Why are they typical?	

Next we need to come up with a contrast. This should be a player with different needs, but who still has good reason to play your game, even though this is different from our principle player.

Who is your secondary target player in terms of:	
Name:	
Gender:	
Age:	
Location:	
Mode of use:	
Motivation to play:	
Reward they seek:	
Why are they different from the primary target player?	

Often two personalities can be enough to help provide contrasting views, but I also like to have a third, the "outlying" player type. These are players who might play your game if only you considered their needs a little more. They should be more different still than the target and secondary players and represent a wider more mass-market audience in most cases (if you have a mass-market concept then instead these should represent more "hardcore" players). This personality should not be the same gender as both the previous personality types.

Who is your outlying target player in terms of:	
Name:	
Gender:	
Age:	
Location:	
Mode of use:	
Motivation to play:	
Reward they seek:	
Why are they different from the primary target player?	
What stops them from playing?	

Finally, let's use these player types to consider how your concept might deliver a unique playing proposition for our audiences. Essentially this is about what makes the game fun for your players (and not just for you!). This might be quite difficult to answer at this stage and you may want to come back after progressing further into the book. Alternatively it might be worth returning to the concept and changing one of more of the features of the concept.

Consider what each player type can get from your game concept that they won't elsewhere.	

Why should each player type download your game and start playing right now?	

For each player type, think about why their friends will care when our players show off your game to those friends?	

WORKED EXAMPLE:

Who is your principle target player in terms of:	Bob is a 40–45 year old male gamer living in the Bay Area with his wife and two kids. He used to play a lot of hardcore games and is quite competitive, but he has lost his edge now due to lack of time to practice and no longer having the manual dexterity. Work and family life get in the way of his time to play so he needs something that can fill the odd few minutes throughout his day. He tends to play on his phone, but occasionally on a tablet, which he prefers due to the scope offered by the larger screen. Game sessions on the tablet normally happen in the living room while his wife and kids take over the family TV. He is no longer a pure "achiever" player, motivated more by exploration and collection. Bob is typical as he is looking for a game that is a little more thoughtful and challenging without manual dexterity being too crucial to success.
Name:	
Gender:	
Age:	
Location:	
Principle mode of use:	
Motivation to play:	
Reward they seek:	
Why are they typical?	

Who is your secondary target player in terms of:	Kevin is a 18–24 year old male living in his parents' house in Guildford in the UK. He plays on multiple devices, but once he starts playing a game he generally sticks with the device he started with (although not always). He typically plays on a tablet for this kind of game, but is also considering getting a microconsole alongside his traditional console. He is a classic hardcore gamer on his PC and console, but enjoys more relaxed-paced playing formats on mobile devices. Despite that, it's all about winning for him—both beating the game and his friends. Ideally crushing them publicly! He is a classic "achiever" with a little "killer" on the side. He differs from Bob because he is more aggressive as a player, but also is a little more flighty so may more easily leave the game for another if he gets bored.
Name:	
Gender:	
Age:	
Location:	
Mode of use:	
Motivation to play:	
Reward they seek:	
Why are they different from the primary target player?	

Who is your principle target player in terms of:	Sumi is a 30–35 year old South Korean woman living in Italy with her American husband and young baby. She uses games to provide her not only with an escape from the day-to-day activity of childrearing but also to provide a much needed social outlet. She roams between different devices freely and gets frustrated when a game's save state isn't consistent between those devices. She has tended to play casual games and particularly likes those that remind her of the Tycoon games of her youth. However, she is open-minded about the genre and will try anything where there is a social context. At heart she is a "social" player. She won't play games without a genuine opportunity to share with her friends; this need not mean direct conversation, but has to offer meaningful reminders of the presence of her online friends.
Name:	
Gender:	
Age:	
Location:	
Principle mode of use:	
Motivation to play:	
Reward they seek:	
Why are they different from the primary target player?	
What stops them from playing?	

Consider what each player type get from your game concept that they won't elsewhere?	This is a game that will have an approachable art style combined with a serious undertone (based on dementia), which is offset against a science fiction backdrop (allowing a sense of distance and at the same time making it easier to create a play mechanic based on memory loss). There is a sense of inevitable doom but this is balanced by the reward from nurturing the family who themselves provide a darkly comic twist as they are mostly ungrateful parasites. Although there will be opportunities to inform players about the real risks of dementia, the focus is to make a playable game, not an educational tool.

Why should each player type download your game and start playing right now?	The game will include strong social elements "connecting" different families and each playing session will have the potential for comical results that can be shared with friends.

For each player type think about why their friends will care when our players show off your game to those friends?	The core mechanic will have the inherent potential for comic effect partly from the way the elements interact, but also through the funnily unpleasant reactions of the family members.

Chapter 3
The Anatomy of Play

Getting to the Bones

In our attempts so far to define what we mean by a game we have looked
at the nature of play and the drivers of fun. We have considered the role
of patterns, rules, victory conditions and, of course, social interactions,
including the role that play takes in forming excusive social groupings.

All of these are lofty concepts and although they are important to
consider they don't leave us with much structure to leverage. If we are
going to actually build a game we have to get under the skin of a game.
We have to get thinking about how to deliver a playing experience.
Those of us who spent too much of our childhood making up games
to play with our friends may have a good instinct for what it fun, but
to reliably make great content we need more solid framework to build
from. That starts by considering the anatomy of a game.

Celebrate Differences

There are huge differences between different games types and genres.
Art-style, controls, genres, even the platform we play that game on, all
influence design decisions. These variations allow us to endlessly come
up with new concepts and ideas and with each one the designer can
communicate something new to their players. However, much of this
variation is on the surface and by looking underneath this skin we see a
great deal of shared common principles.

In this book the model we use is an attempt to make it easy to
consider the flow of play in a game, something that is essential to be
successful when creating games as a service.

Where's Wally?

Before we can start we need some common principles. For this purpose
let's start with the assumption that games essentially break down into
a series of patterns which combine to form rules.[1] Pattern-matching
seems to have been a critical factor in evolutionary success for humans
and as a result it seems unsurprising to me that we gain great pleasure
from being successful at this apparently simple activity. Finding a skinny
guy in a red and white hat and matching jumper is a game, even if one
of limited depth, and it's about finding a known pattern (i.e., Wally
himself) within a complex image.

Humans are also unusual in that we can consider patterns using
our imagination. We can work through different scenarios and

look for the patterns that give us the best outcomes, a skill that has transformed our survival chances. When we play Go we take turns to place our black or white stones in position so that we capture as many of our opponent's pieces as possible, while safeguarding our own position.

Stick or Twist?

Of course games don't just use fixed patterns, they often have some level of randomness. For example, we don't know the original rules for Senet,[2] the oldest known game, but it seems likely to have involved random number generation using thrown sticks or knucklebones (the first dice). Some of the most common modern games use cards to generate a level of randomness, from snap to bridge; even *Magic: The Gathering* uses patterns based on the random selection of individual cards that have different values, suits or rules. We essentially compare our cards with our opponent in order according to the agreed set-up. There are dozens of variations, from Texas hold 'em to Montana red dog, where the winning hands remain largely the same but the betting structure and the process to reveal cards varies. All of these pivot around the principle of players using random results to complete patterns and similar principles apply when we look at dice-based games or traditional board games.

Six to Start

In Ludo[3] I roll a dice, attempting to get a six, which allows me to get one of my pieces onto the starting spot. It also allows me to move any other pieces I have in play across the board, and hopefully I'll get lucky enough to land on my opponent pieces, sending them home. Monopoly uses a similar method for movement, but rather than one die, we roll two and add the total together to find how many spaces I have to move my "avatar" before resolving the actions associated with that space, such as if I land my top hat on Park Place (or Park Lane if you are from the UK) where you have placed a hotel!

The introduction of a second die to determine movement has significance not only on the range of movement of my piece, but also the statistical probability of me travelling a given distance. Monopoly adds to this mechanic further by allowing players to roll again after gaining a double. However, there the game also adds jeopardy by sending you to jail if you happen to roll doubles three times in a row.

Complex Forms from Simple Elements

These patterns form a language allowing us to map the design of game mechanics. At their heart these should be highly repeatable and individually don't usually require complex thinking to resolve. These simple patterns exist in almost every game and combine in unique ways depending on the decision of each player (or indeed to AI response of the game code).

Even chess, a game renowned for its intellectual demands, has very simple rules governing the behavior of each piece. Games like this have a particular characteristic of play that has a profound impact on the flow of the game. They are "games of emergence," where all of the rules and available options are defined at the start of the play. They use essentially simple and consistent rules, but the combinations of each piece and their relative position to each other creates an immense range of variation. They are extremely challenging to create as they run the risk of creating unexpected dominant strategies. For example, when you understand the mechanism of tic-tac-toe (or noughts and crosses) you quickly learn how to always force a draw.

Changing the Rules As We Go Along

The other common type of games are known as "games of progression," which create an evolving narrative, even if like *Tetris* the story is abstract,[4] which is revealed through the playing and which unlocks new behaviors or mechanics over time. These games tend to have lots of stages but only a small range of victory conditions. Quite often the narrative arc is largely fixed by the game designer and merely navigated through by the player. They also tend to require the player to resolve specific mechanics prior to permitting the player to proceed through the story of the game. They need not be entirely linear, however; games such as *Deus Ex*, *Zelda* and *Heavy Rain*[5] famously used a range of interactive techniques allowing the player to influence the outcome of the story. One simple variation includes "forks" in the narrative, which split the path of the player down a fixed number of different outcomes. These forks might over time funnel the player back to the original narrative by presenting them with unpalatable or self-sacrificing options. Other more complex structures include the "hub and spoke" structure where the player has a range of conditions to complete before they can move forward to resolve the next section of the game. Unlike games of emergence, games of progression will have a fixed number of endings because in order to make progress, specific playing conditions have to have been met. Each playing moment is in effect a node for decision-making resolved through play. I am tempted to suggest that games of progression are actually metagames, linking a series of mini-games, but that would be too sweeping a statement.

Getting to the Core

Of course being practical, we know that many games blur the boundaries between these two models of design. Regardless of which type of game we want to make we can still break down the anatomy of the game in the same way. We determine the conditions at the start of the game, the challenges and methods of resolution as well as what reaching the victory conditions actually means, including whether this unlocks further elements for later repetition of play. This is the heart of the core mechanic of the game and it's that which determines what actions are available for players to take, how they resolve the patterns of play, and somehow within these we aim to find the fun.

Let's take some examples. In almost every MMO adventure I have played since *Meridian 59* we start out having to go and kill a virtual rat. When we succeed we loot the rat[6] and then (assuming we have gained enough experience points) we level up. This we repeat, increasing the skill and challenge of the opponent each time to maintain the speed at which we improve our own character. But essentially each of those monsters is simply a bigger rat.

How about a first-person shooter (FPS) game? Well here it's similar. We identify a target, choose the right weapon to defeat them, then we loot their gear. Looked at this way we see that there are lots of similarities in structure to the MMO, but of course the delivery is completely different.

Possibly the purest loops are simple puzzles games. These games are almost inherently self-contained cycles of play. We see an incomplete puzzle, we complete it and gain whatever rewards we expected before moving onto the next.

Even resource management games have repeatable cycles of play. We plant the seeds we start out with in the fields we start with and wait until we can harvest them to get more seeds and of course some in-game reward or currency. However, there are secondary and tertiary levels of cycle. In order to plant more seeds we need to buy extra fields, but extra fields mean that we need extra storage units, which we can only access by selling the plants we harvest. Those plants we harvest can also unlock new types of seed for us to plant, etc. This idea of loops feeding other loops is extremely important and in later chapters. We will also look at how we can use imbalanced economies to balance the interactions between each cycle.

Repetition is the Soul of Play

The repeatable nature of these game loops is essential to how we create entertainment suitable for services. Interestingly, we find this kind repeatable activity intrinsically enjoyable. The more regularly we repeat them the more compelling they become and we create habits through repeated play. There are some models out there that can help us explain how this kind of repetition is enjoyable. The most common example quoted comes from the experiments on operant conditioning by B.F. Skinner.[7] This examines the repeated cycle between action and reward, usually a rat or pigeon pressing a lever to obtain food. Various conditions were applied to the release of the food to create "schedules of reinforcement," which would themselves amend the behavior of the rats. There are of course some apparent comparisons between the ability to manipulate rats using a Skinner Box and the way we affect players' behavior with our games. Indeed there are some who would argue that, because we use these compulsion loops in games, we are somehow "conditioning" players to repeatedly play that game. It's a compelling concept but I believe this falls down in practice. Not least because compulsion isn't the same thing as addiction. One of the key differences is that we aren't restricting players' access to real-world necessities, such as food. The stakes involved aren't equivalent and there are plenty of alternative options for seeking entertainment. On the other hand we never get full of entertainment, unlike our reaction to too much chocolate. However, we do eventually get bored and looking back on our playing history we recognize those games that used operant conditioning too strongly and the resentment that leaves lasting damage for the brand of that game.[8]

Taking Control

Mechanics are more than just the patterns of course. We have to consider the method of play used to resolve those patterns, including the control systems in computer games. In tabletop games we might think about the board and pieces. With a card game we might consider the relationship between the cards we hold in our hand, the remainder of the deck, and the placement of the cards. Computer games—whether on mobile, console, or tablet—have their own considerations. Here we have to think about what the player actually does to move the game forward. Do we move a thumbstick, press a button, shake a controller, type some text, or in some other way direct the movement of an avatar or sprite? If there is some movement involved in the interface, what are the kinetic sensations of the action? How does the game connect the physical movement with the visual and audible feedback? How would that be different if we were to use a touch gesture to slide or spin an object on the screen? How does this action make the underlying experience of play delightful?

The designer has to consider how to communicate the controls system as well as to provide stimulus to inform the player to the actions available to them as well as the feedback from their choices. This has to include any hints, tips or instructions needed to navigate through the game. Will you have pop-up text boxes or "holographic" overlays or perhaps attempt to have all the communication intrinsically contained in the game world itself?

Lights, Camera, Action

We also have to consider what the player sees and how the display responds to their actions. Are we looking at objects in a 2D world? A 3D world? Isometric? You have to consider whether you want the players to be able to direct the camera view or whether you want to fix the camera position within each scene in order to free resources to create the most beautiful visual effects. You might, instead want to have an assisted camera that follows the central character. In some games the designer might also revert to simpler 2D views, perhaps even using parallax scrolling or even Mode7-style effects to create the retro approximations of spatial depth.

The camera view is only part of the visual process. We have to think whether we want our game world to be realistic or perhaps keep it extremely simplified or maybe even quite surreal. The art and audio style we choose will have a profound impact on not only the atmosphere of the game, but to a certain extent the way the players react to specific mechanics and, of course, their emotional responses too.

The Importance of Success and Failure

The core mechanic is like the bones of a game; we can see how a creature might move from its bones, but it's not the bones that provide the source of movement. It takes an understanding of success and failure to understand the equivalent of the muscles. The motivation to play is a complex balance of push and pull from both of these influences, the lure of success and the pent-up frustration that comes from "good" failure.

As humans we crave challenge and actively need the possibility of failure if we are to value what success we achieve. This is more complicated than first appears especially as we start the process to learn about the game. Failure itself is a great motivator, if we cannot fail then there is no challenge. If there is no challenge, there is no fun to be found. Hard games can be incredibly compelling and a real motivation to continue to play. However, there is a downside. Imagine I start a new game, it's a first-person shooter and I'm keen to get going. I find how to move my avatar and make it out of the starting spawn point. I see the bright sunlight of an amazing beautiful world (or, perhaps more likely, the dark brown of some unnatural cave system) and turn to see my friends' avatars charging toward the enemy. Next thing I know, my character receives a head shot. I'm dead. I might get to see a brief replay of my opponent shooting me and perhaps even some obnoxious message to enhance the moment. A few moments after watching one of my teammates playing the game I have the opportunity to respawn back to the match. OK, that wasn't great, but I think I know what I did wrong and decide to get back into the game, a process that often requires about a minute of waiting for the level to reload. This time I'm a little more cautious. I wait till I hear its gone quiet before sticking my head out. Bang. I'm dead again. Another obnoxious message. Another humiliating replay I have to watch, then another minute of waiting for the level to reload. How many times does that have to happen before I stop playing this game? This can be a motivation for some players. But this can't be a good way to build engagement for a mass-market audience.

Don't Punish Players

It doesn't just happen with hardcore FPS titles. *FarmVille*, the classic Facebook social game launched with the infamous "withering" mechanic, where your plants decayed should you fail to harvest them in the allotted time. This on paper is a great concept. We know in advance how long our plants will take to grow and how long they will survive once they are fully grown. It makes sense that if we don't return to a farm that the harvest might spoil. Our friends can restore any lost plants by simply visiting our farm. But a lot people hated this mechanic, especially where the player had spent money on that farm. Coming back to withered plants was something that regularly happened to me and with my odd work/life balance, it was something I could personally do very little about. So I had to either depend on friends coming back to my farm regularly or to pay to fix it. To me, this felt too much like a punishment for not returning when the game demanded it, rather than when it was convenient for me.

In these examples the overwhelming feeling is that the player is being punished for not meeting the games' standards. As designers, it's our job to make sure that we create the conditions where players feel challenged, but not beaten. We want players to be able to reasonably expect that they have a standard to achieve, or they won't feel success when they reach it. However, we don't want them to feel hopeless or so badly resent playing that they never return.

Teeter-Totters are Fun Only When Balanced

Getting the balance between the perceived potential for success and the reality of the experience of failure is extremely difficult and can depend on the mechanic. This is especially true with mass-market audiences where the range of game-playing experience or skills may be very broad. We can look to create ways for the game to assess the rate of learning/ skill within aspects of the game that are less critical to the flow of the game, or allow players to make decisions that let them opt into higher levels of difficulty. It's OK to punish a player's decisions, provided they have the opportunity to change them later. As suggested above, the fear of loss can be an even more effective motivation than the opportunity for gain. Imagine the negative impact of losing $100 compared to the positive value of gaining $100. The same amount of money, but a huge difference in terms of their impact on most people. Because of this effect, loss aversion plays a vital role in decision-making[9] (not always positively) and we should not ignore its importance in gameplay.[10] Being offered the chance to retry a game, without having to restart or lose some in-game treasure can be a powerful incentive to spend money in a game. However, we also should be careful not to overplay this idea at the risk of spoiling the experience for players.

Playing is its Own Reward

Winning is a great feeling, whether that's a small win as we complete a puzzle or a big win as we conquer the game world. This is the "intrinsic" reward for success within the very act of play, even if we don't always succeed obviously. However, we all like to find a way to measure our achievements or to at least be able to find a meaningful comparison so we can feel good about the experience and our abilities. These rewards are highly compelling and provide a lure and motivation to repeat.

Extrinsic rewards, or rewards beyond just the enjoyment of the game, can be very useful to help the game designer demonstrate the players' achievements. Even the anticipation of these rewards can greatly affect our level of performance in a game. These might be shown through experience points, character levels, in-game currency, etc., all of which enable the player to see that their character, vehicle, system has improved (even if this is just in line with the new increased difficulty). Extrinsic rewards can also include badges, trophies, and achievements that I can brag about to my friends—at least the ones who also play the game. The achievement systems on Xbox Live has been a very effective driver to allow hardcore gamers to brag and to reward those players who are motivated to collect every one.

Success is Never Enough

Rewards methods provide the nervous system for a game. These are the tools that provide feedback and affect our playing patterns. The trouble is that repeated exposure to the same reward stimulus has a diminishing effect. We become satiated by the obvious patterns of play that we have already completed and need something more. Building in progression between each repeat of our core mechanic is important to sustain the interest of the player. Progression can take many forms but essentially involve changing the variables in the mechanic gradually each play. This either builds the challenge level as the player progresses through the game or provides variations that stimulate other aspects of the experience from art style, through genre, even different forms of pattern resolution. Largely this can be done in line with the rate of progress of the player themselves. For many of us, we want the difficulty to increase, ideally just a little faster than our ability to play grows, to respond to that challenge.

Measuring Progress

However, we need some way for the game to show us how we have improved and of course our progress in the context of the game. We want small meaningful victories along the way that reassure us of our ability and prove to us that success is not just possible, but something we associate with our own actions. Marking these victories can create anticipation for future stages and show us the measurable value of our investment of time and money in this game so far.

In *Candy Crush Saga*, they have a simple map showing a winding path with stops representing each of the levels to convey a sense of momentum and at the same time to show you where your friends are on this journey. This approach allows you to measure your progress independently of your specific performance on each of the separate stages, making it more accessible to a broader range of players.

Sometimes however, the player may not use the progression mechanic you thought you had set up. Many games prominently display the in-game grind currency within play and reward player success with increases in that cash. All well and good. However, if you are not careful this becomes the principle way that players determine their progress. With games like *Plants vs. Zombies 2* I found this an active barrier to me using that currency to use power-ups like the "pinch," a mechanic I found highly enjoyable to use in the level that introduced these power-ups, but resented using during normal play. Similarly, I found in games like *CSR Racing* that this effect reduced my willingness to spend money in the game as for me the purpose to continue to play was to see how quickly I could earn that grind money.

Telling Stories

Building on this idea of progression provides a good reason to think about why we are playing our game. We can't just have a game mechanic and be able to deliver a great service. There are great products that are simply mechanics that we repeat, however building a service needs more. We need a motivation to continue to play time and again and this often is driven by the context—often the story or narrative of the game.

The context is the circulatory system in anatomy of play. It provides the life and power for the game as well as supplying a sense of purpose for the repeat use of the core mechanic. In *Tetris*, as we have said, this is quite simple and abstract. We have to place the falling pieces carefully so we can clear them from the screen by completing unbroken horizontal lines, getting a high score along the way which we want to beat each time we play. For *Tomb Raider* this is a lot more detailed, but essentially involves the survival of a young Lara Croft, shipwrecked on an impossible historic island, facing crazy gangs of cultist and mythical legends, collecting treasures as she tries to save her largely hapless friends.

Games within Games

Context can also evolve over time, sometimes as part of the narrative determined by the developer, such as in *Deus Ex Human Evolution* for example; do your save the "Thorpe Couple" or not? Do you search to Hung Hua Hotel to find Mei's friend Ning, who had been taken captive "not long ago?" These don't belong to the core mechanic, instead they provide their own tier of gameplay as well as the reason for shooting or sneaking your way round the game.

This opens out an important factor. Creating a context for your game, especially in a service, often requires us to think about the patterns of design that also exist at the level of the game mechanic. Here again we find patterns to resolve. However, rather than creating new mechanics to resolve these, we look for ways to encourage repeated use of the core mechanic.

Through this way of thinking your core mechanic can become a loop or perhaps more correctly a cog cycling forward, triggering the movement of another cog for every complete revolution. This could extend for many different cogs making it easy to extend the potential game experience for ever longer periods of time. It's that thinking that makes it possible for us to create games that can survive not just hours of play, but days, weeks, and even years of play. I'm not suggesting that we shouldn't introduce variation, but there is value in thinking about game design as a series of layers of engagement.

What's in a Game?

The use of narrative or context loops can be controversial and largely this comes down to the values designers place on narrative or gameplay elements. Part of this is the choice of language. The background of the game is part of its narrative, but the flow of play providing context can itself tell a story and it's hard not to call that the narrative of play. However, there is a core issue here too. Is the "story" a designer wants to tell as important as the game experience the user wants to play? The response is of course "It's the gameplay stupid!" However, if we are to make better more repeatable games we need to ensure that we create material that supports our context for our repeatable mechanics, that drives repeat play, and entertains in its own right. Players have to care about that story. Indeed I believe they have to consider that the game's narrative arc as so compelling that they need to return to the game and continue to play because they "have" to resolve that story. Furthermore, I believe that if we are to be a game designer, not just a games player, that we should have something to say about this artform.

Build it and They Will Come?

This sensation is vital if we want success for a game as a service. Only a tiny percentage of games succeed in breaking even and even those games that are downloaded, only a few are played more than once. The volume of games available on mobiles, tablets, PCs, and indeed consoles is so large at this point that we cannot assume that players will find our game, let alone that they will be as keen to keep on playing it as we were to make it. As designers we have to give players both a "pull" to want to play the game as well as a "push" to call them back. This is a critical issue, as if we don't get players back in the game we won't have an audience and more importantly all our efforts to create a great game will be wasted. Of course if we are using the Free2Play (F2P) model this means that even if we have downloads we won't be getting any revenue at all. This is why F2P games have (in the end) to be better than other games. It's a question of survival.

The Gossip Effect

There is a reason why soap operas manage to succeed over decades of daily shows, especially in urban societies. This TV format replicates the human desire to be tapped into the social gossip that we would have experienced in person in the context of village or tribal life. It's linked to social survival that we are on top of the latest news and indeed this can take the form of a game in its own right. Twitter and Facebook fulfill similar needs in many of us, including those who have no interest in the plots of the soaps.

Am I Missing Out?

Similarly if we wish to create successful games as a service we need them to create a sense of activity or change happening inside the world of that game in order to sustain our players' attention over extended periods of time. This means we need a "call to action" that reminds the player to return. This can be a simple notification just telling the player to return, however that quickly gets tiring and can actually be a good reason for many to delete your application. It's much better to have something in the gameplay that we desire that calls us back into play.

One of the most overused mechanics to create a reason to return is the energy mechanic. In this concept, players have a certain amount of energy they can use in any given playing session. Once this has been used up, they have to stop playing and wait till their energy has restored before being able to continue. This model is of course flawed in that we effectively shut players out of the game, requiring them to pay up or wait till they have more energy. However it does offer one really important thing in terms of game design; it created a real sense that the game's world was "persistent" and that while the player wasn't in the game, there was still something happening in that virtual space. There are other techniques we can use to replicate this sense of something mean- ingful happening in the world, including having other players (usually Facebook friends) come into your space to perform some minigame action that rewards both players.

Having a persistent world has other advantages. It creates a context for us to provide regular notifications to the player that relate to changes in that world that become meaningful to the player, rather than just sending sales messages. It also allows us to create stories where the play- ers' actions can contribute to the state of the game world; indeed they can feel part of the ongoing creation of that narrative.

Telling Better Stories

The interesting thing about the latest evolution of games design is that the focus is increasingly on the relationship between the mechanic and context loops that empower players to experience the story rather than have us tell them what's happening. There is some classic advice given to writers: "show, don't tell!" I believe this is just as important in game design. In general, we should avoid exposition and allow players to discover the experiences for themselves, not be told in neat little popup text boxes how their character feels or why they should play more.

Beyond the Context Loop

The concept of cogs driving other cogs doesn't stop with the context of the game. There are other elements that we have to consider which sit above both the mechanic and the context. This is the metagame and provides the last aspect of the anatomy of a game. However, rather than being a physical analogy to a part of the body, this is more like the psychology of the game "animal." The elements are not directly part of the game, but they profoundly influence the performance of the other parts. Indeed the metagame can complexly subvert the intentions of the designer as well as the general flow of the game.

It can be found in the social context that the player exists in while they play or from the "mode of use" of the devices that the player uses to experience it. The metagame can form from the behavior of the super-fans or even from the physical space surrounding the devices used—think of the shared space around a tablet or television set. All of these things remind us that the game doesn't exist in isolation, an idea we will return to in later chapters.

Identifying the Elephant

Throughout this chapter we have tried to break down what makes a game into its component parts. Taken apart, thinking about these elements allows us to get a handle on not only the challenges of game design but also how we can change our thinking to come up with solutions. Thinking of the art-style and game genre as the skin of the game reminds us how important it is for players to see the best of our game and that these concepts allow players to make sense of the shape of the game. Looking at the core mechanic as the bones of the game reminds us that there are "physical" principles at play that have to be highly tuned to support the playing experience. Thinking of success and failure as the muscles is more abstract and perhaps not the best analogy, however I like this way of thinking because it reminds me of what drives the movement of the bones of the game and that, over time, these motivations will tire. That brings us back to the rewards "nervous system," which provides the stimulus and the context, which supplies the "oxygen" to continue.

However, none of these elements alone are the game. Writing this chapter is like the story of the blind men trying to describe an elephant for the first time, where each one only gets to feel a single part.[11] It's only by pulling these elements together that we truly understand what our game looks like.

Notes

1 Although this is the hypothesis presented by Rafe Koster in A *Theory of Fun*, not everyone agrees that it's useful to reduce games to just patterns. However, I think it's a useful place to start so please bear with me.

2   There are modern rules for Senet that can be found online (http://legacy.mos.org/quest/pdf/senet.pdf), which are based on various tomb paintings and the discovery of playing boxes in various burials.

3   Ludo is based on Pachisi, a game from India around the sixth century, other variations include Sorry! http://en.wikipedia.org/wiki/Ludo_(board_game).

4   The idea that *Tetris* has a limited narrative is highly controversial. For me the realization that it has an abstract narrative came to me after a long argument with Nick Ryan and Simon Brislin (PlayStation Home), after a great lecture by Richard Bartle at GDC Online in Austin in 2010 (www.gdcvault.com/play/1013804/MUD-Messrs-Bartle-and-Trubshaw). The progression of colors and shapes to complete rows before our inevitable demise is a form of narrative that for me fairly accurately depicts the concept of mutually assured destruction of the late Cold War, not bad considering that the game's license was allegedly owned by the KGB. For more detailed thought on the argument about the narrative qualities of *Tetris* check out this article from Jack Post, www.ec-aiss.it/monografici/5_computer_games/3_post.pdf.

5   There is an argument that *Heavy Rain* isn't really a game, but is instead is a really advanced form of storytelling; either way its use of narrative flow warrants consideration.

6   I've never really understood where a rat might conceivably keep gold or some of the other curious winnings we find when we loot them.

7   American psychologist/behaviorist B.F. Skinner is widely considered to be one of the most influential psychologists of the twentieth century and invented the Operant Conditioning Chamber, known as the "Skinner Box." Check out www.simplypsychology.org/operant-conditioning.html.

8   There is a great piece on *Penny Arcade* describing the Skinner effect and making the case against its overuse. I think this underestimates the potential positive use of the technique, however the underlying message is sensible, http://www.penny-arcade.com/patv/episode/the-skinner-box.

9   Daniel Kahneman and Amos Tversky talked about the influence of loss aversion on the decision making process in their 1994 work *Choices, Values, Frames*, http://dirkberge mann.commons.yale.edu/files/kahnemann-1984-choices-values-frames.pdf. However, it's also important to note that in recent years the ideas of loss aversion have themselves been questioned. See http://papers.ssrn.com/sol3/papers.cfm?abstract_id=1578847.

10 I talk a lot about using psychological patterns in game design, such as the Skinner Box or loss aversion. This isn't a cynical thing. It's a realization that we need to understand human motivations. Actually, I think it's one of the most amazing things about playing games. We can explore the whole of the human experience and provide a safe way to "practice" our responses. Ignoring how players respond to stimulus would simply impair our ability to make better games.

11 The story of the blind men and the elephant has appeared in many forms but originates from the Indian subcontinent, http://en.wikipedia.org/wiki/Blind_men_and_an_elephant.

Exercise 3: What is the Mechanic?

In Chapter 3 we talked about breaking down the anatomy of a game and in particular about how we develop a language of play from the game mechanics. In this exercise we will explore the concept you developed in Exercise 1 and try to define how the core mechanic will function. This means we need to consider whether you are planning to create a game of emergence or progression, or some kind of hybrid. We need to understand the methods of interaction, what generates the challenges, and how we provide the feedback in terms of success or failure.

While you undertake this exercise I strongly recommend that you take time away from your PC and get your hands on paper, pencils, dice, counters, in fact any material that will help you explore the thought process of your game. Paper prototyping is incredibly useful and especially where take your physical materials (even if they are just scraps of torn paper) and try to explain the game to someone else.

Additionally, remember the target and secondary players you defined in Exercise 2. It remains important to ask yourself how this game mechanic will sustain their interest. How would you answer them if they ask "so what?" to every part of the mechanic design?

Summarize the core loop of your game mechanic:	
Start stage:	
Challenge stage:	
Resolution stage:	
Reward stage:	
Why is this repeatable?	

How will you realize your game in terms of:	
Target device:	
Principle control mechanism:	
Avatar or other focus:	
Type of camera used:	
2D/3D or variant:	
Art style:	
Measure of progress:	
Success criteria:	
Rewards:	
Consequence of failure:	
Reasons to repeat:	

WORKED EXAMPLE:

Summarize the core loop of your game mechanic:	Anthony has to solve a series of missions through the completion of memory matching minigames. The patterns become increasingly complicated to complete as Anthony increases in level (and becomes more confused).
Start stage:	Anthony is informed of a mission, e.g., his child hasn't gone to school or a burglary has gone wrong and he has to cover up the evidence.
Challenge stage:	Anthony has to search the location of the incident and collect items for the memory matching game in order to recreate the circumstances, without being discovered by roaming "enemies."
Resolution stage:	Anthony locates the memory matching objects that relate to the nature of the current mission and places them in the correct order (as required by the specific minigame) in his "brain." There will be many different copies of the same objects that he has to match, but the number reduces each time the player returns to the same location. He can continue to add additional matches as long as he has available "brain slots," but this increases the time taken and the battery life used to follow the player-defined paths.

(Continued)

Reward stage:	Upon completion Anthony is given a reward, typically a power-up or resource that can be used to extend the playing experience and is related to the nature of the task and to the nature of the opposition. Occasionally, he will get a match that relates to his lost girlfriend, helping complete his progression to the next tier of the game.
Why is this repeatable?	Each time Anthony returns to a level, the memory matching variations will have increased and he will have less capacity in his "brain" making it harder to resolve the puzzles.

How will you realize your game in terms of:	Finding Anthony is a mobile game featuring a cyborg mafia boss, played out on fake 3D room layout (2D with perspective). The player controls their avatar (Anthony) by drawing a path around this "room" and Anthony will make his way using the shortest path. When he is close enough to hidden tiles, the player can click on an object to see if there is a tile and what memory image it holds. These tiles will have been laid throughout the space, some more obviously than others. In the room may be other enemies who have to be avoided, something that becomes challenging if they cross the path that you have drawn for Anthony. Bonus points are given for each successful match you place in Anthony's "brain slots" as well as for the length of paths drawn by the player (provided the player doesn't use up all of the allocated battery life to draw them) as well as the time of play and the fewest number of missed clicks. Walking into enemies reduces the number of points you have gained so far and if this reaches zero the game "fails." The art style should be a comic variant of a dark near-future science fiction world. The "brain slots" used in play will use ideas of electronic memory failures, so we need not get too dark and personal, but still be able to use the narrative and playing mechanics to ask questions about living with mental illness.
Target device:	
Principle control mechanism:	
Avatar or other focus:	
Type of camera used:	
2D/3D or variant:	
Art style:	
Measure of progress:	
Success criteria:	
Rewards:	
Consequence of failure:	
Reasons to repeat:	

Chapter 4
Player Lifecycle

Breathe Life into Your Games

In the last chapter I used the analogy of anatomy to describe the component parts of a game. That discussion hopefully helps us think of games experiences as living things and I believe as designers it's our job to breathe life into play. In this chapter I want us to take this analogy further and make the hypothesis that, for the player, their game will go through a lifecycle and that understanding this lifecycle is a defining skill that separates successful games as a service design from box-products. Lifetime value is critical to success and essentially this comes down to sustaining the relationship between the game and the player over an extended time. That means that it is not good enough that a game have sufficient material to play in principle for the lifetime of the player, it has to adapt that content to the player's changing needs as their experience and commitment evolves.

Product Lifecycle 101

Considering games as a service also allows us to look at production as a journey. This means that we can spread the risk and production over an extended time period, initially releasing only sufficient functionality and content to satisfy the initial players.

But to begin to do that we have to know if there are any ways to predict the lifecycle of a game or its players. Fortunately, this is an area that has been extensively researched—the marketing discipline of product management.

The initial stage of any product or service begins with the concept, where we imagine the possibilities and identify customer needs that we can satisfy. There will follow a period of research and development where we test and realize the goods for our intended audience. Next is the "market introduction" stage. This might involve many stages from building the initial hype to creating anticipation to attract the early adopters. Assuming that process is successful the product will reach the "growth" stage. This generally involves broadening the brand appeal, attracting a wider more mass-market audience. Prolonging the growth stage requires ongoing innovation and the identification of new audiences. In time, however, all growth stages will come to an end as products reach the point of "maturity," where the product is established and indeed where further innovation becomes more difficult, perhaps even cannibalistic (i.e., where new adaptations compete with your own core product).

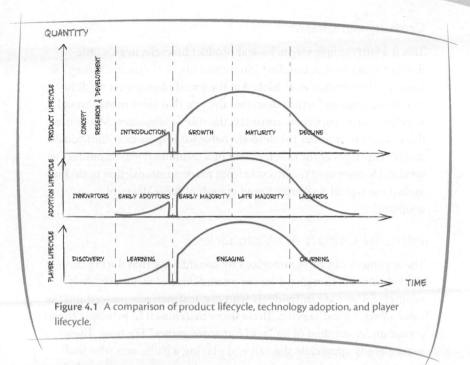

Figure 4.1 A comparison of product lifecycle, technology adoption, and player lifecycle.

Product Extensions

Sustaining the maturity stage is vital to the lifetime profitability of your product. Usually this needs constant vigilance and often involves the creation of product extensions, variations of the product designed to stimulate new interest from its users, as well as to attract any laggard users who have yet to try the product. These product extensions leverage the core product or perhaps the overarching brand and can range from an "improved flavor" to "family sized" packaging, indeed perhaps even introducing new products entirely leveraging the brand's values, such as when Dove, a moisturizer brand, introduced an antiperspirant.[1] Almost inevitably, even with the introduction of product extensions, product will eventually reach the "decline" stage. During this period, only a small proportion of total users can be retained, but if managed well and assuming that the costs to sustain the product are minimal, it is possible to enjoy a great deal of profit out of the long-tail decline of any product. If the decline stage is left unmanaged or allowed to continue beyond the viable lifetime, this can be costly.

Crossing the Chasm

This is a fairly simple way to look at product lifecycle; to go a little deeper we can look at Geoffrey Moore and his 1991 classic *Crossing the Chasm*.[2] This seminal work looked at the social phenomena of "diffusion of innovations," which describes the rate that ideas move through societies and, in particular, considers the role of advocates. Moore used this concept to consider the different behavior responses of individuals at different stages of the development of a technology-based product or service. He compared the lifecycle from market introduction to decline against the typical audiences found at each of these stages of adoption.

Hardcore Gamers Are Visionaries

The argument can be summarized by considering that during the market introduction phase we see an audience of visionary "early adopters." These are individuals who can instinctively understand the value of your good/service. These users match well in principle to our classic understanding of an "avid hardcore gamer" fan base. These users already appreciate the value of playing a game and who find it easier to suspend disbelief in order to play your game. Provided of course the game reaches a minimum standard they will "put up" with some behaviors that more mainstream users might reject. For example, a steep learning curve or frustrating tutorial might be more readily forgiven by hardcore players compared to more casual-minded players.

Casual Gamers Need Permission to Play

As we move from the market introduction phase and our early adopters, we start looking at the early maturity of the product/brand. It is this phase where we see a new kind of user known as the "early majority," who are made up of more pragmatic, often less committed users but who represent the largest revenue opportunity. Like our casual games players, these individuals need more handholding and support than the visionary early adopters (or hardcore gamers). Quite often these early majority users need us to provide safe, clear explanations of why they should change their current behavior and replace that with our product or service. In particular with luxury or entertainment services, like games, this means that they need to have some kind of permission to purchase or play. I use this idea of permission to explain the emotional difference in the decision-making process for mass-market users. They don't have to have a game. They choose to play a game where we have sufficient control over our other needs or (importantly) wish to escape from those other needs. This idea of "permission" for me came out of a research project we commissioned while I was working 3UK[3] running their mobile games portal. A survey inspired by my experience of talking to some of the earliest female only Quake clans back when I had been working at Wireplay.[4] This research looked at the adoption of games by female gamers and concluded that female gamers tended to select game-playing only after they had completed other activities that they felt they "had to complete." That they needed to give themselves "permission to play" and, interestingly, the genre of the game was less important than the "social context." In other words, if they could socialize with others during play, this would greatly increase the likelihood of choosing to play. All of this seems pretty obvious in hindsight, now that we have seen the rise of social games and percentage of female players using those games. However, there was something even more interesting in the survey. Male non-gamers showed almost exactly the same responses as female players.

From Product Lifecycle to Player Lifecycle

The lesson of this is that there is a significant gap, or chasm, between these early adopters and early majority in terms of their needs and ability to accept your product/service. In games, at least, this appears to relate to whether they are willing to give themselves 'Permission to Play'. That "chasm" is shown on the lifecycle curves as a slice cut out of the normal distribution curve. If we want our products/services to be successful we have to cross that chasm.

When you are running services another factor becomes clear. It's not just the services that experience a lifecycle. If you take the data of activity from players themselves and compare them from the date they started, we generally see a comparison which shows that players themselves have a lifecycle and this cyclical behavior also reflects the levels of engagement of those players.

The process for players starts before they are aware of the game itself. This is the discovery stage and the process of how the player engages with the game is crucial. There are many techniques we can use to attract the attention of the player, from advertising to encouraging friends to show their favorite games to each other. During this process we are setting expectations. We need to create a desire to play and create conditions that make it as easy as possible for that potential player to

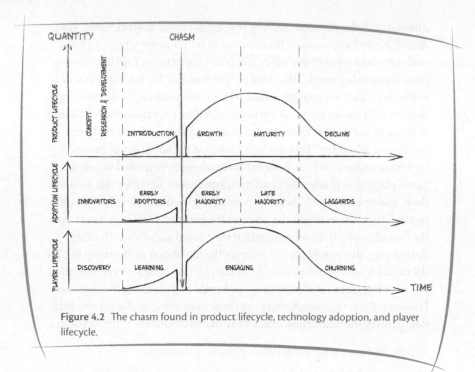

Figure 4.2 The chasm found in product lifecycle, technology adoption, and player lifecycle.

give themselves permission to invest their time and (hopefully) money. Success is measured by the proportion of players we manage to convert to not only installing the game, but also then running it. The limitations of some games promotions, particularly incentivized download, is that—unless handled well—these can trigger downloads motivated only by the reward, where the downloaded app is then immediately ignored or deleted. Our success in the download phase is measured by the number of users who run the application.

Time to Learn in a Safe Place

The next stage is the learning stage. This is where the player has first downloaded the app and is starting to learn about where, or whether, this game fits into their lifecycle. They are also learning about the flow of the game monetization and whether they can see the value in playing on, as well as how much they might wish to spend. This stage is critical and delicate, especially with the freemium model. At least with a paid-for game we have the motivation to get through the tutorial in order to get to the game experience we paid for. However, freemium games have no such invested value or utility to maximize. This means we have no reason to keep with that game other than our curiosity and expectations of entertainment. Anything that doesn't support the enjoyment of the player or their expectation of delight will inhibit their engagement. We have very short time to get them into playing and shouldn't waste that by building in levels of unnecessary menu systems, tutorials or Quick-Time videos. If we don't delight these players the chances are that they will look elsewhere for something to entertain them. This is just the start of the learning process and in later chapters we will go into more detail on how we can evolve the player engagement up to the point where we have built sufficient trust so that they are willing to make the transition to the next stage, "engaging." The learning process is an important stage if we are to convert a player to become a repeat player or repeat payer; just like with Moore's "chasm" we have to help the learning player evolve to the point where they treat our game as part of their lifestyle.

Repetition, Repetition, Repetition

Repetition is vital to building habit and commitment to our game. If we can't create that repetition, we won't achieve the potential lifetime value which is so vital to the success of games as a service. Repetition is only the start of course as during the "engaging" stage we also want to focus on converting players to start spending money on our game. Only if we have demonstrated the value of investing time into the experience of our game will we be able to provide the conditions where they will be willing to pay. We actively want players to feel committed to continue to play as long and as regularly as they feel the game entertains them before we really start to consider asking them to pay. Some developers have been successful in pushing for earlier revenue, however that is often at the expense of the lifetime value. The better alternative is to realize that it is during this "engaging" stage that our players are most connected with our content. They have taken our game into their lifestyle and will happily repeat that experience over their playing lifetime. They already trust and understand the experience and will return our investment with their time and/or money.

Money For Nothing

One of the hardest things to accept about the Free2Play (F2P) model is that the vast majority of players will never pay. This is difficult for many people to understand. The problem largely comes down to the fact that most us assume that the effort we put in has a direct value. Just because we put hundreds of hours into the creation of a product doesn't mean our product is "worth" thousands of pounds to the buyer. The product is only worth what the buyer is willing to pay. This can work in our favor too. A product that is cheap to produce but that everyone wants will be highly profitable. I don't want to go too far into the talk of monetization now, that will be covered later in the book. However, it's important to think of "engaging" as the most valuable life-stage, even though that's not just in terms of direct cash. Committed regular non-payers are as important to the success of any game as the highest-spending users. Without them, we don't create the social context that makes it worthwhile for the high spenders to pay for our game. Additionally, the longer we retain these players the greater the opportunity we will have to eventually convert them.

It Takes 8–12 Days to Engage

During my time at Papaya Mobile we looked at the performance of the best monetizing social mobile games and saw that average a typical high-spending, regularly repeat-playing, "whale" user (which we defined as someone who spent $100+ each month for at least three months) didn't start spending until after 8–12 days had passed. When you look at the data for your game, can you predict which of your new players are going to become these high spenders? If we can't engage players for this length of time, or don't offer enough content, then we are probably missing a highly valuable audience. It's vital to understand and sustain all the different cohorts (or segments) of your audience and look for the best way to maximize their engagement stage. Freeloader players in particular provide a hugely valuable role in the ongoing discovery of your game as they often share their playing experiences with their friends in person and through social media. Finally, freeloaders who have gone past the learning stages of the game are also generally quite comfortable to see advertising within the game—assuming its placement is appropriate. In particular, they may even readily seek out opt-in incentivized advertising, if available, in order to gain in-game currency in order to further sustain their enjoyment of our game. This is a direct revenue source, but more importantly it extends the retention of that player and teaches them to use the in-game currency earned to learn how to value spending money. Making a great game is about engagement not just monetization, and that also brings acquisition and retention.

Mature Content

The earning stage, like the maturing stage of product lifecycle, is essential to the lifetime profitability of any game. Our objective is to sustain the players in this stage for as long as possible and this takes a great deal of effort and development. We need to consider events and activities, as well as the perpetual addition of new content and appropriate new features. Even simple download games feel "dead" if the app hasn't been updated in several weeks, services need to feel alive every day—ideally more frequently. At 3UK we discovered that the average frequency of return to the game store was directly related to how frequently we updated the site. In the end we managed to find a way to update the front page every four hours, significantly increasing our sales. The same affect can be seen in games as services.

Plan for Change

Obviously, with the technical constraints as well as the various platform processes, it's not practical to create a pipeline of new activity to constantly update the experience with new material; that would be both costly and a huge resource commitment. However, it is possible to make the game feel like it constantly changes with a few simple preprogrammed changes. In order to build and reinforce habits, it's useful to consider how you can create regular predictable changes that build delight and then complement these with apparently random moments of irregular rewards, ideally within the context of the game narrative.

All Things Come to an End

However, this won't continue forever. In time players will leave the service, we tend to call this "churning." Managing churning users is just as important as any other part of the lifecycle. We want the best possible outcome for our players, not least as we need to be able to plan our resource commitments and still be able to sustain any remaining players as long as practical. Additionally, if players are content with their experience playing our games, we have a greater chance to bring them back to play other games we make, perhaps even creating a level of anticipation that would otherwise be expensive to reproduce. Also if we manage their departure, we have more chance to turn this into an opportunity for additional revenue through advertising or, better still, convert this into new users through cross-promotion. Ideally, churning players will continue to recommend our game to their friends. If on the other hand we leave players feeling exploited or that we have squeezed every penny out of them they will tell other people about their bad experience. That negative feedback is poisonous (assuming we want to have a long career making games) and players are vastly more inclined to tell people of a bad experience rather than a good experience. This is essentially the same effect that comes from relying too heavily on "Skinner Box"-style techniques; players feel exploited if they feel they continued playing longer than was "good" for them.

The Soul of a Service

Thinking of a game as an organism means we have to take into account the different life stages. These aren't just convenient distinctions to help us think about the strategy of development but also help us in terms of thinking about the evolution of the type of entertainment that those players want to experience over time. It allows us to think of the game as a living, evolving thing that needs sustainable conditions if it is going to survive and thrive. Using the perspective of the player lifecycle from discovering, learning, engaging and churning helps us to apply a different mindset to each stage of the player's experience. It requires us to accept that a player's needs will change over time as their relationship with the game changes and that we have to adjust our approach if we wish to retain them as their engagement evolves. These are factors that we need to take into account not only in the design of the ongoing support of the game, but also in terms of the design of the playing experience itself; especially in terms of the context and metagame aspects of game design.

More than that as we launch our game we will find that it will have to adapt to its surroundings and we will see it change as we adjust the parameters, hone the mechanics, reward systems, and success criteria. Watching the player lifecycle allows us to evolve the game in line with the needs of our players. It's the soul[5] of games as a service.

Notes

1   Technically the introduction of all new products using the same brand is a "brand extension" or "line extension." If you want to investigate this further, it's worth checking out works such as *Strategic Brand Management: Building, Measuring, and Managing Brand Equity* by K.L. Keller.

2   Geoffrey Moore's *Crossing the Chasm: Marketing and Selling High Tech Products To Mainstream Customers* was initially released in 1991 and remains one of the most influential

studies on entrepreneurial marketing. It is one of the few marketing principles I have
continually relied on throughout my marketing career, not just in games.

3 3UK is shorthand for the UK Mobile Phone Operator Three, part of the Hutchison
Whampoa group. I was responsible for the games offering there between 2001 and 2006.
There were a lot of firsts which we were able to do during my time there from the first
mobile in-app purchase solution (Rent Games), first 3G realtime multiplayer games
(a FPS called Lock'n'Load) as well as the first Video game reviews channel on mobile.

4 Wireplay was an online gaming service using dial-up modem based connectivity. The
project led by Colin Duffy and Richard Warren came out of British Telecom's experiments
with video on-demand based in Milton Keynes in the UK. It missed being the world's first
such service by just two weeks when MPlayer launched in the USA.

5 As an atheist it's hard to come up with a good definition of a soul, but for me it's a way of
looking at a thing as a whole, rather than just the sum of its parts. I use it here because
it allows me to propose a difference between the lifecycle and the metagame. The metagame allows us to consider the role of the environment from within the context of the
experience, hence my analogy with the psychology of the game. The lifecycle is a different
kind of design influence. It's about the players' engagement and how the relationship
evolves over time.

Exercise 4: What is the Context Loop?

Following on from Exercise 3, where we looked at the mechanic loop, in this exercise we are going to focus on the context loop. This allows us to think about how we are going to sustain our audience over the longer term and how we give them purpose and progression. To do this well we should try to understand the changing needs of the player and to find ways to encourage them to become even deeper involved with the game experience. The purpose of the context loop is to sustain the life of the game over time, creating reasons for the player to continue to want to return and engage. Ideally we will create a positive form of the "Crack-Berry" effect, where players feel that they might be missing out when they aren't playing the game (for more on this, see Chapter 5).

To help us with this process let's use a cut-down version of the hero's journey[1] as a tool to model the essential aspects of a narrative model. The first stage is the "call to adventure." In this situation it's about how we draw the player into our game and how we explain the mechanics of play and excite them about the possibilities of the game. There is an argument that at each new tier of the game we should introduce new playing methods, renewing the call and reinvigorating the player.

The next stage is the "awareness of challenge." In our case this is about how we introduce the player to new variations and increasing complexity. This is still a handholding process and may include the support of a "mentor" figure if that proves useful. This process doesn't have to lead the player by the nose with a step-by-step path, we can use alternative missions, side quests, even a complete narrative sandbox to play in. But we still want a sense of purpose and progression.

After that the progression commences in earnest and we have a series of "challenges and improvements," which allow us to trace the player's progression and the rate at which they approach the "boss level." That approach should be designed to draw the player ever closer to that larger goal with the knowledge that it will be truly challenging, but with the greatest reward. We need to understand whether our context loop approach will directly signpost the boss level, or if instead we build up the suspense and simply foreshadow the inevitable showdown. The term "boss" is intentionally derivative, there may be no traditional enemies or bosses to beat, indeed the idea of a "level" might have no direct relevance, but that doesn't mean we don't need narrative tension and you should consider this whatever the equivalent for your game. The final stage is the "transformation" of your character, which takes them up to the next tier of engagement. There may be new goals, new abilities and new narrative arcs to follow, but we should relish the moment of triumph after the boss level before moving onto the next step in the narrative.

As I continue to stress it's vital that we consider the replayability[2] of your game. I don't mean just is it possible to repeatable the experience. I choose to define that term in a way where I mean that each return to the experience feels like a new game session. Repetition is dull and lifeless, replay value brings something fresh each time the game is played.

Summarize the context loop of your game mechanic:	
Call to adventure:	
Awareness of challenge:	
Challenges and improvements:	
Boss level:	
Transformation:	
Why is this replayable?	

Mapping out the stages is just the start of course and we have to think about how we will in practice deliver our context loops.

How will you realize your context loop in terms of:	
Sense of purpose:	
Reasons to return:	
Measurable progression:	
Narrative arc:	
Alternative paths:	
Graphical representation:	
Cogs within cogs:	
Why am I missing out?	

WORKED EXAMPLE:

Summarize the context loop of your game mechanic:	Anthony as the boss for his family has to build his reputation in the community and ensure that his subordinate Capos are doing the same. However, his Capos are asserting their own authority and one by one, region by region he has to regain his control over each part of the city. At the same time he is distracted by different family members calling on his time and resources to resolve more trivial family matters. Anthony has to keep earning "happiness" and "status" otherwise for each day that passes his family become more difficult and his status is diminished (locking him out from other districts).
Call to adventure:	Anthony has been in a car crash where he lost consciousness. He has been treated for his obvious injuries, but has lost his memory and has no information about why he lost consciousness. There is an image of a missing girlfriend in his mind, which he can't tie down or shake.
Awareness of challenge:	As Anthony returns to work he has a series of missions that allow us to demonstrate to the player the various ways he can play the game and how these contribute to his control of the city as well as how "happy" his family life is.
Challenges and improvements:	Once Anthony has played through the core areas of the central city district, he start getting an increasing number of alerts for missions all around the district. Some of these will foreshadow a narrative boss challenge to his authority in that district. The challenge might relate to his family, to the family or the civil authorities. New missions will continue to appear on the district map as fast as they are resolved until Anthony defeats the challenge for that district.
Boss level:	The boss level will present a much more significant challenge than usual levels and may indeed consist of multiple rounds as well as different variation of play to resolve. Often these boss levels will introduce a new power-up that can be used to assist the player compete against the boss.

(Continued)

Transformation:	As Anthony advances he start to lose "brain" slots, which makes it harder to get bonus scores by exceeding the number of matches needed to complete the mechanic. However, these "lost" slots can be filled instead with the "power-ups" they get as a reward during play, but making them permanent (at least till they are removed—which destroys them). The power-ups can be collected and multiple duplicate cards sacrificed to obtain more powerful boosts (which can of course be purchased in booster packs).
Why is this replayable?	Defeating the boss challenge for each district not only unlocks the next neighboring districts but it also unlocks a clue to the mystery surrounding the missing girlfriend; there will usually be 3–4 clues to unlock the next part of her story, but these have to be pieced together by the player like a jigsaw puzzle.

How will you realize your context loop in terms of:	The context loops for Finding Anthony is a series of maps showing locations related to potential crimes, family incidents and civil authority. Each accessibly location will have a ticking clock showing how much time remains for Anthony to resolve the problem and how much "happiness" or "status" he will obtain if he completes that puzzle in time. Some puzzles will pop up with special daily bonuses including unique daily missions with unique variations of play. These elements all create reasons to return or miss out on an opportunity to reach your score faster.
Sense of purpose:	
Reasons to return:	
Measurable progression:	
Narrative arc:	
Alternative paths:	
Graphical representation:	
Cogs within cogs:	
Why am I missing out?	
	The art style of the game is a kind of retro science fiction; slightly dark with Blade Runner-like qualities and the maps and location interiors will reflect that. Anthony gets to see how much "happiness" and "status" he has, which measures his progression and how much he needs in order to access the boss challenge.

(Continued)

| | The context model is scalable for each new district although there would be limits to the scale of the world based on the number of "brain slots" and the narrative arc for the "missing girlfriend." |
| | Once a district has been completed, there will still be missions you can return to in order to ensure that you maintain the "happiness" and "status" in that district— like maintaining the spinning plates. |

Notes

1 The hero's journey is a tool widely used by writers as a template for the progression of their characters through their stories. It's a deceit on the principle of the monomyth, the idea that all heroic stories are essentially variations of the same story, http://en.wikipedia.org/wiki/Monomyth.

2 Not everyone likes the word "replayability," http://iam.benabraham.net/2010/09/replayability-is-not-a-word.

Chapter 5
The Rhythm of Play

Finding our Rhythm

In the last chapter we tried to identify the soul of games as a service and we postulated that the player lifecycle helps us to differentiate this approach to games design. The next question is to find a practical application of this thinking and to see how this can help us provide a framework to improve our designs.

The problem is that we can only really understand the specific details of the player lifecycle for our game if we stand back and look historically (and dispassionately) across the collective behavior of our players. That's not particularly useful as long as the game remains actively played and, worse still, the very act of analyzing requires us to change our attention from the detail that makes up the player experience, instead looking to the higher level patterns of flow through the game.

Focus on What Matters

A more practical approach is to look for the transitional phases such as the move from discovering to learning that is found in the data from access to our page on the app store to the initial download and in the first moments of play. Then we can look at the transition from learning to engaging, where we see how the player goes from playing the precarious first time (perhaps even the first few times) to the point where they are playing regularly and ideally multiple times per day (depending on the device they are using to play). As part of this stage we can look at the process by which players convert from playing to paying. I'll come back to that in the last few chapters of the book. Finally, I want to consider the end-game, where the play moves from engaging to churning. How they leave the game as positively as possible matters if we want to sustain our brand and be able to re-engage that player for different games.

The Player's Journey

In these places we find patterns of behavior that help those players move more easily onto their next stage. When we look through the player's journey, particularly the first-time user experience, it seems to me that these have a rhythm that we can build on. There seems to be a series of cycles that repeat and layer upon each other to create a composite experience, ideally one that reinforces habitual play and deeper enjoyment of the game. I like to call these habit-forming patterns the "rhythm of play."

The rhythm has to start quickly if the player is going to get a chance to become entranced by your game. There is a tentative delicate moment that begins at the first point the player encounters the game. The name of your game has to quickly define their expectations about the game that, combined with the icon you use, has to be instantly identifiable. These two simple things have to be compelling and memorable, not just to download the game, but to ensure that it will be clicked a second and third time once it has been downloaded. This isn't an easy task when there you have only 11 characters and a 57×57 pixel icon (114×114 on HD devices), especially given that there are over 900,000 existing variations. We have to think of reasons for players to want to press that icon the first time; of course much of the reason they will press it time and again will come down to the game itself.

First Impressions

The first time the player launches the game is a kind of exploration where everything is new. Every click, every splash screen image, every inconsistency compared to their expectations will jar and risk them going off and playing something else instead. Unlike a premium game, players have not spent any money yet. They have no investment or "utility to maximize" in the game at this point, just the effort they have so far taken and the anticipation they have for our game. Any undue effort they have to go through undermines even that limited utility and you risk them getting so frustrated that they don't give your game a fair shot.

This is the equivalent of the first date. You can't expect them to make a commitment at this point. Don't ask them to change their Facebook status or otherwise register until you have at least taken them out to dinner . . . I mean, until you have made sure that they enjoy the game.

There is no clear evidence over how long is too long. Personally I like to say that we have about six seconds to grab a player's attention or we lose them. This isn't particularly scientific, however, it does reflects the kind of design guidelines used when you create direct mail or newspaper headlines. Headline writers know the importance of catching attention and drawing people in and we have to learn to do similar thing with the way we create our user interfaces. Ideally players should not be faced with choices they don't yet understand or which present dilemmas, like having to play with other real people before they understand the rules of the game. We need the transition from launching the app to starting to play as quickly and as comfortably as possible if we want to build up retention rapidly.

Measuring Your Heartbeat

Getting players started is just the opening bars of our rhythm of play, but allows us to introduce them to the principle underlying beat. The first play needs to introduce them to the core repeatable mechanic of play, the heartbeat of play if you like. We start with an objective, act upon it, and gain a reward; this is a pattern we then repeat throughout the game. There are alternative methods than just loops, for example the hand-crafted one-time-only puzzles used in classical adventure games. However, the loop is particularly effective for freemium as its repetitive nature helps create positive reinforcement in terms of play.

This Isn't About Addiction

We mentioned the idea of Skinner Boxes and operant conditioning in Chapter 3, which looks at the idea of creating schedules of reinforcement of behavior. This type of thinking while hugely useful is also quite controversial and makes some people think that Free2Play design can become manipulative. I largely disagree not least as there is firstly an assumption that "entertainment" has the same compulsive effect as addictive factors such as food, sex, money, and drugs—all of which affect the lower level "need states."[1] There is the suggestion that higher need states like entertainment don't (by and large) have a limit by which we can satisfy our appetite, unlike our consumption of food for example. However, as we also discussed in that chapter, the form of entertainment we are offering through pattern-matching does indeed tire over time. If we know how to solve the pattern so well we can do it subconsciously then we stop getting the same enjoyment. Because of this I disagree that we are attempting to create some kind of a Pavlovian response[2] in the same way that ringing a bell starts a dog salivating. But that doesn't mean we don't want to recognize the way humans react to conditions that encourage the player to want to make our game a regular hobby.

The First Minute

The early pattern of play for games as a service is often most successful when featuring short repeated plays through the mechanic itself. This lets the player quickly get feedback on their performance and allows them to learn and get the positive payoff from their initial success. That doesn't mean we can't have longer loops of play that may themselves repeat several times in order to resolve a larger section of the game narrative. For example, I may have to battle many waves of enemies or plant and harvest several items before I complete the objective needed to move to the next stage of play. However, if we are going to respond to the needs of the "learning" user then we need to appreciate the benefits of having an immediate sense of meaningful reward, directly attributed to their actions, within the first minute or so of playing. This ability to complete actions within short periods is particularly important with mobile device games. We commonly use our phones in circumstances where we are at risk of being interrupted. If we can't have satisfying bursts of entertainment, or if our expectations are that the playing cycle will take too long to get into, this will limit the audience accessing our game. Although it might seem less relevant for tablet devices, which are less prone to interruption, or consoles, where we deliberately set aside hours to indulge, these short loop cycles are still valid as they provide a limit to the duration of intense focus needed to compete each puzzle or obstacle before moving on to the next. Otherwise it can get to be a bit much for some players. We all need save points or moments when we can relax a little in the game.

Building on Success

Once we have succeeded in giving the player a positive sense of success with their first play through our game loop, we have to build on that to progress. We need to move on to the second or third cycle of play, building on that initial engagement and foreshadowing the delights that the player can enjoy if they continue to play.

Although these loops are easy to repeat in principle, if we don't adjust them over time they can quickly become boring if we can consistently solve them. We need these puzzles or loops to evolve as the player becomes more familiar with the style of play. This typically means we introduce a sense of escalating challenge that builds on each subsequent loop, adding either greater difficulty or some other sense of progression. This can include the use of stronger opponents, new level designs, greater complexity, or new characters to encounter.

Making Progress

However, we should not just focus on the increase in the resistance of the mechanic to the player's increase in understanding; we also need to present a sense of advancement or progression to the player. This often takes the form of introducing new tactical options, the use of new weapons or moves that allow them to solve different puzzles, or perhaps just introduces choices that add dilemma to the outcome. This is particularly effective if the progression of the player introduces ambiguity into the strategy for play, such as choosing where to spend any experience points you gain.

Don't Be Greedy

The important thing is that we don't have to rush into making money out of our players. Indeed it could be counterproductive to try to monetize the wrong things too early. We need to build up confidence in the game and a desire to continue playing as a lifestyle choice, a hobby. This kind of habitual behavior only comes from players returning to the game repeatedly and feeling that they can both trust the service and see that value of spending money in that service. We can't afford to be discordant or otherwise disrupt the rhythm of play. Instead we have to foreshadow reasons why buying goods in the future would be a good investment in the game the players are enjoying.

Playing the core loop several times in the first playing session is important in order to ensure that the player fully understands how to play the game and so we know that they find it suitably enjoyable. However, if we want to build a sustainable game as a service, this is just the first step forward. The next challenge is to find a way to keep players coming back to the app time and again. This is not a task to be underestimated. This is why we need a rhythm of play to create cycles that effectively demand the player restart our app again and again. Just having a "nice" game isn't enough. Looking at the behavior on mobile platforms as well as on PC with stream, even if a game is downloaded, there is no guarantee that it will be played. Even if it is played there is no guarantee that it will be used twice. Very few games are ever played multiple times. Think about what that means. Unless you charge upfront, something that always impacts the proportion of people who download your game, you are dependent on repeat use in order to be commercially successful. If only a tiny proportion of games are every reused at all, you need your app to be one of them. That means we have to stop being squeamish about encouraging repeat play.

The "CrackBerry" Effect

So what can we do to create reasons for the player to return after their initial playing session? A compelling narrative or context can help, as can the desire to complete the next puzzle or to progress your character through different levels. These are important ideas, but they are hard to make truly compulsive, especially with all the noise out there from other games, media, and, of course, real-life pressures.

If you had a BlackBerry when they were at their peak of popularity you might already be familiar with the kind of experience that truly compels the user to return to an experience. This device was the first to actively use the buzz feature to alert you whenever a new email, meeting, or event was happening. The term "CrackBerry" became commonly used to compare the behavior of BlackBerry users, unable to resist any incoming message, with users of crack cocaine. Not an entirely flattering idea, however, it does reflect the very human response to partial knowledge and the importance of resolving patterns as well as information. When that little device buzzed it might be a spam email or a summons from my boss at the time. The only way to tell was to pull out the phone and check. Doing this while out on a date with my wife never went down well and I quickly learned to turn off the notifications that weren't important. However, despite the negative description, having this tool was an amazingly positive thing and vastly improved my ability to keep up-to-date with what was important to me. It just happened to also mean that I couldn't be without that device.

Am I Missing Out?

We need something about our game that taps away in the player's subconscious like that old song we hear on the radio and find ourselves humming all day long. Something that at the same time reminds us of the fun we are missing out on. The feeling that there is something going on inside the game world helps encourage us to return, knowing that otherwise we might be missing out. This is of course a fine line (as with all of these concepts) because if I feel I have missed out too much then I won't return, and if I feel that the game is nagging me to return at its convenience not mine, I will simply turn off the notifications or, worse still, delete the game.

Building Compulsion into Play

There are many different approaches to how this can work. It can start in the core mechanic, be part of the context of the game or even part of the metagame. The most common way technique we have seen in social games so far is the use of energy. What if the player has a limit to the number of actions they can perform in a given period of time or for some reason (as suitable for the game) they have to wait before a tool they are using will recharge.

Either method creates a time delay or "friction" to the way the players progresses. The influences the player's decision-making process in the game and creates a playing mechanism in its own right around which action is best. All good. However, it also happens to create a moment that stops their ability to play further, at least until that energy replenishes either by paying or waiting. This also happens to cover up when the developer doesn't have enough content to satisfy the lifetime of the player (but that's not something I'd recommend).

The Friction Factor

Friction is a normal factor with a game design. It allows us to managed the pace and flow of a game and where this is "player-directed"[3] it can be a powerful tool to enhance the game, but there is a very fine line between friction and frustration. Knowing that the energy will recharge over time means that in order to maximize my utility (existing investment) in the game so I need to return just as soon as the recharge has completed. Missing this timeframe has an opportunity cost but usually doesn't actually cause me to lose any gameplay asset. However, it has become overused and many players can become cynical and lose trust with the developer when they see it in a game.

An alternative to energy, and one famously used in social freemium games on Facebook, is the "harvesting" mechanic. In this case the player decides which crop (it could easily be a car repair or tower defense building) to plant in their farm (or garage, or defense base) and knows that this will take a predictable period of time to complete, making it available to harvest or use. As we talked in Chapter 3, *FarmVille* included a "withering" concept where, if the object has not been collected in a specific time-frame, this becomes useless or requires me to pay or get intervention from a friend. If you want to use this technique, you need to think carefully about how to communicate this to your user base and find a way to make sure this is seen as a part of the tactics of play rather than just a frustrating experience that punishes the player, encouraging them to lose interest and churn early. It is a natural for designers to look to monetize energy or friction, but it's a pretty transparent technique that players have come to deeply resent.

Are We Running Out of Energy?

Despite how unpopular it has become to use energy and friction to monetize your game, I argue these techniques still have real value to create the sense of activity in the game which the player is missing out on, something I believe is more valuable than the money they can earn. There remains a debate over whether you should stop your players playing or not. This might seem obvious, but stopping your players playing when they want to is generally a bad thing. However, managing their access to engaging with the game can intensify the experience and create a compelling driver to repeat play, particularly if these restrictions are highly targeted.

Take for example a *Monkey Island*-style classical adventure. What if clue objects could only be used three times every ten minutes?[4] This would transform the way that you try to solve puzzles in a point-and-click adventure and encourage a more thoughtful response to the puzzle rather than having players depend on the brute force solution of repeated clicking on every aspect of the screen.

Alternatively, take *Real Racing* 3 from EA. It takes time to service your car and, although you can pay to speed this up, it's often easier to simply switch to another car while you are waiting. That encourages me to vary the style of play and the nature of the experience I have while playing. It does more than leave me aware that my car might be fixed when I stop playing, it also reminds me of the other races and playing values of the game.

Of course this kind of approach is not for every game or every player, but I'm sure as a designer you can see the potential benefits of using friction wisely from a pure gameplay perspective.

I'm Not in the Mood

At this point it's probably worth discussing mode, mood, and pace. The flow of a game is rarely static and when we look at the playing experience we are trying to create in mechanical terms such as "loops" or "cogs," it's hard to remember the importance of the intensity and emotional experience we are trying to create. This isn't strictly part of the anatomy of the game, it's more about the rhythm, which is why I'm bringing it up here. Personally I happen to play lots of different games, almost at the same time.[5] Mood often drives my choice of game as well as the "mode of use" I am currently in. Mode being the relationship between where I am, what devices I have access to, whether

I am connected or not, as well as the impact my physical location has on my playing choices, e.g., in the living room with my family. Mode determines largely practical considerations while by contrast my mood reflects the emotional decision-making, which is largely drawn to less obvious conclusions. For example, subject to my mood, the cathartic gloom of a horror story might well be more rewarding than a high-octane rush or the sweet indulgence of a candy-colored world. Mood often makes us behave is a way different from our usual approach, making us appear to behave like a different user-segment (or cohort) than we would usually expect. For example sometimes I don't want highly intense experiences, sometimes I am looking for trivial distraction. Much of the time I am not directly aware of my mood but this will still be reflected in my game choices as well as how I respond to the way the game delivers content. Curiously, although we often want a game to help us journey through a particular mood state, this is rarely a static proposition, and where the game takes us forward emotionally we often find ourselves lost in its story. I suspect this is part of why games are so powerful at engaging us.

Pace is directly connected with the rhythm of play and has a musical pattern to its design. Many equate the patterns of building tension, harmony, energy, or relaxation to concepts from music theory. Pace has a role in sustaining interest as well as punctuating the narrative or context, but it also acts like a mirror to the mood delivered by the game. More than that, it helps players push forward on their emotional journey.

Different games will have different patterns of play peculiar to the context of the experience but what matters is that this pace should adjust as the play continues. Players will become bored if the pace and mood of play don't vary, just as much as it will alienate them if the pace and mood vary too greatly and clash with the context of the game.

Keeping Up the Pace

Pace relies on forces which direct the player's attention. This might start with the stick of an enemy behind them or the carrot of a reward they can acquire just ahead. This is important as there is a great deal of difference between the way we make decisions while calm and logical, as opposed to when we are hot and under tension. Stimulating players' emotions[6] can impact the way that they act during play and this can make for deeper enjoyment and a greater opportunity to fail. A great example of this is the tongue-twister, as many of us know how infuriating these can be when we are rushing or under the influence of alcohol. Time can also play an important factor, just as a limitation in the number of moves (or indeed energy). On the other hand, pace can be reduced to enhance the relaxation derived from a game. Creating a sense of awe about the location where the play takes place or a building an impression of upcoming dread, perhaps of a known enemy just up ahead, can do wonders to slow down the pace of a game. Even the simple mechanics involved in different action mechanics can influence the pace and mood of a game. Even the smooth movements used when harvesting goods in *HayDay* contributes to the pace of the game that players experience and this technique affects the game for the better. I'm less interested in story exposition, which although can help slow the pace down, often does so at the expense of the game. I believe we should try to "experience not tell" in games.

Pace, like mood, needs to vary throughout play in order to sustain the interest of the players. This means we need to take note of the patterns of interaction, how consistently we repeat them and what patterns we can create that take the player on an emotional journey while they enjoy our game.

A great example of this for me is the way *CounterStrike* plays through the intensity of a counterterrorist action, with forces moving rapidly toward choke points in order to take out the enemy, followed by a few minutes of downtime between battles which allows them to chat and re-equip before kicking back into the intensity. There are musical parallels here for me with the Soft>Loud>Soft>Loud associated with grunge rock. Of course different games resonate with different musical forms. It's too complex a subject for us to cover in enough detail here, but it's worth checking out various articles and books on the subject.[7]

The Lure of Other People

Sometimes it's not the game mechanics themselves that encourage us back into the game. The biggest compulsion can come simply from the knowledge that our friends (and other people like us) are coming back to play. Social play has been a big influence for many computer games. Games like *Singstar* encourage shared play in the same room, while games such as *Quake* or *Counterstrike* thrived on real-time connected servers.[8] Social Facebook games like *FarmVille* and *Zombie Lane* encouraged asynchronous connections that had a simple low-level of interaction that benefited both sides. Even relatively simple web games like *Tribal Wars* from Innogames[9] include a level of persistence where the actions of other players can have a direct effect on all the other users in due course. If you know your game might be affected your fellow players—whether they attack your village, water your plants, or tune the engine of your car—it creates a reason to return. Again we have to be careful about the type of consequences we want to build into our games, but the awareness of other players acting on the game world while we are not there can be quite compelling, especially if those people matter to us.

Social play is more than just a reason to return. It helps reinforce our expectations and values associated with playing a game, and it can in the end become a driver for deeper engagement in its own right.

Don't Let Me Forget

Although there are many more techniques out there to build reasons to return, do not underestimate the value of the appropriate use of the notification system. Add to that the impact of regular predictable new content releases or functional updates to trigger a desire for players to re-engage. We should use every technique suitable for our game and create an appointment mechanism to encourage players to regularly and predictably return to the game, as long as it remains meaningful to the players.

Stop Nagging

We have to create this as a benign process designed to encourage repeated play. We can't afford to do this in a way that upsets or annoys players. The last thing we need is allegations that we are being manipulative. Long-term lifetime value depends on trust and if our objective is to get as much money as possible, rather than to make a better game, we will be found out and lose out.

If we get the balance right we will have succeeded in building the rhythm upon rhythm. This starts with the core mechanic, building with the minute of play, further building with the context loops. We have to keep our interconnected rhythms going and harmonious so we can help players fully realize their enjoyment of our game over an extended period of time.

Patience Will Pay Off

We need players to keep playing our game for days or weeks to realize the full benefits of their engagement. The biggest spenders in social mobile games seem to take between eight to twelve days before they start spending any money and if we get the model right they will continue to spend over many months.

Eight days of repeat play for a mobile game is a massively long time and we can't just rely on escalating difficulty or simple appointment mechanisms to guarantee that players will sustain their interest in our game. To achieve this we need to build a rhythm and progression that provide ongoing purpose and drive for the player to continue their game over the longer term. This generally uses that part of the anatomy of the game I described as the "context" but the specific tools we use can vary widely.

Wheels within Wheels

The basic principle is to build up mechanics as cogs, feeding into the next tier of cog in line with the context of the game or the overarching metagame, giving players a sense of narrative or progression along the way. This typically means we find a reason to repeat the Core Mechanic as separate steps building up to another cyclical objective but at the context level. One example of a context loop might be found in an MMO quest where an non-player character (NPC) asks me to obtain an item for them. Each step to complete that quest involves me encountering a number of enemies who I have to dispatch until I finally reach the boss encounter and resolve that. This mission could easily be a series of connected puzzles or even a series of different layouts of a casual match-three game. Each stage is a separate use of the core loop mechanic with its own rewards, but if all the stages are complete I gain an extra reward from the context loop. This is potentially endlessly repeatable, but will often form parts of a finite ladder of progression or in the case of *Candy Crush Saga from King*,[10] a lengthy fixed path of separate puzzle levels that show your friends' progress and success at each stage. Importantly this path isn't just static. At each stage a new variation to the mechanic is revealed, building on what has gone before and increasing not only the challenge level, but also the variation and uncertainty within the gameplay.

Another example would be where there is a puzzle or natural barrier that requires a player to repeat the core loop in order to gain the right equipment or skill level required to beat that barrier. For example, if you have to build a bridge to cross into a new area you might have to find all the raw materials and then practice your blacksmith skill until you were able to create that bridge. This feels like a natural process in the storytelling but requires ongoing repetition of the core game mechanic to complete that task and, once complete, opens up a new chapter in the story, which may itself have a further context loop.

One of the best lessons I learnt about creating natural barriers comes from the game *Galaxy on Fire Alliances* from Fishlabs. While playing the beta version of the game, I found that the experience was missing what I can only describe as the "Middle game." This is a sense of purpose that we are trying to build with the context. However, rather than adding a new feature, the designers cleverly increased the difficulty to create some of the more valuable items in the game; in this case a Mark III Carrier. Having to invest much more effort to raise the rating of your HQ, Laboratory, and Starbase by spending your grind resources and waiting for the process to complete transformed the playing experience. As a player I had the tension of having to wait, with the potential risk of being attacked during the process, to build my most effective defense. There was no need to add new features or complications on top of an already complex game.

Creating Special Events

There are other methods that are less integrated with the underlying concept of the game. For example we might introduce a series of daily rewards or challenges that are only available if the player returns to the game each day (perhaps even more frequently) as well as less predictable "special events," which subtly subvert the rules of play in a way that adds an interesting challenge, such as a boss opponent who is invulnerable to "water" effects. The original *Plants vs. Zombies* and *JetPack Joyride* both include these kinds of disruption to the normal play. To gain certain achievements in *Plants vs. Zombies* the player has to change their approach to specific levels, such as not using any "mushrooms" in a night scene or not using any catapult plants on a "rooftop" level. Similarly, *JetPack Joyride* challenges the player to deliberately die at a specific distance—something that is trickier to achieve than you might at first think.

These kind of challenges need not only be about avoiding using certain items, indeed there is no problem having some of them benefiting from the player using temporary boosts, additional energy, score-multipliers, etc., provided that these can reasonably be obtained without paying. Otherwise it might be seen as a cheap trick to obtain money from the player.

The rhythm of play continues beyond the context level and can also reside up in the metagame level. Metagame loops can include a range of behaviors that interact with the game, but are not necessarily tied directly into the game mechanics. The most obvious of these is the playful involvement with others. Socializing games mean more than just connecting people through a social graph such as Facebook or Twitter. They require that we create both reasons to share and meaningful interactions. We should not underestimate the personal effort and risk involved for players who don't know what their friends' reactions might be. It takes energy to maintain active relationships whether that is in person, over a real-time game connection, or even through playing asynchronously via social games. The latter of course requires much less effort on the part of the player but still provides emotional engagement and shared experience. If designed well, social interactions within a game can become a conduit to help maintain relationships we might otherwise lose.

Making Metagames

Metagames can involve almost unlimited options, and this is an area I believe the potential is only just being considered. Think about what patterns we can create by leveraging the real-world location of each of the respective players. What about the physical space around the device we are playing with, from augmented reality to shared-screen multiplayer experiences? How might we use each player's connected devices to generate new patterns of play, which might deepen our relationships with the game and its other players?

Fundamentally, any game is enjoyed for the rhythm of how it is played, from challenge to defeat to ultimate success, whatever that might look like. Designing a game as a service means that we can't take these patterns of behavior for granted. We have to pay very close attention to them and find ways to enhance the delight that these can bring so that our players engage more deeply and build utility into the game itself.

Notes

1 It's worth investigating Maslow's hierarchy of needs to understand the different levels of engagement, http://en.wikipedia.org/wiki/Maslow's_hierarchy_of_needs.
2 Pavlov famously rang a bell in his experiments on classical conditioning before giving his dogs food and discovered that the ringing of the bell itself could elicit salivation, even without the presence of the food. However, there are those who question whether this response was conditioning at all, http://en.wikipedia.org/wiki/Classical_conditioning.
3 By player-directed I mean that the player makes the decision to select how they use their allocation of actions, any mistakes or limitations are by association their choice— provided the player considers that they had a fair allocation in the first place.

4   This was an idea suggested by someone in the audience during a panel session at Game
    Monetization Europe 2013 in London.
5   In case it's not obvious, playing lots of games is an absolute must for a game designer. This
    shouldn't be limited to computer games. There are lots of amazing mechanics out there
    from card, board, dice, and RPG games, and I once arranged for bridge lessons for all of my
    team at BT. Personally I also enjoy LARP and pub games like Shove-Ha'Penny, although
    pool and billiards don't do it for me. Even mechanisms such as old-school Play-By-Mail
    influences my design thinking. All that being said, probably my biggest influence is a
    business learning tool called the Balloon Game.
6   This form of cognitive bias is based on the hot–cold empathy gap and we will discuss this
    further in later chapters, http://en.wikipedia.org/wiki/Empathy_gap.
7   There is a great *Gamasutra* article looking at pace in games at www.gamasutra.com/view/
    feature/132415/examining_game_pace_how_.php?print=1.
8   In 1998/1999 I worked for Wireplay from British Telecom and we operated numerous
    online games including first person shooters like *Quake* and *Counterstrike*, which were
    played over dial-up modems—hard to imagine now in our permanently connected wire-
    less broadband world.
9   This is a city-building and conquest game that requires a certain aggressive mindset to
    play and which can be quite brutal and unforgiving.
10 King's *Candy Crush Saga* reached over 70 million users in April 2013, http://www.tuaw.
    com/2013/05/16/king-claims-70-million-daily-active-players-pet-rescue-saga-com. This
    game features a lengthy path showing all the levels and each players progress so far.
    At Level 35 it introduces a barrier where you have to introduce friends or pay in order
    to progress further. Since then they have also introduced "Quests" that allow you to
    continue provided you come every day and complete a special level over three days.
    Although fiendishly difficult at the higher levels, it is possible to play endlessly if you are
    prepared to go back to the earliest levels again.

Exercise 5: What is the Metagame?

In this exercise we are going to take a look at the outermost cog of the game, its metagame. This is the level where we think about all the elements with which we interact with the game from the role of the social graph, superfan styles of gameplay, the behavior profile of the device we are using, and even the physical space around us when we are playing.

We are looking here for ways to develop a deep level of engagement with the player and ensure that our game fits comfortably in their lifestyle and natural community. This is all about turning our game from a means to passtime to an experience they will remember and talk about in years to come.

Let's start by considering the environmental context of your game and how your metagame uses those elements to help deepen your engagement with the players.

Summarize your metagame and how it operates its environmental context:	
Mode of use:	
Reasons to share:	
Opportunities to collaborate:	
Creating appointments:	
Superfan game:	
Social connectivity:	

A superfan game is essentially a high level mechanic that is intended to sustain the most engaged players even further, and ideally encourage them to want to invest more time and money in the game than they might have otherwise done. This variation of the mode of play will be for the most dedicated players who will be more willing to spend, however, they also expect a high level of return on that value. They also expect something that allows them to maximize their potential in the game and be able to gain recognition in the games community.

In this exercise we will look at the superfan game using the same principles of the core loop mechanic we looked at with Exercise 3.

Summarize the core loop of your superfan game:	
Start stage:	
Challenge stage:	
Resolution stage:	
Reward stage:	
Why is this repeatable?	

WORKED EXAMPLE:

Summarize your metagame and how it operates its environmental context:	Finding Anthony is a memory game that uses a narrative context to ask questions about memory. It needs a science fiction concept in order make it easier to ask these questions without them becoming too dark and personal. The metagame will have two components. The first is the creation of families, which allow players to cooperate with others and compete in terms of the family with the best control over their districts. The second component explores the search for Anthony's missing girlfriend, who doesn't actually exist. The objective is to locate her, before she disappears. Once the Player has unlocked at least three districts of their map they start to collect more fragments of the puzzle that provides clues about the whereabouts of the girlfriend. These clues are time-stamped in allowing you to work out where she will be at different times during the day. The more team-mates (family) you can have ready in that location at the right time, the bigger the value for everyone and this contributes to your "family" controlling that district.
Mode of use:	Finding Anthony is a game that has short bursts of concentrated but not intense play. It is ideal for mobile and tablet play as it can provide ongoing engagement and still be easily interrupted. The selection of the most

(Continued)

	efficient paths by drawing on the screen also perfectly suits this experience. The game would also work well on a second screen-supported experience, such as using an Android Phone with an Android based UnConsole; PSVita as a controller for a PS4 title or the WiiU.
Reasons to share:	The style of play combines quick spatial thinking, which can easily go wrong as the avatar bumps into moving obstacles or worse still enemies, creating funny moments.
Opportunities to collaborate:	The metagame will allow players to join "families" where their performance manages their districts.
Creating appointments:	Returning to the game becomes important if you want to avoid missing out opportunities to gain "happiness" or "status" by completing missions, but there will always be more missions even if that means it takes you longer. Additionally, the collection of the puzzle pieces provides an opportunity for the most engaged players to arrange to collectively gather at the point where they believe that the girlfriend will appear, granting a special bonus.
Superfan game:	The principle superfan Game is all about building up your "family" and trying to dominate the districts. This is accelerated by finding the girlfriend.
Social connectivity:	Compare your performance in each district with friends. Collaborate with other players by joining their family. Work with fellow family members to locate the girlfriend.

Summarize the core loop of your superfan game:	Superfan game 1: friends and family.
Start stage:	For each location in the district that your Facebook friends have completed you can see the "Facebook" avatar of the highest performing player.

(Continued)

Challenge stage:	Once you have completed the level you see how your performance compares with your friends. Select one of your friends to access a link to the video playback of their performance and see what paths they took and whether you can beat them. Additionally, players can invite their friends to join their "family."
Resolution stage:	The game will collate the combined performance in each location in the districts and record that as the performance of their family. Families will be managed by the community and have roles that grant advantages but where you can be replaced by being outbid by spending "status" to obtain that role.
Reward stage:	All members of a family should gain rewards for their contributions and those families that are achieving the best scores will be displayed on the district map.
Why is this repeatable?	Your contribution in terms of score only persists for seven days. This means that you have to continue to play in order to sustain your faction's dominance over a district.

Summarize the core loop of your superfan game:	Superfan game 2: the girlfriend.
Start stage:	During missions you will obtain puzzle pieces that provide clues about Anthony's missing girlfriend. These clues can lead to a prediction of where she will appear.
Challenge stage:	Collect and decode all the puzzle pieces to work out where and when the girlfriend will next appear. Alternatively the player can spend "happiness" to get more clues.
Resolution stage:	Arrange for as many people in your faction to turn up at that location at the designated time to get a sighting of the girlfriend and a significant bonus.
Reward stage:	The animation for the sighting of the girlfriend should be haunting and fleeting, but what she leaves behind is a minigame where instead of collecting memory tiles, each object hides a power-up and the combined scores of the team are multiplied to help your team dominate that section of the map.
Why is this repeatable?	This happens every day—perhaps more frequently—and can help smaller families displace larger, but less unified factions.

Chapter 6
Building on Familiarity

Finding the Fun

In the last chapter we started to move our focus away from the structure of a game and towards the behavior and needs of the player. "Identifying and satisfying consumer needs" was described to me as the definition of marketing and I have since found that it equally applies to product development and design. Commercial game design is no different; we use the expression or application of human creative skill and imagination to create engaging experiences.[1] That means it is important to us to satisfy our audiences as well as to understand what attributes those players will value.

The simplest way to express the desire of players comes down to "fun," an attribute we tried to define in Chapter 2. We talked about fun being an emotional response to play and that play was a free activity with no care for material profit, with commonly agreed rules as well as some level of uncertainty. This isn't a new thought. Mihály Csíkszentmihályi[2] proposed that happiness comes when people are in a state of "flow," a state of concentration that completely occupies the mind between the challenge of the task and the skill of the performer. Looking at games as a service means that we have to be interested in the whole lifecycle of the player. When they start to play, they essentially have no "skill" (or at least have yet to learn how to use that skill appropriately for the game) and we have to illuminate them and bring them to the point they can leverage their potential ability to maximize and sustain that flow state. It takes time to reach the point where a player can slip into that state of flow and an essential aspect of freemium game design is to help them through that process. The good news is that players don't come to our game in isolation. Games build upon familiar patterns and concepts.

Familiarity Breeds Trust

We need to use playing mechanics that are familiar enough so they can quickly make sense to the player with as little explanation as possible. This doesn't just make it easier to get started, it actually engenders trust and confidence. Familiarity is important to shortcut communication about the values of our offering in order to attract an audience in the first place as this makes it easier for gamers to decide to download our game. However, as we looked at when considering the rhythm of play, we know players can quickly become bored if they pattern is too familiar. Players need our game to bring something special, even unique, in order to attract their attention or satisfy their craving for something more.

Familiarity Breeds Contempt

Familiarity is a compelling concept. The trust this engenders can motivate people to download games that share concepts with games they
already love. However, the fatal flaw with clones is that in reality we don't
"just" want to play the same game with a new skin. Any duplicate will
always fail by comparison if they fail to take the concept forward as the
very act of playing the original has already altered our perceptions from
the original game. Instead we want to recapture the feelings we had when
we first discovered the great games that inspired those clones. Indeed
you could argue that often players are seeking to recreate the emotions
that first triggered their appreciation of interactive entertainment, something that is essentially impossible to achieve as we are no longer that
original naive player. If we rely too heavily on the familiarity of game
design this will feel shallow and inevitably fail to meet gamers' needs.

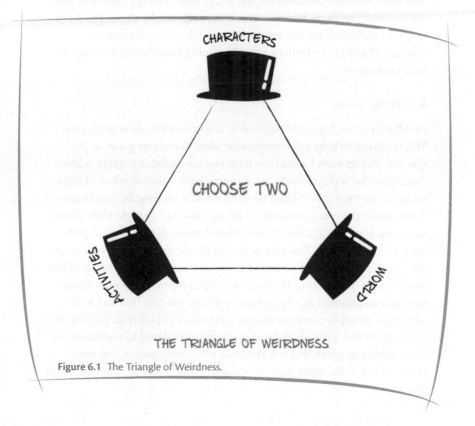

Figure 6.1 The Triangle of Weirdness.

A Little Disruption Goes a Long Way

Disruption only comes when we are brave enough to challenge existing preconceptions. But be careful not to try to remove all familiarity. Scott Rogers talks about the Triangle of Weirdness[3] where you could change the nature of any of the three elements of "character," "world" or "activities" around a familiar concept; but not all three. If you change every element then it upsets the frame of reference for the player and becomes problematic to sustain their attention.

This model seems to work, look at the some of the most disruptive games we have seen from *Angry Birds* to *Walking Dead*, *Portal* to *Candy Crush Saga*; all of these took a previous concept into new territory by radically challenging specific areas of gameplay without breaking an overall sense of familiarity. Games that balance the new and familiar like this often manage to obtain a large passionate fan base who become advocates for the wider mass market audience that can catapult the game into success, often without the developer having to spend too much money on marketing. We will talk more in Chapter 10 about the importance of building brands and leveraging your community.

So Little Time

Familiarity as we have said helps us to communicate ideas to players. This is critical to help us communicate ideas about our game to prospective players even before they have any idea what our game is like. Assuming that a player finds our game we have a tiny window of opportunity to get their interest and we can't waste it on lengthy explanations. Think about the space available on the app store or Google Play, where we essentially have just the thumbnail and name of the game to grab the players' attention. This gets worse on the device itself because after the game is downloaded we only have a 12-character app name and the 96×96 pixels of the icon.[4] We have to think extremely carefully about how we can best hint at why our game will be the one that will best satisfy the entertainment needs and aspirations of potential players. We can only do that with a high level of attention to detail to communicate ideas about our game that will resonate with other games that went before it, but at the same time we must still find a way to stand out from the crowd.

Great Artists Don't Copy, They Steal

It's important that we don't rely too heavily on the experiences of previous games, even if our own is deliberately intended to stir up feelings of nostalgia, such as with the modern-classic 8-bit game art style.

There is a fine line between healthy borrowing from previous games and outright copying. I don't just mean in the legal sense (although a breach of copyright is a serious consequence that I assume we all want to avoid). However, creating a game that is little more than a derivative version of an existing title without adding something is bound to end poorly. As I have already stated, most players who are familiar with the original will eventually feel cheated with your version if you don't take the concept in a new direction.

So how do we deliver on the promise of the new without removing the familiar values of the experience that we are building on? I believe successful game development is very much like standing on the shoulders of giants. We try to understand the games that formed our thinking and look at how we can build higher still. This may sound lofty, but there is something in reminding us that that we aren't (usually) creating from a blank sheet and that this is OK. When we want to build a game in the style of one of our own great influences we need to start not trying to copy, but instead trying to recreate the objectives of the game's original creator. We need to consider what they originally wanted to deliver (or at least your own approximation of that) and understand what compromises drove them to build that experience. Then we need to consider how the resources, platforms and technology have changed and whether we can use these to get past those compromises. More than that, we want to consider how we can apply our own values and creativity to those objectives in order to make something completely new and unique to you as its creator. You need to take ownership of that idea for yourself.[5]

The Story of *Arkanoid*

One of the earliest examples of this principle is arguably Taito's *Arkanoid*.[6] On the surface this game looks like a simply copy of Atari's *Breakout*.[7] However, there are differences. First, the bricks have rounded corners. I know this seems trivial, but it does mean the art style is different, something that was vital in the accompanying court case. Second, *Arkanoid* had a story. The rectangle you used to bounce the balls was actually a space ship, the Vaus—that had escaped from the doomed mother ship, the eponymous Arkanoid—which you have to steer through all the levels until you defeat Doh.[8] OK, the story, like *Tetris*, was fairly abstract, but it existed. *Arkanoid* also offered power-ups, which it granted on completion of levels.

Don't get me wrong, building on other games is a murky area fraught with problems. Look at *FarmVille*, which was accused of being a clone of *MyFarm* and *Farm Town* among others. I'm not going to enter the debate about whether those claims are right or wrong. Instead, in order to talk about how we can discuss how to build on familiar concepts, let's look at the more useful comparison of *Harvest Moon*.[9] *FarmVille* and *Harvest Moon* are clearly not the same game, but both rely on relatively cute characters managing the resources of their respective farms. There are many unique aspects that *Harvest Moon* has to offer that never made it into Farmville,[10] and I know that some designers who say that Zynga's breakthrough title was missing any gameplay. I don't agree, but I do accept that the game did very much simplify the playing process, which made it much more accessible to people who were not established game-players. The most important contribution this game introduced (compared to Harvest Moon) was asynchronous social play with Facebook friends into that design. Your friends could meaningfully interact with your farm.

Social Interaction is Playful

The idea of using the Facebook social graph was not new. Playfish, one of the first teams to successfully work with the early Facebook APIs, had started experimenting with this approach as early as 2007.[11] However, after its launch *FarmVille* quickly became dominant, and I suspect this was due to the combination of simplicity, schedules of reinforcement,[12] and social play. The thing that impresses me most is that—more than any other Facebook game of the time—*FarmVille*, through its social elements, managed to transform the appeal of game to a truly mass-market audience who had previously rejected computer games as too geeky for them.

Building on Expectations

I argue that disruptive creative change is most successful when the design builds our expectations, rather than simply confounding us. We can create startling new stories or playing mechanics provided we do so from a place of comfort. If we can foreshadow expectations of the changes that players are able to reveal, this will empower them to enjoy the game more. Better still we should try to make the most of how we reveal these elements by creating moments for the player to remember and share that makes the experience their own story.

The disruptive elements you introduce to your game have to make sense in line with all three tiers of what makes the game work: its mechanics, context, and metagame. The underlying flow of play in terms of usability, immersion and narrative are equally as important as whether the handling of the mechanic feels right. I believe that this is a critical issue for game designers to consider and it will come up again when we look into monetization in Chapter 13.

Too Much Disruption?

We should also be aware of the risks that bringing disruption into a game can cause. The flow of the game needs to carefully balance the mechanics and context, as well as the monetization. Adding new features to existing concepts can accidently cause us to breach the delicate boundaries between the reason to play and the objectives of the game. This topic is the subject of a wider industry discussion known as "Ludo-narrative dissonance." The term was introduced in 2007 by Clint Hocking in his critique of *Bioshock*.[13] He used it to describe the conflicted demands of the gameplay against the demands of the narrative. He argued that the needs for character progression worked against the narrative structure to prevent the player from connecting with either, leaving players unsatisfied with both. As designers, we have to pay attention not just to good gameplay and good story, but also to ensuring that the underlying player objectives pushing forward the gameplay are aligned with the objectives that support the narrative (or at least context) we are creating for the game. This seems on the surface to be a fairly obvious thing, but in practice it's more difficult to avoid than you might think. To help find these problems, it's essential to test out all of the potential game strategies, not just the most instinctive ones. Perhaps there are dominant strategies or hidden consequences that lurk below the surface creating a dissonance that destroys the intended harmony between game and story.[14]

Lucre-Ludo-Narrative Dissonance

This idea of the conflicts between conceptual elements in a game isn't restricted to the narrative and the mechanic. Within freemium monetization we have to also consider the impact of virtual goods sales and advertising as a factor in this balancing act. When this goes wrong it creates a similar imbalance in gameplay focus as Hocking described. A Lucre-Ludo-narrative dissonance if you like. OK, it's a bit of a joke term, but we do have to consider the impact of commercial elements in a game with the narrative.

There is a relationship between the decision to sell a consumable virtual good or place an advertisement and the way that the game plays. This might affect the flow of the game, our ability to suspend disbelief, but the more interesting effects come when they impact the tactics or strategy of play. Think about a resource management game where we spend in-game currency to build up our farm, city, or units. We can earn that currency by harvesting things or perhaps playing some kind of minigame. How we use spend that currency might affect the rate at which we earn additional currency and that in turn affects our strategy of play. But if we can purchase additional in-game currency then this removes the resource restrictions that made the game challenging, it fundamentally changes the game. It's not my intention to go too deep into monetization at this point, something you will hopefully notice is a trend in the way this book is written. We will come to that topic in time at the end of the book in Chapter 13.

Understanding Reward Behaviors

Understanding the motivations for playing or paying for games content, indeed why particular games have been successful is something that returns us to thinking about the needs of the player. As we mentioned when talking about the phenomenal rise of Facebook games from 2007 to 2011, games now have for the first time a truly a mass-market audience. This means that we can't just assume that all the players are like us anymore. Indeed I would argue that we never could and that this has always held back our potential as designers. We can look at demographics and other traditional marketing theory about consumer segments, however, in games I believe that there are more relevant techniques based on the concepts of "mood" and "mode" as we discussed in Chapter 5. Here we look at the behavior of the player to provide us with insight on the segments.

Richard Bartle's[15] work on player types very much reflects this kind of thinking, each type responds to the different objectives of each segment that arose in the *MUD* virtual world and each represents a different reward behavior. While we can't assume that these types will exactly match the player needs we will discover and satisfy in our games, they remain a useful tool to allow us to consider who is playing our game and what they will want from the game.

Mass-Marketing Means Targeting Everyone

Trained marketing people like me will usually tell you to identify your target audience and then work out how to satisfy them. The trouble with selling a mass-market product is that everyone is your target player, and you don't want to ignore potential players. This makes things more complicated as we can't target everyone. That's why we have to identify different segments and look to see how we can satisfy their player needs differently. If you complete a puzzle to release a magical sword that automatically kills all the monsters in your path, this won't be particularly satisfying for an "achiever" player. In fact you will probably be undermining the very thing they thrive on, their ability to beat opponents despite the odds. However, an "explorer" might find this a tremendous benefit as it frees them from the trouble of perfecting their fighting techniques, something they might not be as good at or enjoy. Instead, unlocking this sword allows them to spend more time working on puzzles and finding new secrets.

Players Aren't Static Types

Of course looking at player types isn't enough. As we have discussed, players are rarely one "type"; although they will usually exhibit a dominant one. Mode, mood and of course player lifecycle all affect their attitudes and behaviors within and between different games over time.

This was my experience playing *CSR Racing* from Boss Alien/ Natural Motion. Around the third tier of the game, I found that the core drag-race mechanic transformed for me from being the whole point of the game to simply a minigame that allowed me to earn money and gold faster. Instead I discovered a new game. The "real" game for me became selecting the right upgrades and races that would get me the most income fastest and with the optimal use of fuel. Of course I could buy more in-game money, fuel, gold or indeed better cars but that would defeat the purpose I had found in playing the game and my personal narrative as I attempted to rise up the ranks to defeat the other racers.

Don't Make Your Currency the Performance Metric

A common mistake made by designers is to fail to recognize what players choose as their performance metric. Grind currency can be an incredibly powerful way to gate content access, provide friction, and importantly demonstrate a level of progress in the game. However, if this is the only or best way to measure our success, then we are creating a problem for later. Why would I spend in-game currency if it's the only way I can measure my ongoing success? If I want players to progress in my game and to become repeated payers then I need them to be able to feel free about spending that in-game money, and not create a disincentive to spend it.

If we are aware of this effect we can look for other ways to motivate the players and find ways to ensure that the both the friction mechanics and monetization approach works in line with the flow of the game, rather than against it. Friction and monetization methods are design tools, they are not compromises we have to throw in to frustrate players. There is no need to create a "lucre dissonance" in our games when with care we can use these elements to simply make a better game.

Monetization as a Design Tool

One of my favorite examples of how this might work came during a panel session at Game Monetization Europe conference. The panel was moderated by Nicholas Lovell and included myself and Patrick O'Luanaigh of NDreams. We were attempting to show how one could turn any game into a Free2Play model. One of the suggestions was the classic point and click adventure, *Secrets of Monkey Island*. After a series of discussions including turning the world into a sandbox and the introduction of repeatable minigames to complement the mission system, we asked the audience for their ideas. One of them suggested that you could restrict the number of times per day you could use puzzle objects. That might sound like sacrilege to the purist, but if we think about it as a disruptive technique it could have a genuinely beneficial impact on how we play the game. Rather than clicking everywhere on the screen, having a limited number of tries per day makes us more cautious about how we control Guybrush to find the solutions to puzzles. How might this affect the way we locate a file from inside the piece of carrot cake from Otis? Would this add to the emotional intensity of the research we might so in order to find out that the file is in fact intended to shave the rhinoceros toenails and open the idol's case? This might cause some frustration of course, but it contributes to the game, rather than taking an approach like selling "hints" where spending money simply defeats the purpose of playing the game. Not to mention that there are probably all the answers we might want freely available on the internet. Thinking with this approach to monetization means we can create game mechanics with real-world consequences associated with each attempt to solve a puzzle. In reality, the risk is that this particular mechanic would be too heavy-handed for some players and of course its introduction makes for a different game experience. The point is, however, that we can use virtual goods in many different ways to create new strategies and consequences that can positively contribute to the experience. The limitation is only in how we approach the design. The presence of virtual goods can and should be entirely beneficial to the gameplay, as long as we think about the consequences and use them as part of our palette of design tools.

Notes

1　The expression and application of human creative skill and imagination is the very definition of art, http://oxforddictionaries.com/definition/english/art. However, we are making more than "just" art, we are creating experiences for paying players.

2　Mihály Csíkszentmihályi has been described as the world's leading researcher on positive psychology. His seminal work is *Flow: The Psychology of Optimal Experience*, http://en.wikipedia.org/wiki/Mihaly_Csikszentmihalyi.

3　Check out http://mrbossdesign.blogspot.co.uk/2008/09/triangle-of-weirdness.html for more details on Scott Roger's Triangle of Weirdness.

4　The app name is actually based on a maximum length rather than the number of characters on iOS, 12 (including a space) will often work, but sometimes 11 characters is safer. Android uses character length of 12 and the pixel limitation described above refers to the higher resolution screens for Android; in practice you have to be able to create your icon using 36×36 dp for the lowest resolution. On iOS this resolution is (at the time of writing) 114×114.

5　Pablo Picasso is often quoted as saying "Good artists copy; great artists steal." The argument being that inspiration may come from external sources, but it requires the artist to take ownership of the idea; to make it their own.

6　*Arkanoid* was Taito's response to *Breakout* and was very similar, http://en.wikipedia.org/wiki/Arkanoid.

7　*Breakout* was originally conceived as a successor single-player mode version of *Pong*, http://en.wikipedia.org/wiki/Breakout_(video_game).

8　I was personally never patient enough to play through the entirety of the game.

9　*Harvest Moon* or *Farm Story* was originally produced by Victor Interactive Software; later purchased by Marvellous Entertainment and first released on Nintendo's SNES in 1996, http://en.wikipedia.org/wiki/Harvest_Moon_(series).

10　*Farmville* was introduced in 2009 by Zynga and as well as winning the GDC "Best Social/Online Game" in 2010 was also described as one of the "50 worst inventions" by *Time* magazine, http://en.wikipedia.org/wiki/FarmVille.

11 I was lucky enough to be one of the first 100 people sent an invite to the Playfish game
    Who has the Biggest Brain? in 2007, which was one of the first games to reach millions of
    daily active users.

12 We talked briefly about schedules of reinforcement and the Skinner Box in Chapter 3.

13 http://clicknothing.typepad.com/click_nothing/2007/10/ludonarrative-d.html.

14 I strongly recommend that you try paper prototyping techniques to stress out the prac-
    tical details of your design before asking a coder to commit to writing the game software.
    It's much quicker and cheaper to iterate a design with your imagination, some paper
    designs and physical playing pieces to represent what the game will do and you almost
    always learn something about the properties of the gameplay.

15 We mentioned Richard Bartle, his work as co-creator of MUD, and the analysis he did on
    different player types in Chapter 2.

Exercise 6: What is Your Bond Opening?

In Chapter 9 we are going to explore a number of themes that will help us think differently about our game and that reflect the transitional moments between each life stage. The first of these themes is the "Bond opening." Think about any movie featuring James Bond and how the first ten minutes sets up everything we need to know about the movie,— who Bond is, how amazing he must be, and something about the world he lives in—all without revealing the main plot for this film. It will usually introduce at least one of the bad guys and sow the seeds that foreshadow the plot to come. The point about this moment—and why I believe it's a useful metaphor for games design—is that it gets everyone up to speed, not by telling them who Bond is, but by showing them. It reminds the old die-hard fans how great Bond can be at his best while at the same time explaining his character to any new viewers. It also sets up the context to show just how terrible the opponents that he encounters later in the film really are; because if Bond can't beat them, and we know how good Bond is, they must be really scary!

In this exercise we need to work out what is your equivalent of the Bond moment for your game. This is not about creating a tutorial; if possible we should find a way to never have one. It is about conveying the most essential elements of the experience clearly, quickly, and in as an engaging manner as possible. We need to focus our attention on getting our players into the game within just a few seconds of launching the app. Then we have to explain the core game mechanic as simply and safely as possible, making certain we don't scare them off with the complexity. This includes providing real clarity over the control mechanisms themselves, which have to be entirely obvious and joyful to use. Next we have to make sure that we reward our players for their understanding of the game and ensure that this isn't a patronizing thing, it has to be meaningful and based on a real achievement.

We have some more long term goals too. How do we introduce the driving motivation from your context loop. How do we communicate it and its benefits to them as a player? The same questions apply to the various aspects of the metagame especially the social interaction and the superfan game elements you plan to introduce. The point here is to foreshadow the value of remaining in the game and demonstrating that they can have fun playing the mechanic, but there is also a purpose associated with it that will give them even more long-term enjoyment.

What is the Bond moment for your game?	
How many clicks till you start playing the game?	
How do you introduce the core gameplay mechanic?	
How will you explain the control mechanisms of the game?	
How will you meaningfully reward your player within the first minute of play?	
How (and when) will you introduce your context loop?	
How (and when) will you introduce your social elements?	
How (and when) will you introduce your superfan game?	

WORKED EXAMPLE:

What is the Bond moment for your game?	Anthony waking up in the hospital. This will take the form of an interactive comic, which in each cell explains not only the narrative but also introduces a new interactive moment. Players will be able to go back to this "tutorial" later, but in doing so the narrative will have changed slightly to reflect Anthony's growing understanding that his memory is affected.
How many clicks till you start playing the game?	Upon starting the game the player is presented with splash screen with an image taken from the last mission they player participated in, or the starting image from the comic. There is also a Start button and the logos of our company and any partners as required, these logos link to mobile web pages about those companies. Selecting the Start button triggers a new game, if the player has never played or restarts the game from a point where the local save state determines the last play. If a connection is available, this save state will be cross-referenced with server and a tamper check will be performed based on the upload of any cached play data from the device. Players will immediately go into the game.

(Continued)

How do you introduce the core gameplay mechanic?	When Anthony wakes up in his hospital ward, the player will be asked to draw a path to the door. When he reaches the door a nurse will check him over and ask if he is alright and the player will be asked to open his "brain slots." When the surgeon comes in to talk to him, he will be asked to locate the first matching pair of tiles and place them in his brain slots.
How will you explain the control mechanisms of the game?	Before he leaves the hospital ward, Anthony will have to search the ward for a number of additional matches and this will introduce the battery mechanic, the score bonus and the time factor in play. All of these stages are treated like comic book cells, but played against the background of a real level.
How will you meaningfully reward your player within the first minute of play?	At each stage the player gets a reward (a power-up and score) for completing it.
How (and when) will you introduce your context loop?	The context loop will be introduced when Anthony leaves the hospital ward. There will be two additional cells of the comic tutorial. The first will introduce him to his unpleasant family and demonstrate the "happiness" resource. The second will introduce the wider district map and the family as well as the "status" resource.
How (and when) will you introduce your social elements?	After a few successful missions the player will be told that if they login to Facebook they can compare with their friends and get free in-game currency. They will also be told that we won't post to Facebook unless they initiate it. Once they sign-in they will then see their highest ranked friend's face for each mission as it appears.
How (and when) will you introduce your superfan game?	Once the player has cleared their first district and demonstrated their ability to complete a "boss level" they will be able to invite friends to join their "family" and align their family with a "faction." This act will grant both parties a free "power-up" and grant them access to the social controls for the superfan game, including a view of the different districts that shows the current state of control among the factions.

Chapter 7
Counting on Uncertainty

Strong Foundations

As we have previously discussed, familiarity is a vital foundation for
any new concept. However, with a game as a service we have unique
challenges that were not seen as important historically. The ability
to sustain an audience through hundreds, if not thousands, of plays
is something that needs special attention in the design. We need to
balance both repeatability and uncertainty if we are to sustain our
audience.

This is a topic that many designers completely miss. Too often I see
games which are little more than instructions dictating how the player
has to complete the puzzles as defined by the designer. Jump precisely
'here' to get the gem & avoid the monster. This is a terrible idea for
repeatability. What is the player's contribution to play, other than completing what you created? Don't get me wrong I appreciate this can be
a fun model for some games, but unless there are other variables than
success or failure, repeatability becomes impractical. Level designs can
take months of effort to perfect and if our players complete that puzzle
within a few minutes and never want to go back and play that level, then
it's going to be extremely hard to make a sustainable service experience.

Sources of Uncertainty

Instead we need to find ways to build into our games a level of unpre-
dictability or a variable strategy that will encourage repetition. But
where does this uncertainty come from and how can we use it to make a
better game?

Without wanting to go into too much detail on specific examples[1] you
can essentially break down the sources of uncertainty to five key areas.

Taking a Chance

The first source of uncertainty is found within chance and probability.
For the purposes of this book, let's consider these to be two separate
things. In this definition, we will consider "chance" to be an unchanging
randomness, that crude but conceivable obstacle where the roll of a die or
some behind-the-scenes random number generator determines the outcome. This is an inflexible, but "honest" or "fair" approach to introduce
randomness. Traditional games such as Ludo and Monopoly use this to
mix up the opportunities for players to succeed and players can always
blame the roll of the dice. This can be a great leveler, but when you are the

player on the negative side of the lucky rolls, it can get tired very quickly because there is no opportunity for the player to influence the result.

What's the Probability?

On the other hand, if we define "probability" to mean a random attribute that may be influenced by other external factors, this gives us a useful comparison with chance. For example, as I improve the skill level of my character in a role-playing game the probability of my success with that skill will improve. Here the player (and the environment) influences these random factors. It becomes possible to select the best conditions and invest in the associated variables that will affect the outcome I want and, as a player, I may decide to advance those variables over time. Using this technique to inject uncertainty into a game introduces not just a sense of risk, but also a sense that the player has some level of control. It introduces a level of strategy in the game and creates a reason for players to invest in repetitive mechanics to increase those abilities or to accept that any failure during play can be traced back (at least partially) to their own decisions. However, this can be problematic, especially in the early stages, as it can appear to punish new players who have yet to learn the process. It can also lead to an emergent problem where players unduly focus on a narrow range of variables, creating a range of dominant strategies that reduce the enjoyment of play if overly relied upon.

The Skill of the Player

A second source for uncertainty can be found within the ability of the players themselves, which we know will vary for everyone who engages in the game. The idea of player performance is particularly important for games that have some degree of multiplayer behavior, but can also be used to add uncertainty or choice in single player games. Not every player will have the best thumb/eye coordination. Others might be better suited to special awareness or logic-based puzzles. Being aware of these differences, the designer can introduce obstacles that require different problem-solving abilities or alternative strategies. The problem is that too much emphasis on player performance tends to punish players who lack the prerequisite skills. Going back to Csíkszentmihályi's concept of "flow," this imbalance between the skills of the player and the challenge of the task can lead to anxiety; or, in the case where we "dumb down" the puzzle, it can lead to boredom. On the positive side, however, the mistakes I make are my own. Repeated failure, especially where the player considers the problem to have been their own fault can be incredibly compelling to some people. *Demon Souls* by From Software and SCE Japan Studio is a classic example of a game so fiendishly difficult (largely due to the "permadeath" model the game uses) that it makes me want to throw my controller out of my living room window . . . moments before I press the button to restart.[2]

Leaving Room for Interpretation

The third uncertainty source comes from ambiguity. A lack of clarity regarding how to apply the rules of the game can be particularly powerful, provided that there are still consistent rules. For example, is there is an imbalance of information between the game and the players or between opposing players? This often arises when you have rule elements that combine to create different effects. For example, with a collectable card game, each card can introduce new rule elements and the associated strategies can greatly affect the style of play we adopt. My favorite analogy for this can be found with the Californian fast food chain In-N-Out Burger.[3] Rather than simply ordering off the simple menu in the restaurant you can order from the "Secret Menu" with special terms like "Double Double" (two Burgers with two Cheese) or "Animal Style" (a mustard-cooked beef patty with additional pickles, cheese, spread, and grilled onions). The system is quite flexible and you can discover different ways to customize your meal, which adds a delight. For example you can order a 3×3 (three burgers and three cheese) or a 100×100 (although they don't server this anymore apparently).

Dilemma Brings Meaning to Choices

Ambiguity is not about a random consequences, it's about decision-making without access to all the necessary information. Part of this is to build in a level of dilemma: a concept rarely used to its full potential in games, but used for marvelous effect in *The Walking Dead*. Do you save Doug or Carley when the drug store is attacked?[4] Of course dilemma doesn't just have to apply to a life-or-death decision. Having a limit of two weapons forces me to choose which are going to be most valuable to me in the upcoming plot. That's a dilemma and it's based on ambiguous information. These less critical decisions can be an incredibly important opportunity for the creation of depth in the game and of course monetization. The decisions can impact different parameters than the success or failure in the game. We can look for secondary goals or alternative ways to achieve the principle objective. I like to call the non-essential decisions in a game "soft variables," and these soft variables can add creativity as well as reasons to rewardingly repeat otherwise static game mechanics.

Complexity Creates Emergent Behavior

Our fourth source is derived within the nature of any complex system. We may have simple rules, like with chess, but the way that the pieces interact with each other and their respective positioning introduces dozens of potential alternative moves. Thinking ahead compounds the difficulty, but to be at least reasonably proficient we need to try to think at least three moves ahead,[5] which can introduce thousands of potential moves. Of course we mitigate this by focusing our attention on only the most beneficial moves, which are often the most likely ones. However, this very act of selection means that we can miss a pattern and find ourselves in trouble. Using complex systems in a game design can create a barrier for users who may struggle to learn these rules and how they interact with each other; rules affecting rules. In particular it becomes possible that a player will inadvertently make a simple mistake early on, which will come to punish them later. An example of this can be as simple as the "interest" mechanism used in some tower defense games.[6] If I spend all my construction money early on in the game, I never get to gain enough interest to build the bigger turrets I will need to survive later waves of enemies in the game. This can absolutely add dilemma or ambiguous uncertainty into the game, but if it's not clearly communicated or if the conditions aren't perfectly balanced this can quickly become annoying if the player isn't given some hint about what the dilemma means early enough in the process of play.

Feedback Loops

Probably the most powerful aspect of a complex system comes when you start to look at the way different rule interactions can create feedback.[7] This is a causal relationship where one action had an impact on an outcome and it becomes particularly interesting in games when this forms loops. If in our tower defense game we have "build money" and an interest mechanic, then there is a positive feedback[8] if we choose the tactic of not spending all our money. The interest mechanic increases both the pot of build money and any interest we had previously earned, the interest becomes an amplifier of itself. If the interest level is set too high, the rate of gain of resources can quickly get out of hand and thereby eliminate the challenge in the game. So we need something that can return the balance. This is where negative feedback comes into its own. Perhaps the more build money you have, the larger the attack waves that come each round. There quickly reaches an equilibrium point where you have to put more of your build money into the game to offset the additional forces attacking you. The study of feedback loops in game design deserves a lot more attention than I can give it in this book and I strongly suggest that you take time to research this in more detail. They can be incredibly powerful tools to help balance your game mechanics and to build engagement and strategy. However, you have to be extremely careful that their use doesn't introduce unintended consequences. It's not unusual that games fall into a trap where there is a hidden dominant strategy that ruins the game, even if to use it the player has to do something contrary to the game's ideology.

Reality Gets in the Way

The fifth and final source of uncertainty comes from the real world. This is the area that many designers simply ignore, after all if you are designing a game, why would you care what players do outside playing that game? However, I argue that if you are building a service that you hope will persist, you can't afford to make that mistake.

Real life creates demands on your players and this can prevent them from ever returning to your game. More than that, there is the potential that the influences of the outside world and the social relationships of the player can impact on their playing decisions. If you are supposed to be meeting your friends or spending time with your family, or perhaps in a meeting with your boss, the last thing you need is for a game to be prompting you to return to a game to harvest your plants.

If you are worried about when you are going to be paid, the last thing you want to think about is having to spend another $0.99 on a virtual lollypop. We can't (and shouldn't try to) know the minutiae of our players' lives, but ignoring that there might be external pressures will eventually lead to your app being deleted.

The Importance of Culture

Cultural context can also play an important part in the behavior of players. This includes the differences between players from different countries with different values, religions and politics—indeed even different perspectives on history can have huge effects. At the same time, cultural impacts can also apply to demographic groups that, despite being located in different countries, can in some cases have more shared values internationally than within their own country. Something that I suspect is becoming more common as the reach of the internet allows us to share more diverse experiences.

There is also an interesting argument that sometimes the cultural differences can be a reason for players to actively seek out your game. Many Chinese, Korean and Japanese players like specific Western games and consume them specifically because they are different from the local content; similarly many Westerners enjoy Asian content, in particular Japanese RPG games.

Physical Presence

There are other real-world considerations we should consider. If we are playing a game with other people, are they in the same room as us? If so, how does that space between us influence the experience itself? How does the game take advantage of that? At Game Horizon 2013, independent game developer Alistair Aitcheson[9] talked about the process of creation which went into this shared screen (iPad) multiplayer game *Slamjet Stadium*. Key to the design was that the device didn't know whose fingers were flicking which players' pieces, and it is that fact which makes the game so compelling. You are encouraged to use the space on the tablet and around it in any way that helps your gameplay. In short, you are encouraged to cheat. We should think about the way the real-world impacts our players. Multiplayer gaming isn't just about real-time connections, we have to consider the moments where players are going to be comfortable to take the social risk to show off their skills and the conditions where they can rely on the connections. Asynchronous games are not just about how we use Facebook (or other social graphs) to connect with people. The experience has to be genuinely meaningful to the players and their friends who they might reach out to and encourage joining in the game.

With a little thought about the real-world context we can create disruptive experiences, just by considering the environment that the game will be played in and what other forces might be acting on those please. During my time in Sony London Studio working on PlayStation Home, I remember that the EyeToy team was particularly interested in how multiplayer games worked when all the participants shared the same screen. Imagine what that might do to the way you design a game.

Social Bonds

Awareness of these forces means that we can both work with them and look for ways to use them to help us create deeper bonds within the game experience. We can use social experiences to build deeper bonds between players by creating a context within which they can share things they all value. Games like *Words with Friends* and *Draw Something* both leveraged the social bonds that already exist with people to create reasons. They were also sensitive to the cycle of play, allowing player to have short intense bursts of enjoyment that need not happen at the same time. Their asynchronous playing style worked ideally to allow the player to enjoy a shared experience without the burden of having to plan to be in the same place or even online at the same time. These solved the problem of creating a meaningful shared moment, resolving the damaging uncertainty and replacing it with the positive surprise that comes from seeing what other players do with the words or puzzles they are presented with. The reactions and responses of other people to gameplay never gets boring and we are usually more forgiving if a person beats us than if we are beaten by the game itself (to a degree at least).

Practical Applications

All this theory is useful, but we need some practical direction on how we can use this concept of uncertainty usefully in games. To help with this I've looks at three approaches of how we might bring uncertainty into a game and in particular how we might use this to create reasons to repeat play our games. They aren't the only techniques out there, but they do provide strong examples worth considering.

Easter Eggs

I use the term "Easter Eggs" to describe the first of these techniques. But don't be fooled, it's not just about hiding lots of meaningless little prizes around your game. We can be more imaginative than that. The key is to create a series of secondary goals that do not contribute to the core success criteria of the game. Indeed they can be alternative goals with their own objectives, which may even be at odds with the ultimate goals of the game. I don't suggest you take this too far, but they can introduce a level of dilemma in play. Typically they involve the placement of incongruous items in places that players need not explore to complete the game or in places that require extra skill to access.

An Easter Egg is a great way to satisfy different reward behaviors than the rest of the game fulfils, for example in a game where players are expected to compete for speed they can adding in a "collecting" element. Alternatively, having a monster you can kill or rush past can add tension to a player's decisions especially if there might be an extra reward to be found if they make it to the goal early. And of course even the classical egg hunt brings additional pleasure if you are able to be the ones to locate all of them. There is an interesting dynamic which happens when players complete these "side-goals." It seems to instill a sense of "being on the inside," especially if they have the means to share their success with others. It can build on their personal identification with the experience and other players like them, marking them out as special, especially if it's known that this takes skill and ingenuity to find.

Emergent Behavior

The second technique relies on building emergent behavior onto the mechanic. I'm not really sure if it's even fair to call it a technique, as this often arises by accident rather than design. These are really alternative applications of the rules of the game that create new ways that the game can be enjoyed. They are typically tangential to the normal way you can play the game but somehow retain a level of enjoyment, even if differently from the way the designers had intended.

Some of the best examples are the most surprising. Think about how players decided to recreate the Mona Lisa in *FarmVille*.[10] This wasn't the original intention of the game, and there are some who argue that it happened because there wasn't enough gameplay in the game so players made their own. Finding something to do, when there is a problem in the game but still pent up demand, is a common source of inspiration for players to find these emergent behaviors. We saw this in the early days of PlayStation Home before there was much in the way of playable games. We saw players trying to exploit the tiny snags in the collision-layers that had been missed in the initial testing. This allowed their avatars to popup into the air as if they were defying gravity. For a time it was quite an enjoyable activity but it didn't take long for those spaces to be cleaned up and, of course, there were soon lots of games to play.

Soft Variables

Despite being largely an accidental phenomena, we can find ways to use emergent principles to introduce new strategies, especially if we use those "soft variables" not directly to influence success, but to add flavor or alternative strategies. In a level-based puzzle game we win by completing the level and lose by failing. However, how fast we complete the game, which path we take, and whether we use any boosts or power-ups are all soft variables we can measure. *Plants vs. Zombies* from Popcap used this principle to beautiful effect by introducing achievements if the player chose to restrict their options when completing a level. For example, I would gain an achievement if I chose to not use any mushrooms during a night scene, or to not use a catapult in a roof scene. *Jetpack Joyride* uses challenges to create a similar effect, for example, asking the player to die at exactly 1,000 yards to gain a reward.

Strategic Choices

Emergent properties can also come into effect in the choice of virtual items a player uses to interact in a game. Take the example of a weapon in a first-person shooter. A shotgun and sub-machine gun (SMG) may deliver the same damage per second, but the shotgun does this in infrequent bursts while the SMG delivers a continuous stream of bullets that instead increases your chances to hit. The shotgun might do more damage on flesh, but an SMG might do more damage against armored opponents. The soft variables don't affect the basic principles of play, but each weapon creates a different strategy of play, either of which may better suit the player.

Imbalanced Economies

The last technique uses the relationship between different playing resources and their affect on the progress in the game and considers how these can be used to create an imbalanced economy.[11] The idea is that the creation of new resources requires resources of other types and effort on the part of the player. In any resource-restricted game we might start with a given amount of money, things we need, and a method to allow us to earn more money. As we play the game we earn grind money we can spend on gathering or improving our playing resources, which allow us to earn money faster. However, the rate at which we can interact with the world limits how quickly we can gain resources. This restriction might be a practical issue because of how long it takes to play the core gameplay mechanic or it may be "artificially" restricted through the need for a fuel or energy, or perhaps some cool-down process. However, we can free up those restrictions if we spend grind money (or alternatively real money) on upgrades that affect our performance. In some games this might be complicated by other tools such as storage space, which again needs money to improve. What makes this an imbalanced economy is that every upgrade we take requires more resources to resolve and puts a demand on the player to invest in another aspect of the game.

The principle can be used in any game. We have a tradition of using XP/equipment/potions in a RPG and combat games that serve this exact purpose of creating a level of friction (and achievement) to the progress of your character. Games such as *Clash of Clans* have perfected the use of an imbalanced economy to create deeper engagement for players,[12] making it so that each success introduces a new challenge for the player, which continues their desire to play.

Game Theory

Imbalance becomes even more interesting when we throw in other players, especially if we allow the players to exchange goods with each other. That process is extremely complex, especially if we try to model precisely the economic implications of trade with supply and demand impacts on price. More complex still if we insist on a '"zero-sum gain"— the principle that there is a finite supply of goods so if a player takes more than their share other players are left with less. This starts entering the economics world of game theory, rather than games design using "economies" (two very different things).

Summing Up Uncertainty

All of these concepts deserve much deeper analysis but are presented here to encourage you to think differently about the way you look at game design. My objective is to encourage you to consider how these ideas might be applied to almost any game and deliver greater longevity to your title. Most importantly I believe they can help to create moments that make the game special to each player. In particular I believe that it's essential to consider how we can use soft variables to give meaning to every play of the game and to open out the opportunity for mistake and error and those crazy moment of genius where everything just works. That's why uncertainty is important to me as a player, it makes the gameplay mine, not just what the developer decided I should experience.

Notes

1 Go check out Greg Costikyan's *Uncertainty in Games* if you want to see a breakdown of different sources of uncertainty with a wide range of games from *Super Mario* to rock/paper/scissors, http://mitpress.mit.edu/books/uncertainty-games.

2 Yes I know that quitting the game and restarting is cheating. But it's a cheat I would have happily paid for after my 200th death on the first section of the game, mostly down to my lack of concentration or mishandling of the controller.

3 You can find out more details of the In-N-Out Burger online, but to be honest that takes away a little of the fun of the process, http://en.wikipedia.org/wiki/In-N-Out_Burger_products.

4 If you haven't checked out the amazing *The Walking Dead* from Telltale Games I strongly suggest that you do, and if you want to relive that moment check out www.youtube.com/watch?v=au09wFtbS3k.

5 This is why I will never be a decent chess player, I lose focus after just thinking two moves ahead and quickly get bored. I once hired Garry Kasparov to help promote a chess service we launched for Wireplay and watched him playing four tables at once, four times over in just a few hours. Unsurprisingly, he won every match easily but it was amazing to watch. There are some great sources out there if you want to improve your game. This one talks about how to train yourself to think three moves ahead, http://antheacarson.hubpages.com/hub/How-to-Think-Three-Moves-Ahead-in-Chess.

6 Don't get me wrong, I much prefer tower defense games that include an "interest" mechanic specifically as a tool for dilemma that gives me more to think about than to just trying to build the most efficient maze.

7 Feedback is a very important phenomena in economics, biology and, of course, games, http://en.wikipedia.org/wiki/Feedback.

8 There is a great blog post by Daniel Soli based on observations by Jesse Catron, Jay Barnson, and Kyoryu that looks at the use of positive and negative feedback looks in a series of different games, http://danielsolisblog.blogspot.co.uk/2012/05/feedback-loops-in-game-design.html.

9 Alistair Aitcheson was also behind the game *Greedy Bankers* and he had previously explored same-screen multiplayer through the tablet version of his game called *Greedy Bankers Against the World*, www.alistairaitcheson.com.

10 There have been an amazing range of art pieces created using the *FarmVille* game, it was a bit of a meme in 2009. This link contains a selection of 21 of the better examples, http://reface.me/applications/21-farmville-art-masterpieces.

11 There is an interesting blog post by Ian Schriber that looks at the use of economies in some detail, http://gamebalanceconcepts.wordpress.com.

12 Personally I find the model used in *Clash of Clans* to be too steep and I haven't chosen to spend money in that game, despite my deep longstanding affection for the guys at Supercell. I admire the game and its revenue potential, and appreciate their dedication to making the best possible game, but in this case the combat system doesn't work for me as a player. I suspect that's because at heart I'm still a table-top war-gamer and want to control the troops more directly.

Exercise 7: What is Your *Flash Gordon* Cliffhanger?

Following on from the last exercise we will continue to explore the themes from Chapter 9. This time we will look at the "*Flash Gordon* cliffhanger." This is taken from the classic Saturday matinee film series of the 1930s and 40s. My favorite was Buster Crabbe and his version of *Flash Gordon*. Each episode was a self-contained story that fitted into the wider narrative, but at the end there was a moment of disaster. Flash would be fighting one of Ming's henchmen when the Princess would slip and fall off the cliff to her almost certain doom and Flash jumped after her to try to save her; or some such fancy. Come back the same time next week to find out if (or more likely how) they survived! Why did they use this formula each time? They did it because it gave their audience a reason to return next week and part with their hard-earned cash.

In this exercise we will explore how these ideas can help your game design and what techniques you plan to use to create reasons to return to the game rather than just assuming that because the game is enjoyable then this will deliver you retention. We need to create a sense of activity happening in the game, even when the player isn't connected. We have to decide if we are going to use an energy mechanic or some other time-based resource that has to be used up or takes time to refresh. We also have to notify your players when something interesting happens that might affect them or simply comes from social sharing, how do we find our when our friends leave "footprints in the sand?" We also have to work out which channels we will use to communicate with our players and how we can avoid that becoming annoying—we should never nag our users! Finally, we have to think about the different notification process for your more engaged players and whether we need to create some specific social tools to support that experience.

What is the *Flash Gordon* cliffhanger for your game?	
Which happens in your game while I am not playing?	
Which resources are real-time dependant?	
What asynchonous social events can happen when I am not playing?	
How will you communicate reasons to return?	
How frequently will you notify users about changes occurring live in the game?	
How will you avoid the game "nagging" players?	
Is there a separate notification cycle for the superfan game?	

WORKED EXAMPLE:

What is the *Flash Gordon* cliffhanger for your game?	Finding Anthony has a low-impact twist on the "energy" mechanic in that missions appear in the game for limited periods of time and reoccurring at a set rate depending on whether the district they take place in has been cleared or not. Players waiting to play can always use boosts to spawn new missions.
Which happens in your game while I am not playing?	If I don't check the game regularly I may be missing new missions, each of which might have unique rewards, such as a puzzle piece about the "girlfriend".
Which resources are real-time dependant?	The missions themselves are real-time dependent and the rate at which they can be completed is dependent on whether the district is cleared (slower) or not (faster).
What asynchonous Social events can happen when I am not playing?	My friends may complete a new space or beat my scores and send me a direct challenge to try to beat them back.
How will you communicate reasons to return?	The game will allow the player to switch on or off notifications when there are ten or more missions available to complete. Player challenges can be sent via Facebook messages or Email as well as via an in-game notification. The receiver can decide how the game should deliver this and messages follow the same rules as a poke—namely I cant resend a poke until the player concerned has returned the poke.

(Continued)

How frequently will you notify users about changes occurring live in the game?	Each day players will get a different free boost, the value of which goes up for each consecutive day returning (up to ten days). Players will be notified to collect them as they become available.
How will you avoid the game "nagging" players?	We only send out gameplay messages, not marketing messages. Additionally, they will be alerted within the game that they will get notifications and we will highlight how they can cancel these alerts (opt out). This process will not be hidden.
Is there a separate notification cycle for the superfan game?	Family members will be notified (opt out) when other family members have taken new locations in your districts or when other families take control from yours.

Chapter 8
Six Degrees of Socialization

Playing With Others

Some people think of social games as a new phenomenon because of the introduction of Facebook and the way this changed how players shared their experiences. However, over millions of years of evolution, mammals have been playing with others as a way to learn new skills and to test their social position. It's really only in recent history, with the arrival of the computer game industry, where we started playing alone. Even then, with the arrival of connected computers, Trubshaw and Bartle introduced the first virtual world or *Multi User Dungeon* (*MUD*).[1] This text-based experience was profoundly different because the world contained real people, people who could type for themselves and communicate (or more likely fight) with you. For those with an imagination and willingness not just to suspend disbelief but to accept the limitations of the technology this was incredible. This also provided an amazing reference point for Bartle to find insight into social playing behaviors as we have talked about in Chapter 2.

From Small Beginnings

Online gaming continued to grow as the quality of connection and games experiences grew. Services such as MPlayer, GameSpy, and British Telecom's Wireplay used different approaches to provide a central hub for players to help them find and share their online gaming experiences; in particular games such as *Quake II* or *Unreal* and, my personal favorite, the groundbreaking *Counterstrike*.[2]

However, these services were flawed for many reasons, not least that the technology meant that you had to download a specific client, you couldn't run them in the browser, and on top of that they usually needed some form of direct integration into the game—something that most developers didn't have the resources to do.

The other problem is that these games were particularly niche. Only people with the technical savvy (and resources) to link their computers to the emerging internet as well as to troubleshoot these temperamental connections could realistically play.

In 1999, Wireplay had 50,000 monthly active users with more than 1,000 simultaneous peak connections over dial-up (typically 28k or 56k baud) modems. That was one of the largest games services in the EU (probably the largest) at the time, but if you compare that with the 70 million daily active users of *Candy Crush Saga* it pales into insignificance.

Even with the rise of broadband and connected console games with Xbox Live and PlayStation Network, I would argue that this kind of play remained niche. Of course it grew, but the idea that it might be enjoyed by mass-market players was almost laughable. The growing audience of MMOs was probably as important as the impact of console players in terms of the range of audience. More so if you consider that these games were probably the first to be able to locate significant numbers of female players. People wanted a social context to enjoy games playing together and titles such as *EverQuest* and *World of Warcraft* offered that to large communities of both gender.

Footprints in the Sand

However, it took the introduction of social games on Facebook to herald an unprecedented increase in the size of the audience for online and mobile games, bringing for the first time a truly mass-market adoption of casual games. These games picked up on something which in the old days of online gaming we missed: asynchronous play. This was the idea that I don't have to be online at exactly the same time as you in order to enjoy the experience. I could leave "footprints in the sand" for my friends to discover and these would allow them to feel like they had shared in my experience and enjoyment.

Yes we know that more recently, the social games pioneers such as Zynga, Digital Chocolate, and Playfish have stumbled, but rather than signaling the end of the line for social games, I believe this is just a stumbling start. We have seen a "gold-rush" of developers discovering social values and using data-driven techniques but it has broken the trust of players and left them wondering where the fun went. Something that I hope this book will help you, as a designer, address.

The trouble is that getting under the skin of social play requires that we turn upside-down our expectations of what we currently call social games. Instead of looking at games as single player or multiplayer, we should look at how people behave socially in games and look for patterns of engagement that build trust and confidence. Understanding the role of social elements in games ultimately comes down to understanding people and relationships, not in trying to build on the technical implementations used in games such as *FarmVille*, *World of Warcraft* or *Call of Duty*.

Understanding the Facebook Poke

When considering social play, it's hard to break things down into simple processes. However, Facebook has a core element that, although it has fallen out of favor, does allow us to get to the heart of what happens emotionally when we use the internet for communication.

The Facebook "poke" is a little more hidden than it once was, but it remains a very simple way to connect to your friends. Poking someone is a transfer of information; it says: "Hey, I thought about you today." It doesn't require reciprocation; it's not demanding. You can choose to respond, inviting further interactions, or you can hide the notification. Facebook even has a simple and effective anti-spamming mechanism included in that you can't resend a poke until the other party responds. If I poke you and you don't poke me back, that's that. This kind of message doesn't need words, it communicates simply through the action of its use. Receiving this message gains our attention and compels us to find out more if we want to—but the only pressure to respond is internal to ourselves.

For me the most profound realization was in the meaning a poke conveys to its recipients and that this intrinsic "message" is entirely subjective to your relationship with its sender. Think about the different meanings associated when you poke your lover if you are in a new relationship. What about if you have a wife/husband/partner? This message might be flirtatious or even a deep token of love. That message might be completely different if this was to my child or perhaps a close friend. If it's someone I've only recently met, this might have an entirely different context still. A poke can convey other information, for example if we have an arrangement to meet at a pub that day, it can act as a reminder to leave on time; or perhaps if they owe me money, a reminder to pay.

Of course there is a darker side to this kind of communication. If you receive an unwelcome poke, perhaps from a stalker or bully, that can be deeply disturbing.

The point is the message and the medium are not necessarily connected directly. Playing games allows us to see other players who matter to us, whether or not we actually communicate in person. If I know that you can see the purchases or playing decisions I make then that will directly affect my behavior, making me more or less likely to interact in the game depending on the context.

Interdependence Matters

To understand this effect it's useful to think about how relationships work and consider how players might look at your game as a medium for communications with their friends and other players. This will allow us to find ways to help build deeper engagement as well as to reinforce the positive values that make it more likely that players will gain the emotional engagement with the game as well as to feel safer about spending money with us.

There is a concept called interdependence theory that is used to help us understand interpersonal relationships and in particular why some relationships are stable and others aren't. For me it also provides a useful way to consider how the social elements in our game can contribute or detract from the interaction with other players. This theory considers why some people have happy relationship experiences and yet have unstable relationships, while other relationships can be stable despite the unhappiness of their participants. This concept was first introduced way back in 1959 by Harold Kelley and John Thibaut in their book *The Social Psychology of Groups*.[3]

Measuring Love and Friendship

Defining your relationship with someone is problematic. However, if we take an objective, utilitarian view, we can theoretically compare the love, friendship and affection gained from a given relationship with the effort we expend to maintain it and from this we know if the relationship is "worthwhile." Of course that's not something we can do in practice, partly because we are too close to that relationship, partly because all relationships are in a state of flux (we feel different needs at different times) but mostly because we fail to correctly perceive the true value or effort involved. However, for the purpose of this exercise, let's assume we can make this calculation and let's call this the "outcome" of the relationship. Of course that's not all. We also bring to each relationship a set of "expectations." This isn't usually a consistent thing. We don't expect as much from some friends as from others and in some relationships (with family members in particular) we are often willing to put up with a reduced "outcome."

I Can't Get No Satisfaction

According to interdependence theory, "satisfaction" with a relationship comes when the "outcome" exceeds the "expectation." To complicate matters, we inevitably compare the outcomes we are getting from our relationships to the outcomes that others are getting from theirs, and those comparisons affect our expectations as well. This shouldn't come as a surprise; we are social animals and, in the end, social position is part of the motivation for play in the first place. Because of this we can easily find that we set our expectations so unrealistically high that it seems almost inevitable that we will be unhappy with what otherwise might be the best possible relationship; only to discover the truth too late.

Playing Together

This way of thinking is very relevant to social games. Our players have a relationship not only with the game but with the other players of that game. Each player will have a set of expectations that will create an outcome for each game session that may have little to do with any success they associate with the essential play of the game. Whether they continue playing is dependant not just on players' satisfaction with the game itself, but on their social relationships and their expectations of alternative services, which might otherwise satisfy their playing needs.

Is it any wonder that this social games market has proven to be more complicated that just having a game that sends "gifts" to your friends and that encourages you to "sell" the game to your friends in return for a few virtual resources?

Other Sources of Emotion

This kind of analysis is all well and good and gives us a sense of the dynamics of social influence on play. However, it can't of course help us isolate the specific emotional drivers of the players. This matters for games as it's a key aspect of what we try to engender in terms of play and how we use mood and pace as discussed in Chapter 3. So as designers we don't just need to think about how players emotionally respond to the gameplay, we have to consider how the gameplay will affect the social context in which the game is played. There are internal forces built into our game design as well as external forces from the social context. Player satisfaction will also be influenced by practical factors such as the ability for players to use our game to fill unoccupied time, the ability for the game to be interrupted, and how others, especially friends, can participate in our shared experience. At the same time satisfaction may also be influenced by opportunity factors such as what the player should be doing instead. Each of these may positively or negatively affect a player's commitment to playing our game. If we fail to consider these issues we will fail to reach the potential value that socialization can have for our game.

Don't Be Complacent

There is of course a darker way to view this interdependence model. Does the player's experience have to be entirely positive? If the outcome exceeds their expectations (and especially the expectations from other games), then this model tells us that they player will keep on playing. There are some grounds for thinking that this might be the case, if our players are new to gaming and their expectations of other available games are sufficiently low, perhaps they might keep playing our game.

I'm not suggesting that anyone deliberately sets out to make a bad game, but it could be argued that there have been some prominent examples of complacency among the original wave of social games. I suspect that this might be a contributing factor to why some of those high-profile early-mover Facebook games lasted as long as they did; in the absence of better gameplay, their players' expectation of value wasn't very high due to their relative inexperience in games. The trouble is, you have to ask yourself why new games didn't just come along to fill the void of quality or at least depth of experience. It's not like there weren't other "better" games—whatever that means—available. However, this market was one where the big publishers and developer were spending lots of money[4] to acquire users and often were spending a vast proportion of their earnings to simply retain their position. In that context it's not surprising that other games had little chance of being found.

What Can We Do About This?

When we think about the forces at play in socialization of games it's clear that we can't easily affect the expectations a player has about our games. We can try to create anticipation as well as brand values and that will help, however, players will still have their own thoughts and ideas. There are two factors we can genuinely control when it comes to thinking about our game: how entertaining the game is, and how easy it is for players to share and communicate in the game. The more we reduce the effort required to socialize, the more we have a chance to increase the engagement with our audience.

However, thinking about communication brings us back to the "soul" of games as a service. Player behavior evolves as their engagement builds. This concept directly affects the social needs of players as much as their playing needs and it's important to consider how the social forces adapt as the player lifecycle moves on.

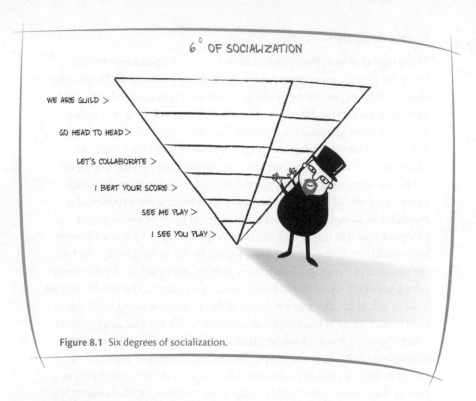

Figure 8.1 Six degrees of socialization.

Six Degrees of Socialization

To help us understand how this works, let's consider social interaction in different stages, I call them the six degrees of socialization—six core differentiating levels of social interaction that give us a way to examine the engagement needs of players and how we can use this to help sustain and build the audience for our game. More than that, this model helps us think about how to avoid problems that arise when you try to build a critical mass of players by reducing the the social effort expected of your players.

The First Degree—"I See You Play"⁵

When a player downloads your game for the first time they are in the "learning" stage and generally this is the most vulnerable time from the perspective of sustaining their interest. At this time they have not decided if they are willing to associate themselves with the game and they may have a level of concern about their ability to perform in terms of game skills.

This stage of socialization is passive, almost voyeuristic. First degree players need the reassurance to know that they are not alone and that there are others playing this game. This voyeurism is vital to sustain expectations and to help players overcome the initial disillusionment that comes after the initial download. Other players can provide the vision of the potential of the game and help foreshadow the benefits that the game has to offer in a way that no tutorial or developer-led process can. The point is at this stage that there is no risk to the player. There is only the opportunity to feel welcomed into the community.

The Second Degree—"See Me Play"

Once players become comfortable with their initial experience of the game, and often still within the learning stage, they will become more open to sharing their experience with other players as well as their friends. This requires a little more effort on their part, but provided that the experience is positive for the recipients of these messages (other players, friends, etc.), that's OK. For example, a simple Facebook post or perhaps a video post of my gameplay (such as Everyplay from Applifier) provides a way for me to share a positive moment from my gameplay, likely an achievement or high score that I've achieved. Perhaps even a funny moment that I managed to capture. The payoff comes if others follow me to join the game I am playing and if I get to show off moments of success.

The Third Degree—"I Beat Your Score"

The third degree, appropriately perhaps, is where we start to interrogate our relationship with the game. By this point players have probably crossed over from "learning" to "engaging" and their relationship in the game is now deeper and they are probably playing regularly, perhaps even paying already. At this degree the social elements are more direct where players are deliberately comparing their performance and behavior with their friends. Their relative progress starts to matter. This is not always directly competitive, indeed this is still largely about communicating their experience to each other than directly getting involved in each others' games. There is almost always a bragging element to this (imagine that) from high scores to leveling up, however this is more about players giving themselves a reason to keep returning, playing and interacting with other players in-game.

The Fourth Degree—"Lets Collaborate"

As our confidence with both the game and the social tools grows we start becoming more open to deeper forms of collaboration and even start to expect a level of reciprocation from other players. In some games this can start quite simply, such as visiting a friend's farm or playing the same map of an FPS game. There may well be competition between players and indeed the purpose of play may even be to beat others. However, the point of this degree is that we increasingly rely on the involvement of others to get the enjoyment out of the game. Indeed some level of collaboration is often vital in order for each player to progress further in the game. This builds stronger bonds and long-term loyalty for our deeply "engaging" players. Of course there are games out there which jump straight to this form of collaboration in games; think about games such as *Battleships* or *Call of Duty*'s online play. These are all about playing together. However, these always do this by creating a barrier to entry for some players. The question to the designer is how great is that cost and are the players who might be put off sufficiently important in terms of cost of acquisition? On the other hand, there are games that have tried to offer single-player versions and have then found that converting player to multiplayer or social versions has been problematic. These problems are usually caused by a lack of focus on communicating the values of transitioning to social play. Building strong fourth degree socialization requires a much greater level of effort than that in previous degrees, and requires that players (and the game developer) spends some time nurturing those relationships. Otherwise these communities can quickly collapse.

The Fifth Degree—"Go Head-to-Head"

After the initial level of collaboration we find that the degree of engagement accelerates further and usually the focus will be more directly competitive. This usually requires a considerably greater level of commitment and indeed to extent training. The offline experience becomes essentially irrelevant and the core enjoyment is found entirely through the interaction with other players. This is largely a phenomenon associated with real-time play, but there are some examples that leverage asynchronous play as well. A critical mass of users is essential to sustain an experience like this and this will inevitably skew your user base toward players already predisposed to the game (and genre). However, building this kind of interaction from the perspective of the metagame or indeed as a superfan game can be quite effective. *Clash of Clans* is a great example where the superfan nature has brought together collaborate and competitive elements within an asynchronous game.

The Sixth Degree—"We Are Guild"

The final degree takes socialization to its ultimate level where the social experience becomes more important than the specifics of play, indeed where the game becomes merely the chosen method of communication. That's a great thing to achieve and something that actually gives the developer a degree of freedom because they can often take that fan base with them into other games.

At this level, players use social tools in the game to manage and schedule their experiences together. They actively plan to participate synchronously, perhaps at regular times of the week, or even daily! The best example of a game that has achieved this status is *World of Warcraft*, but other examples also exist, notably first-person shooters such as *Quake, Counterstrike*, even *Tribes*. For players the real-world connections they make through their clan or guild can be highly rewarding, but the effort needed to sustain them is equally high. It's probably not a surprise that many a divorce, marriage and affair have happened as a result of people connecting through playing with guilds. Only the most dedicated of player groups will sustain them, but these are the same groups who'll be your greatest asset, if you let them. Given the right in-game tools, loyal players will provide the social "glue" you need to sustain interest from less committed players.

It's the Journey, Not the Destination

What I have tried to do through these six degrees is to show that, just like the player lifecycle, social engagement is a journey not a destination. By understanding the concept of interdependence we can try to understand the forces that sustain or break these social groupings. Social forces are, however, different and less controllable than player lifecycle. It's like trying to build a pyramid out of sand, sometimes the pressure of being at the top of the point causes the grains to fall out of shape. It takes effort to sustain a community. They are the most loyal, but you can't assume they will be around forever. You need to find ways to not only allow others to take over the positions of your most loyal fans, but to actively reward those who take on those roles.

A Social Pyramid Scheme

One of the lessons of managing online communities is that there is no way we can ever have enough staff to engage with the community as directly as we would like. However, by understanding the six degrees of socialization and providing the right tools we can put the power to recruit, manage and engage with the audience in the hands of our play-ers. This takes a different way of thinking than most social games have taken to date. First we have to remember that guilds and clans tend to be fairly small in terms of their immediate members but they leave a much greater shadow on the community. The people who coordinate the play of their guilds and clans have a particularly vital role and we should find ways in the game to reward them for their effort. The more we value their contribution and find ways to return their investment through gameplay, social prestige and, to be frank, love from the developer team, the greater their commitment will be back to the game.

There is a risk that this kind of thinking could get us in trouble, especially if we look at the way pyramid schemes work. Even organiza-tions such as Amway that use the relationships of their sellers to recruit others to promote their goods have a negative perception. However, we have an audience who love our games and it is only reasonable that we should find ways to reward players who genuinely help us retain or acquire users; provided we don't resort to cheap, brand damaging tricks.

Notes

1 *MUD* was the first virtual world, although my first experience of text-based virtual worlds came in 1985 when I first played *Shades* (a later descendant) on my Apple IIE with a coupler modem. This was the first time I realised the importance of lag; it turns out that it's difficult to fight in a text based game with a 9600 baud connection. Wireplay still sup-ported *MUD2* in 1998 and I had my first contact with Richard Bartle over support calls for that service. I know I've already provided this link earlier but this presentation is definitely worth checking out, www.gdcvault.com/play/1013804/MUD-Messrs-Bartle-and-Trubshaw.

2 *Counterstrike* remains one of my favorite games of all time. Indeed I would claim that Wireplay helped "save" that project. OK, that's a bit of an exaggeration. We bought the original mod team a set of new computers when they were low on cash and in return the fifth beta release of *Counterstrike* was branded "Wireplay." One of the best decisions I ever made. Sadly, it was only years later that Adrian Manning (one of my former col-leagues) owned up that he and two others managed to get their names in the credits. I've not forgiven him for not getting my name on that list, despite it being my decision and budget that paid for it. Adrian—consider this my revenge, mate.

3 Interdependence theory is largely about social relationships, rather than the relationship between a player and a game, however, it has great parallels for social games, http://en.wikipedia.org/wiki/Interdependence_theory.

4   It's hard to nail down exactly how much people were spending on user acquisition at the peak of Facebook games but the Fiksu reports suggest that $1.18–1.81 is the typical range for a "loyal user" on mobile, http://www.fiksu.com/resources/fiksu-indexes.

5   This model is an update of the one presented in my article in *Casual Connect Magazine*. I have adjusted the first degree to reflect players who want to see others who play but are not yet ready to socialise themselves, http://issuu.com/casualconnect/docs/winter2013/3.

Exercise 8: What is Your *Star Wars* Factor?

This is another exercise where we will continue to explore the themes from Chapter 9. On this occasion we will look at the elusive "*Star Wars* factor." This is about how users separate their identity from others using your game as the vehicle. It's the principle behind why some people will understand what I mean when I say "Han shot first,"[1] and why others don't really understand *Star Wars* (in my opinion of course). There are special rules and experiences that allow us to include some people while excluding others, especially the more we seek other ways to identify with people than just familial bonds. We naked apes are a funny lot when it comes to socializing.

In this exercise we will explore what elements in your game are designed to create a sense of shared experience and therefore to leverage the retention and monetization benefits as well as, importantly, the viral discovery opportunity that comes from effective meaningful social-ization. What social media will you support? Facebook and Twitter are common in the West but what about China, Japan, South Korea, Indonesia, India—all huge games markets. Just as importantly you have

What is the *Star Wars* factor for your game?	
What mechanisms do you support to connect to social media from your game?	
Why should I trust your game with my Facebook/ Twitter/Weibo details?	
What advantage do I get by connecting socially in your game?	
Why would my social media friends care about what I might post?	
How frequently will you notify my social media friends about the game? * The right answer is only at player request	
What makes these social connections meaningful?	
What social tools will you be making to support the superfan game?	

to think about why these have meaning, and not only to the player who wants to share but also to their friends, the recipients of those messages. They may not care about your game but the last thing you want to do is put them off because they feel like they are being spammed by their friends, your players. Finally, do we have to build some special experience, perhaps an open application program interface (API) to enable the superfans to make the most of the higher levels of gameplay?

WORKED EXAMPLE:

What is the *Star Wars* factor for your game?	There are two social aspects to *Finding Anthony*: the ability to compare your play with your friends and the superfan game, which allows players to collaborate as a "family."
What mechanisms do you support to connect to social media from your game?	We will support all Facebook, Twitter and other localized social platforms such as Sina Weibo (China), GREE (Japan) and Kakao (South Korea). Additionally we will leverage Everyplay to offer access to gameplay recordings of every play, including an incentive to upload and share the video each time you beat your friends' high scores.
Why should I trust your game with my Facebook/ Twitter/Weibo details?	The game encourages sharing of gameplay videos alongside playing achievements as well as incentivizing players who agree to connect with their social media. It will provided moments to share throughout play but the principle access will be through the player's activity, namely the gameplay video.
What advantage do I get by connecting socially in your game?	Connecting to Facebook allows me to compete and collaborate with friends. The completion comes from outperforming my friends as well as learning from how they played the game via their video replays. Additionally, I can invite my friends to join my "family" and this adds two new dimension to the game. The first is the shared endeavors of our family (something that can be quite bonding). The second is the coordination required to locate the appearance of the "girlfriend," creating personal shared moments. We all are in the same space at the same time.

(Continued)

Why would my social media friends care about what I might post?	Watching the gameplay of a game my friend loves is a great way to discover new games content, plus it's personal to their experience. It's not about the game, it's about what they did in that game. That might be funny/silly/dumb. But because it's your friend, that's entertaining in its own right.
How frequently will you notify my social media friends about the game? * The right answer is only at player request	We only notify when the player wants to and we only suggest connecting or updating when the player has done something meaningful or when something meaningful happens to that player's "family." They have to confirm the action and in doing such updates we offer players the chance to share a free item with that player.
What makes these social connections meaningful?	The posts about achievements are connected with personal challenges to "beat" the score for that level. Whereas other posts will relate to the superfan game
What social tools will you be making to support the superfan game?	Players in the superfan game will be allocated a URL for their family that includes a template page with wiki-links, forums, and a live chat system. All of these will be mobile friendly. The site will leverage a OpenMap API, which allows players to track family members' performance and allow competition between clans within the family to be measured separately from the overall family performance.

Note

1 If you don't know what this means, just type the phrase into Google or ask someone with a copy of the original *Star Wars* film (Episode IV)—not the special editions . . . definitely not the special editions.

Chapter 9
Engagement-Led Design

Getting Engaged

In Chapter 4 we talked about how understanding the "soul" of games as a service comes from thinking about the evolution of a player through their different life stages. We continued this theme in Chapter 5 when we tried to not only map out that the changing nature of engagement by thinking about the different cogs and loops we use in games to maintain and sustain the interests of the players over that lifespan.

All of this has been an attempt to get you thinking about player engagement and to understand that by acknowledging the player flow we can build on their engagement without accidently breaking it when it is at its most fragile, by asking for money or social sharing at the wrong time.

Thinking Differently

In this chapter we will explore the concept of engagement-led design in more detail and look at some specific tools we can use to build mechanics that respond to the player's evolving needs. This isn't intended as a prescription to define a formula for game design but is intended instead as a tool to help you review your game designs and to identify potential problems as well as ways to punctuate each stage of play with experiences that can help build deeper engagement, perhaps even to "upsell" players to the next life stage, to spend money, or simply to keep playing.

In Chapter 5 we identified the need to grab the player's attention in just six seconds and lead them to a meaningful success within the first minute. But how do we do that; what design principles can we use to deliver on something like that?

The Bond Opening

Let's take an analogy from the film industry[1] and look at the James Bond movies, which always deliver a spectacular opening moment.[2] Within the first ten minutes or so we are treated to a condensed experience with all the guns, girls, chases, cars and, of course, quips that we expect from the genre. This isn't a random indulgence. This reintroduces us to Bond himself, what he does and, importantly, just what he is capable of at his best. It's a benchmark against which his abilities are measured, allowing us to understand the difficulty to overcome his opponents later. The story of that opening is separate from the rest of the plot. This moment is about setting up the conditions that allow us to make sense of the plot later in the story, hopefully without giving anything important away. This is about explaining the environment of the world Bond lives is. Then it ends with a classic staged moment, we look at the archetype "licensed to kill" spy down the barrel of a gun. This reinforces the continuity between the films and whoever is playing Bond on that occasion. It's a level of familiarity that creates a concrete connection between the viewer and the film, settling everyone into place for the journey that is to come. This approach makes us willing to forgive all kinds of incredible or flawed plots as it gives us permission to turn on our "suspension of disbelief" and turn off our critical thinking.

What has this got to with games? Well it provides us with a perspective we can apply when we look through the first moments of our game. We should try to work out what qualities the opening experience has to delight players and importantly whether they foreshadow[3] the value of playing our game. This starts from the moment that the player selects the icon. We are setting expectations with the art style, the UI and how smoothly this functions. The way we explain to players what they need to do to play the game matters and should feel part of the experience. In fact I'd go further: it has to delight the player. If we have a boring, frustrating tutorial, this risks setting an expectation that we have a boring frustrating game. Instead we should try to eliminate the need for a tutorial and use play to educate the player in the ways of the mechanics as far as possible.

A Core Experience

The early stages of a game should clearly communicate the core mechanic (what we earlier called the "bones") of the game and this means we have to also clearly communicate the success criteria (the "muscles"), which at the same time means we have to explain the values of the game, which are intrinsically linked to the reasons why we should keep playing. Games such as *Assassin's Creed* take a very direct approach to this by giving us the chance to play a fully equipped and skilled avatar in the first stages of the game, only to take away much of those perks so that we can earn them back again. On the other hand, *Plants vs. Zombies 2*[3] uses a pattern of play that starts simply and draws you across the map for each level, allowing you to quickly unlock a series of new seeds you can use. This demonstrates the route map through the game, before you are informed that to proceed to the next "world" you have to collect a specific number of stars. This asks you to repeat the journey you have already made, but with a new end-goal as well as new twists to each stop on your journey. Both these techniques provide the player with a degree of freedom, a sense of purpose, and the opportunity to take a step-by-step journey of discovery that gives them the opportunity to learn and perfect the controls without this being too scary. Further, they use these steps to create entertainment, genuine fun as well as genuine progression punctuated with regular and early playing rewards. These are not just meaningful to sustain every player, but they also set up the expectations for later in the game. From this groundwork, the player will understand whether, for them, the game is worth spending money on later. Don't ask players to spend money at this point, however; the point of this stage is to demonstrate the value of the game to them so they are much more inclined to buy at the right stage in their engagement. That being said, this is an opportunity to lay our cards on the table; that our game is worth spending money on. We want to make sure that even in only the first minute that we are explaining that we have a great game, that there are things about this game that are worth spending money on, but only when the player is ready to do so.

Reasons to Trust

Let's also not forget the importance of communicating the core values of our game's brand and that we should ensure that our use of art style, the emotions of our story, the way we sound, and, of course, the core game-play combine to set expectations that will be lasting. Part of the reason why it's so important to paint such a good picture of our brand is that these first impressions last. James Bond is a brand, he represents specific qualities and an identity that, despite the terrible things he has to do, remain something to aspire to; admirable despite his attitude towards women. It doesn't matter if he is being played by a different actor or if the role takes a comic or dark tone. Bond is an idea that goes beyond a logo or icon. Like other strong brands, Bond has become shorthand for all of the qualities we want people to think about when considering the ultimate, elegant spy. What is the equivalent for your game? What are the qualities you want to communicate about your game? How does each element from art to camera, from mechanic to narrative all help to build up this identity? And why would your players think of your game when reminded of those qualities in the rest of their life?

Easier Said Than Done

Building a brand is not an easy thing to pull off. There are very few truly famous games brands out there. However, those that exist carry with them values and expectations of a playing experience that we understand instantly. I only have to say "Lara" and most gamers know exactly who I am talking about, and I don't mean the classic cricketer.[4] Don't expect that you can create a brand that will be the next *Sonic the Hedgehog* or *Angry Birds*. That kind of brand requires an incredible alignment of luck, timing and usually a huge and well-spent marketing budget. However, thinking like a brand is still really important and its impact on the quality of your game and the expectations of your player will be enormous, as well as helping you to coordinate your promotional messages about the game.[5] The required consistency of art, design, writing style, PR messages, etc., will pay dividends and should be rooted deep in the concept of your game and what makes that unique and compelling to players.

The *Flash Gordon* Cliffhanger

After the Bond moment, and assuming that we succeeded getting our audiences' attention, we then have to consider how we will encourage them to keep playing. I can't stress too strongly that the core differentiation between a product and a service is about "repeated engagement." So what can we do to build or better still consolidate that repetition? Let's take another analogy from the film industry. The Saturday matinee serial was the mainstay of the 1930s with actors like Buster Crabbe, who played eponymous classic characters from Tarzan to Flash Gordon and Buck Rogers. The writers of these classics knew that they had to satisfy their audiences with incredible, self-contained stories that would not only delight them, but keep them coming back each week for the next episode. The writers had to leave the audience desperate for more each week. The trick of having a never-ending story goes back at least as far as *One Thousand and One Nights* and continues to be used in many modern TV series,[6] perhaps most notably the original *Dallas* when we all wondered "who shot JR?"[7] You could arguable that the Kiefer Sutherland-fronted series *24* turned this into a fine art, with every moment created to deliver a new and deeper twist.

Gordon's Alive?

There are so many alternatives but, although I'm tempted to bring up *Doctor Who*, it will always be *Flash Gordon* that sticks in my mind. I remember as a kid watching reruns on a Sunday afternoon of Crabbe's famous character in glorious black and white, fist-fighting with one of Ming the Merciless' henchmen only to fall to his apparent death from the spaceship. Then in the next episode he would have suddenly have grabbed some protruding pipe and survived. It was all a bit ludicrous but finding out how he survived and how badly that scene was put together[8] is all part of the fun. However, what's important here is the build-up of tension and the creation of a perceived peril. We might have known that Flash would survive, but our suspension of disbelief allowed us to the luxury of wondering how he could survive the latest death-defying moment. This format didn't just have to be about life or death, the writers could mix it up with love interest (would they kiss or not?); would the hero kill his enemy? Was the enemy really dead? Leaving an ambiguity about the end of an episode meant you could revitalize any subplot in later episodes and has been the model for soap operas around the world.

We need to look at each playing session within our games as if they were a *Flash Gordon* episode. That means that they have to be inherently satisfying and make sense to the player. The activity in the session needs to draw the player inevitably onwards towards a greater objective (such as defeating Ming the Merciless) while dealing with the current goals (such as negotiating with Prince Vultan of the Hawkmen). However, we need to end the session with the player wanting more and giving them a reason to return for the next session. Indeed we could use this concept to help us mix up the rhythm of play, creating the gameplay equivalent of a musical "bridge." This idea of a contrast to the overarching composite of patterns of play is an appealing idea as, while it shakes up our preconceptions of the game, it still remains intrinsically integrated into the experience as a whole.

Building the Arch

So what is your equivalent of the long term story arch? With a game like *Candy Crush*, not only is the narrative journey literally drawn out as a pathway for you, it also has an "energy" mechanic variation that uses up lives every time you fail to complete a level. Each playing session has a unique layout and rule variations that challenge you in different ways and of course you recover your lives at a slow rate. We can continue to play levels we know how to solve as long as we want, but to move on we have to risk our "lives." In Firemint/EA's excellent *Real Racing 3* we are drawn forward by our ability to progress through numerous race courses and access more cars and different races. However, racing has a natural consequence, causing wear and tear to our vehicles, which impacts their performance. Both of the game examples I have given you are using a variation on the concept of "energy." However, as I said before I don't want to focus on that from the point of view of using it to earn money. At this time I don't even want us to consider these techniques as a way to introduce consequence for "failure." Instead I want you to think what this means from the point of view of getting the player to come back to the game after playing it for some time.

The BlackBerry Twitch

Getting players to come back to the game can't just rely on whether they enjoyed the initial session or not. There have been many stats quoted about this, but sadly I can't find a reliable source to quote. However, something like 85 percent of apps never get played twice. If I am waiting for my lives to replenish or for my repairs to complete, that makes the time I wait part of the strategy of play. The more I return to the game, the more I engage with the game, and the greater likelihood that I will want to invest in the larger story arch of the game, whether that's making my way to the Lemonade Lake or becoming the best racer in the Muscle Car category. These techniques rely on the subconscious awareness that something is going on inside the game and I'm not getting to be part of it. This sense of "missing out" particularly applies when a game has strong and meaningful social interactions. The use of notifications can provide a great reminder of activity in the game, but you have to be careful to make sure that this is valued and appreciated, otherwise it can become a little like a "CrackBerry" and become annoying. Having too many nagging notifications is a reason to delete an app, not to return to it.

Real-Life Interruptions

While we want player to return, we can't control the frequency at which they do so. Indeed we can't control the circumstances when they quit playing any given session. Players don't even have the same needs every time they pick up our game and the differences in their mode and mood will (as we discussed in Chapter 5) have implications on the duration, focus, and flow of each playing session. Sometimes the player will be looking for a quick fix or an excuse to escape from the circumstances they find themselves in, such as boredom on the train or perhaps a mind-numbing activity at work. Of course that would never be to avoid having a conversation with their partner . . . honest. To cope with all of these external needs, we have to make sure our game has natural moments where the session can end and still be left in a way where it matters that I come back later.

The *Flash Gordon* cliffhanger is a great tool to help us think about how we can help each playing session to deal with these differences. This is particularly important for mobile or tablet games, but thinking about this can benefit all game designs. If we know that the flow of play might be interrupted and we still deliver the means to lure the player back then we will end up with a more compelling experience. The methods we use to draw players back might use narrative, be based on a game mechanic, even be socially driven. But the important thing is that we think about how we get players to come back to the game. That's imperative.

Never Seen *Star Wars*?

The next movie analogy is a little less directly about the film itself, more about the subculture that has grown up around a blockbuster series of movies. The original *Star Wars* had as much as cultural influence on my generation (and many that followed) as any other movie, indeed it's hard to find many equivalents in any media. Its influence on games players is probably due to the coincidence of the timing of the market introduction of video games in a similar timeframe as the release of the original movies. *Star Wars* captured my imagination as an eight-year-old sitting in the cinema and to be honest it still does, despite the damage I would argue Lucas has done to the brand over the past decade. I'm not alone. Indeed almost every aspect of popular culture has been affected in some way by the events in a galaxy far, far away. But there are many people who have never seen *Star Wars*. Including my wife. Yes, as shocking as it sounds, my wife has never seen *Star Wars*. It simply doesn't interest her, largely as she knows there is no way it could live up to the expectations I have set up in her imagination. Yet she loves *Lord of the Rings* so all is forgiven.

Why is that important? Well, if I say that "Han shot first,"[9] I know that there is a percentage of people reading this book who will laugh or cheer. OK, maybe a small percentage will actually do that out loud, but the world is divided up into those who understand what I mean and those who don't. The people who don't have never seen the original *Star Wars*.[10]

Why does this matter? Well this is a clear way for particular *Star Wars* fans (like me) to self-identify using the particular shared moments of interest that only other like-minded fans understand. We talked about the importance of using rules to "belong" in Chapter 2. This is all tied up with that sense of secret knowledge that we share with other players. It's not limited to games. This is also why we stand around the water cooler talking about the latest TV series or football game. This is part of our shared identity and it allows us to separate ourselves from those who "just don't understand." Personally, I enjoy watching football, but simply can't be bothered to spend time learning all the intricate details and history of every game for all the teams. That leaves me outside the more mainstream conversations about sport. I'd personally rather spend that time trying to understand how and why games work better. I'm just that kind of geek.

Most people have their own "geek" areas that they love and want to spend more time indulging in. It might be music, history, even tinkering with model steam railways. Each of them has its own language and secret history shared only by the participants. This is the same instinct which Johan Huizinga's described when he tried to define play in his *Homo Ludus*.[11]

Understanding Social Consequences

So with the "never seen *Star Wars*" model we need to look at different and competing factors within a game to understand the social implications of play. First, we want to understand who else cares about the game we are playing. If there are thousands or millions of other people playing this game every day what meaningful impact can that have on the way I'm playing the game? At the very least, does the presence of all those players allow us to reinforce for us that playing this game was a good idea and that spending money will be good value? More than this, as designers we need to consider how we instill meaning into those interactions. While we can enjoy a game on our own and find that deeply rewarding, a game matters to us most when we share that experience with others, particularly people we have a relationship with outside the game. We can of course also gain considerable pleasure from simply playing a game with another person who shares our values, or who at least is compatible with the way we play.

Meaningful Moments

Meaningful moments are about the stamp we make on the game, either for ourselves or for the other players we interact with. The more we can directly influence this behavior—such as the way we control a physics game or the soft-variables we exploit to complete the success criteria faster or with some alternative strategy—the more meaningful the inter-action. We need to identify where these moments occur and think about how that can be shared and retain its meaning.

Introducing social aspects into play isn't about blanket-bombing of Facebook walls as was once thought. Services such as Facebook, Twitter, Sina Weibo (China) and GREE (Japan) remain vitally important as a forum for communication and to find existing connections between players; indeed new services such as Kakao Talk (S. Korea), Line (Japan) continue to grow. However, they should be used carefully. Let us not forget that part of what makes a game playful is our ability to self-identify with a secret experience. We don't want to share all aspects of our gameplay with everyone and when we do want to share, that post has to make sense and be meaningful to those people who don't play. Everyplay from Applifier[12] is a great example of a tool that can record your gameplay and that then shares that with your friends. When Rovio updated their *Bad Piggies* game with Everyplay this radically changed the emotional engagement with that game. For me at least it gave me a sense and purpose for playing with all the experimental pig-engineering projects and I found myself actively seeking out the *Bad Piggies* chan-nels on the Everyplay site so I could watch the funniest clips.

I believe by considering what we mean by "never seen *Star Wars*" and applying that sense of shared experience to our games I believe we can find the meaningful moments of play in our game and find ways for players to share that with people who matter to them. This doesn't just create a deeper bond in the mind of the player, it means that the recipients of their Facebook updates and Tweets have a vested interest in discovering what about your game matters to you. At this stage it's not advertising, it's a genuinely viral force for good and through the social sharing services this creates a natural form of advocacy, genuinely rooted in the playing experience. That trustworthy communication makes the people who receive the social game posts much more willing to accept that the player has a genuine love for the game and that itself is the most compelling reason for anyone to consider downloading your game.

The *Columbo* Twist

There is one last model I believe players should consider with engagement-led design (and we have yet to start considering the monetization pro-cess in earnest). And it comes from television rather than the movies.

There was an American detective program that started 1968 starring Peter Falk called *Columbo*.[13] In case you don't know, the main character was an apparently bumbling detective in a shoddy old long coat; it was his task to work out who had committed the murder and to bring them to justice. The trouble with the format was that we already knew who did it! Every program opened up with all the circumstances of the murder quite obvious to us as viewers. There was no mystery! However, the show performed a magic trick on us all; instead of trying to work out who did it, the point was to watch how Columbo solved it. We saw him stumble his way through and wanted to shout at the screen that the murderer was behind Columbo, like some kind of pantomime. Then as the show came close to the end, as the detective was questioning the murderer for the second or third time, came the immortal words "Just one more thing . . ."

Just One More Thing . . .

That was the point where the show revealed that Columbo wasn't an idiot unable to see the obvious in front of him. That's when he revealed not only that he knew who the murderer was, but where the evidence was and, most importantly, why they had done it. You knew the twist was coming, it was a formula. You knew who the murderer was. But it was still a delightful moment, because you didn't know why or how Columbo would solve it.

In terms of game design, this idea of looking at the satisfaction inherent in the final twist that concludes each episode of play is just as important. But the *Columbo* twist can help us to consider the longer lifecycle of the player too. What new extensions can we deliver to the story or the gameplay that makes us look at the playing experience in a different light? These processes are not for the initial product development phase—we will talk about minimum viable product delivery later in Chapter 12—however, it's very useful to have at least thought about the potential scope for product extension early in the design. If there is no scope to extend the design or to accommodate some extension, perhaps even an ongoing release of content that will continue to delight your audience, then maybe your concept has a problem. If we can't sustain our development over time we haven't built a service, just a product. Our game will feel dead and quickly lose players. We need to find our equivalent of that *Columbo* twist to make sure that even the most familiar players still have an opportunity to be entranced by the game.

The Most Important Question: "So What?"

There is something else that the Engagement Led Design model can help us with. It forces us to ask a really important question, possibly the most important question of all: "so what?"

I can't stress how important this question is for any designer to ask every time they write down a new idea, mechanic, plotline, etc. So what? Why should your player care about that?

We mustn't forget that we are at the end of the day making a game for an audience and although I totally understand the desire to stay true to your art and personal vision (indeed I insist upon it), to do so without considering the effect of that idea, mechanic, or plotline on your player is folly.[14] We are creating an experience that, unlike film or music, uniquely asks our audience to immerse themselves inside the world we have created. We need to understand, satisfy, even confound their expectations. However this only happens when we take the time to consider the consequences of our design choices and whether any player will care. We should always ask "so what?"

The Director's Cut

This chapter has been about getting down and detailed with the way you think about the design of your game, particularly in the transition stages. The Bond opening is about looking differently at the transition between discovering and learning. Where the player has already made the decision to install the game, but where we know many simply don't proceed. The *Flash Gordon* cliffhanger is about creating the conditions to support regular playing habits, especially as we move from learning to engaging. It reminds us that we have to build up the habitual lure of our game and to give reasons for players to return to that game. "Never seen *Star Wars*" asks us to think not only about why we "belong" with a specific game, but how social interactions influence our playing habits depending on our engagement, whether this is conscious or subconscious. Finally we come to the *Columbo* twist, which reminds us to ask that last question "so what?". This question is vital to our ability to fairly review our designs as to ensure that we do our best by our players not just in the short term but throughout their lifecycle, allowing us to look for ways to extend the engaging life stage as long as possible before our players reach the churning stage.

These techniques are all focused around building deeper engagement and, importantly, trust between the game and the player. The value of that trust cannot be underestimated.

Notes

1 Personally I dislike the fact that game designers too often try to replicate the qualities of films in games. They are different media and offer different qualities of engagement. Books, music, film, and even TV formats all bring different constraints and opportunities and we should embrace their differences. However, I have found some of these film/TV narrative tropes to be useful tools to help explain some specific design concepts.

2 Time Entertainment did a list of the top 25 Bond openings in case you feel the need to check out some examples, http://entertainment.time.com/2012/11/09/every-james-bond-opening-scene-ranked.

3 I use the term "foreshadowing" a lot. It's a term used a lot in narrative or theatrical writing. The idea is that we don't tell the audience what is going to happen, but we set up the circumstances that means that they might work it out for themselves, or at least that they won't be entirely surprised when a circumstance happens in the later part of the book or play. For example in a Bond movie we might see a character in the background observing Bond's activity in a bar. This could easily be an extra just stealing the scene, however, when that character turns up later and is revealed to be Bond's CIA contact we feel good as an audience—we noticed that character and just "knew" they would be important. My favourite way to define it is "pre-emptive hindsight."

4 In December 2013 an update to Plants Vs Zombies 2 removed a number of core mechanics which simplified the progression mechanic but arguably limited the sense of personal choice.

5 *Brian Lara Cricket* was a classic hit for Codemasters on the Sega Megadrive in 1995, http://en.wikipedia.org/wiki/Brian_Lara_Cricket; very different from the original *Tomb Raider* heroine from Core Design and Eidos in 1996, http://en.wikipedia.org/wiki/Tomb_Raider.

6 Every game designer can learn from the basics of marketing. Check out the Chartered Institute of Marketing (CIM) guide for some of the basic principles if you want to know a more, www.cim.co.uk/files/7ps.pdf.

7 If you want a list of some of the best cliffhangers from TV, this list might provide some inspiration, www.hollywood.com/news/tv/7808358/greatest-television-cliffhangers?page=all.

8 It was Kirsten apparently . . . http://en.wikipedia.org/wiki/Who_shot_J.R.%3F.

9 These Saturday serials generally had very low budgets and of course they were filmed at least 30 years before man landed on the moon. But I delight in them because they still have that sense of hope about science and space exploration.

10 If you expect me to explain this line then obviously you have never seen the original version of the *Star Wars* movie, only the special editions. You need to find yourself an older version of the film and watch it. Seriously! Put this book down now and watch it! Still here? Oh well . . . I never convinced my wife to watch it either.

11 As I have already said the special editions don't count, not because they are intrinsically bad, just that there were editorial changes that profoundly changed the nature of the story, particularly for Han Solo . . . and I told you go watch the original movie . . . it's worth it . . . honest.

12 Check out http://en.wikipedia.org/wiki/Homo_Ludens_(book) for more information on that book.

13   OK, I know (at least at the time of writing) that I am the evangelist for Applifier, but this isn't included as a sales pitch for that. I started working for Applifier as a consultant because I believe in this discovery and social sharing model.

14   *Columbo* is considered by some to be one of the best television programs ever made and takes a fascinating approach to mystery drama where we already know who did it, but we still want to see how he solves it, http://en.wikipedia.org/wiki/Columbo.

15   The driving principle behind marketing is "to understand and satisfy consumer needs." This might seem at odds with the creative drive to realise your vision, audience be damned. However, I believe that asking questions of our vision that relate to the satisfaction of the audience is extremely useful, especially if you want a commercial success as well as an artistic one. However, I don't think we should ever sacrifice the vision to the mercy of the revenue. That way no one is satisfied.

Exercise 9: What is Your *Columbo* Twist?

This is the last of the exercises from the themes of Chapter 9. In this section we ask "just one more thing" and look at our game from the perspective of the *Columbo* twist. This is about the character played by Peter Falk as the bumbling detective in the eponymous TV series, *Columbo*. We all knew how the murder was committed as we got to see it at the beginning of the program—including who did it. We then got to watch this ramshackle sleuth fumble his way through apparently failing to see what was obvious; until he said those immortal words, "just one more thing . . ." This is what we were waiting for. Now we would see why the crime had happened in the first place and, more importantly, how he had worked it out. We would realize the character's genius and delight in the result. As a program format it should never have worked but remains, in my view, one of the finest detective programs of all time. The magic trick was creating a format that we felt comfortable with, that we could trust and that told us what was going to come, but yet still left us room to delight in the results. That's a neat trick that you need to bring into you games if you want to sustain play for more than 100 days.

In this exercise we want you to think about what about your game will keep your audience coming back over the 8–12 days which is how long it takes for the people who will spend $100+ per month on your game to start spending at all. What will keep those players (as well as the freeloaders who we also need) to stay for 100+ days of play? Think about the ongoing events you plan to create that will create a sense of life for your game and can further build anticipation and ongoing excitement for the community as well as how they can create their own events/experiences. It's also vital to think about how quickly players will take to perfect (or grock) the mechanic so it becomes second nature and how to avoid that becoming boring. Indeed how can we instill a sense in the mind of the player that the game always has new secrets to reveal only to the most dedicated players, foreshadowing ongoing value that is always yet to be revealed in full?

In essence this is about how we can sustain the level of interest as far and long as possible; evolving the experience along the way so the players feel there is scope to continue playing, perhaps through product extensions.

What is the *Columbo* twist for your game?	
Why will players keep coming back to play every day for 8–12 days?	
What will keep players coming back for 100+ days?	
What ongoing events/ activities will the game include?	
How will you leverage community to sustain longevity?	
How do you play to stop players from "grocking" the game?	
How will the game foreshadow the value of keeping playing?	
How will you provide ongoing predictable value?	
How will you introduce a sense of anticipation of uncertain value?	

WORKED EXAMPLE:

What is the *Columbo* twist for your game?	In *Finding Anthony* we are playing with a mechanic that is designed to make people think about mental illness and the increasing difficulty that comes as our faculties diminish. This is reflected in the increasing complexity of the memory tile game in each lesson as they are repeated as well as the "failure" of brain slots that happens as we move into other "districts" in the game world. Each district will have different locations in it and each location type will have a variation of the puzzle, but because the complexity setting is specific to each location there will be huge replayability. Add this to the superfan games and there is no end to playable content.
Why will players keep coming back to play every day for 8–12 days?	The game tantalizes the player with the promise of ever more districts for them to control, perhaps even different cities (servers?) that can be explored and new communities located. Missions will appear in each district only for limited windows creating a reason to return in order to advance as quickly as possible. Each time you repeat a mission in the location mechanic will get gradually harder. The appearance of the "girlfriend" is designed to deliver a narrative element

(Continued)

What will keep players coming back for 100+ days?	The social elements including competitive scores as well as becoming part of a family (indeed having the potential to run your own) will help build longer-term commitment for play.
What ongoing events/ activities will the game include?	The platform will include the ability to offer special missions that will be managed by a web server. This overrides the standard missions and replaces them with reskinned versions of locations with an alternative look tied into the theme; e.g., Christmas, Halloween, Golden Week, Star Wars day, etc.
How will you leverage community to sustain longevity?	The social structure of the families will create a sense of cooperation internally as well as cooperation externally. The most committed player will have an advantage if they can recruit new users to their club/faction, perhaps even getting to be the ultimate boss.
How do you play to stop players from "grocking" the game?	Each playing location has a level of increasing difficulty as well as roaming enemies whose paths can be programmatically generated; making each mission slightly different. As the player progresses, their "brain slots" start to fail, which hinders the choices of play but at the same time offers the opportunity to create permanent versions of power-ups, each of which can be improved by "burning" duplicate power-ups.
How will the game foreshadow the value of keeping playing?	The ongoing appearance of the girlfriend will provide a narrative arc which will last longer than 100 days of play to fully tell and which continues to offer a reason to gather online at the same time as other players from your family, creating a genuine shared experience.
How will you provide ongoing predictable value?	The family system combined with the girlfriend narrative create a sense of both ambiguity and foreshadowed value. The control of the metagame story arc is to a large extent in the hands of the players themselves
How will you introduce a sense of anticipation of uncertain value?	The same source of predictable values drive the anticipation from the uncertainty as I cannot predict (as a player) the outcome for me. I can set up my own clubs and get a position of authority, but how that influences my profile in the community is a reflection not just of the gameplay performance, but also my social savvy. More practically, I never know when the puzzle fragments for the girlfriend will appear and how each encounter with her will reveal new information about what she represents.

Chapter 10
Delivering Discovery

Age of Digital Discovery

The digital distribution age we find ourselves in has created amazing opportunities for games studios to self-publish their content without needing the intervention of third-party publishers or wholesalers. Indeed, as I have often argued, Apple's genius is the way it completely opened up the mobile market and set an incredible precedent for other platforms. However, this process has meant that there is no filter (for good or ill) over what content is available and indeed the fact that the market is so open has meant that by the time you read this there will probably be more than 1 million apps available on the app store.

The consequence is that we have a real problem getting our game discovered. Don't get me wrong, this isn't Apple's fault or the fault of any of the other app stores. Their objective is for users to be able to find a game to play, not to find yours. They will promote content and that's a vitally important channel. But you can't rely on Apple to promote your game. Hope is not a strategy.

We Live in Interesting Times

The other problem is that this very age of digital distribution has also brought with it a revolution in marketing channels. Social media has changed the way we communicate with our potential players and this has affected the effectiveness of more traditional media. For example, TV and magazines simply don't have the same level of audience they once had; by contrast games have become a highly effective medium for advertising, particularly for other games.

Traditionally, the game designer has had nothing to do with how the game is sold or marketed. We designed a game, helped make sure that the development team made what we had intended, and then passed our masterpiece over to those "awful marketing people who have no souls as far as games are concerned."[1] If the game made money it was because of our genius, if it didn't it was because the marketers didn't understand it. OK, that's a terrible simplification, but we can't work like that anymore. Since 2011 and the seismic shift Free2Play[2] has now put the focus of monetization on the designer. More than that, increasingly the marketing of a game is dependent on the design and flow of the game to create moments worth sharing.[3] Personally as a marketer and designer I believe this is just a reflection of our industry maturing and realizing what ever other industry has had to do, to become marketing-led.

Marketing 101

Having a marketing-led business essentially means that you need to have a focus on your customers. Indeed I was always taught that the very definition of marketing was the identification and satisfaction of consumer needs. Marketing is not about fancy adverts and expensive parties, although there might sometimes be good reasons for both. There are some more fundamental principles at work and I strongly believe these can help us with our design process and help us to build discovery through the game itself.

This all starts with the 4 Ps;[4] four simple words that help us think about what we are making and why, as well as how much we will charge, who our audience is, where they can be found, and how we are going to talk to them.

The first P is product and there are several questions we have to ask ourselves when considering our product (in this case service also applies). What are we making? How will it be used? What does it look like? How do I consume it? And so on. It's important to fully understand what it is we are selling and what it is we are using to attract and retain our audience. We also have to consider the market context for our game including the competing forces[5] that affect its reception by players. The list doesn't stop there, we also have to understand the costs of production and distribution. Marketing-led products aren't just looking to sell as many units as possible; they seek to find the optimum balance between costs of production, price, and volume of customers. We have already talked about how important a repeat customer is in Chapter 4, and this becomes critical for a marketing-led business if we are to create a reliable and sustainable income stream over time.

The Fifth P

All important stuff, however, I must admit to a personal twist on the traditional approach. I believe that products are really about people (the fifth P, if you like). If you reduce all of the decisions and creativity we need to deliver a great product it comes down to understanding people. Obviously we have to first consider the customer or player of our game. This audience used to be as simple as "someone like us to plays our games." When we believe our customers are like us it makes a lot of things easier. We already instinctively understand their motivations and likes (they are like us after all). Unfortunately, this has never really been true. Even among the hardcore games audience there are variations in terms of reward behaviors as we talked about in Chapter 2, when we briefly outlined Richard Bartles' "player types." The other reality is that by building games we want to play, we have been self-selecting an audience who would be interested in the same things that we are. We have not been trying to create experiences that other people might play, because we believe that they "didn't buy games." Social and mobile games have shown that to be a lie. OK, maybe that is a little too strong, but it is clear that there is now a bigger audience and they are not all just like me. Accepting this means that we have to spend more time looking at the different drives and interests of each player. But with games like *Subway Surfers* gaining 26 million daily users and *Candy Crush* getting over 70 million, it's not possible to understand every view or need of every player. So instead we have to find some way to generalize by differentiating or segmenting players into coherent types.

Who Are Our Players?

There are many approaches to how to do this. The first and most common method is demographics. Here we attempt to identify the age, sex, and location of each player, perhaps also their cultural or occupational context. However, these attributes are both very difficult to verify and increasingly are not proving to be particularly useful. Assuming someone will behave in a particular way because of their age or location is not very sound. A much better way is to look at how people actually act. This is something we can do really accurately in online game services but it does take time and lots of AB testing[6] to understand the types of average behavior. There are some variables we can know, such as how often they play, how successful they are with the game, how much they spend, what virtual goods they buy, how often they interact socially in the game, or how often they share material through the social graphs. Of course this doesn't tell us what why people don't do certain things or how many people might have played if you had changed something about the game. There are some high-level segmentation models we often fall back into with F2P and they are the whale, dolphin, minnow[7] and the freeloader (non-payer). I find that approach unsatisfying. It assumes that the objective is just how much money you spend rather than what motivates you to play. I prefer to consider factors that are likely to affect adoption, retention and monetization. However, how do we identify players who have qualities that can help us improve performance in all three metrics?

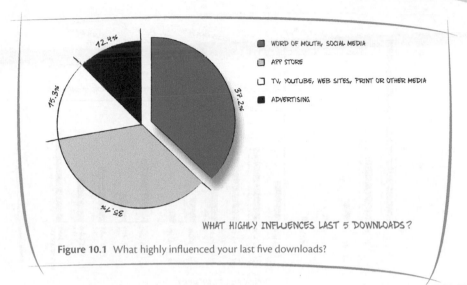

Figure 10.1 What highly influenced your last five downloads?

Stop Hunting Whales

In February 2013 Applifier conducted a user survey, asking what influenced players' decisions to download their last game. This showed that the principle influence the participants reported was "word of mouth and social media" at 37.2 percent. This included personal recommendations from friends in person or via some social media, including videos of play. You'll notice that this is slightly greater than the impact of the app store itself, including features as well as the search process. The role of advertising was reported as only influential in 12.4 percent of the responses. There is room for bias here.[8] Users are notoriously reticent to accept the influence of advertising and in these responses most players declared multiple influences.

Sharers Stay, Share and Spend

Social factors turn out to be more influential than even this result shows us. We discovered that 20 percent of the respondents self-identified as a segment group we called the "sharers." It turned out that this segment downloaded more games, spent more and played more than other players.

What is also interesting is that the playing behavior of "sharers" tends to reflect a better balance of interests than the "whale" players. This can be extremely valuable as it means their interests provide a better

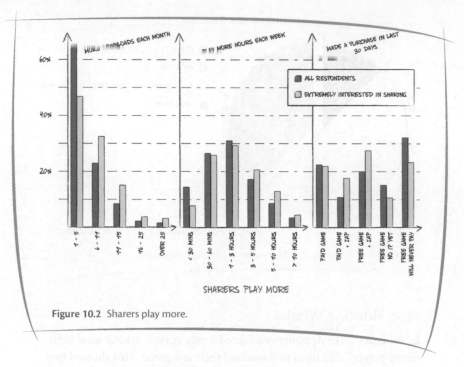

WORLD + DOWNLOADS EACH MONTH   PLAY MORE HOURS EACH WEEK   MADE A PURCHASE IN LAST 30 DAYS

ALL RESPONDENTS
EXTREMELY INTERESTED IN SHARING

60%
40%
20%

1 – 5   6 – 11   11 – 15   16 – 25   OVER 25   < 30 MINS   30 – 60 MINS   1 – 3 HOURS   3 – 5 HOURS   5 – 10 HOURS   > 10 HOURS   PAID GAME   PAID GAME + IAP   FREE GAME + IAP   FREE GAME NO IP YET   FREE GAME WILL NEVER PAY

SHARERS PLAY MORE

Figure 10.2 Sharers play more.

perspective of overall playing interest, which creates the conditions to allow whale users to bubble up. While it's very hard to generalize across different games, it seems that the highest spending users appear only when there is a strong pool of other "engaged" players.

All We Need Is Love

Of course don't take my word for this, find out for yourself and check with the data you can obtain and confirm how universally this applies to your game by asking your players and checking the accuracy of their responses by looking at their actual behavior. The key thing we want to learn is what will make people care about our game enough to play regularly and even pay, but we want this information broken down into each of our segments. A lot of this comes down to how much they trust you and how you show them in the game that you love them back.[9]

Heaven and Hell Are Other People

Potential players are not the only people that we have to consider. Think about the people in our team who are making the product, as well as the partners or colleagues involved at every stage of the project. If our team doesn't fully buy into the product we are making then there is no way we can deliver the right product (or service). Understanding how those people work at their best is just as important if we are going to make our game experience as efficient as possible, and I suggest that this shines through in the end experience itself.

If we understand the people elements of our game, this will vastly help to make sure we have the right product. Then we can start looking at the other 3 Ps.

Putting a Price On Success

The second P is price. There are many different pricing strategies, each of which applies to different games in different ways. Premium pricing is used to refer to games that are charged upfront, rather than necessarily being a measure of quality of experience. Paymium takes such a paid game and includes additional material within the game for players to buy. Freemium removes the initial pay-way presented with a premium game and concentrates on the in-app revenue opportunities including virtual goods and advertising while ad-funded games rely only on advertising revenues. We will talk about monetization strategies in detail in Chapter 13, but when we want to create a game as a service the answer is usually freemium. We have so much to gain if we have the mindset that makes it free to access our service and create a market of goods within our games that continue to add value over the complete user lifetime. However, making this realty is not easy of course. The trick comes down to working out what we are actually selling and what we are using to attract and retain an audience. With Free2Play we aren't selling the core gameplay anymore, that's what we use to attract our audience and to try to retain them. Instead we look to added-value services to deliver us some income.

Kids and Credit Cards

Considering price is more than just the business model. We also have to look at how easy it is for our players to pay for goods and how much they understand the value of what we have to offer with our added ser-vices. Most payment services rely on credit cards but what about people who don't have them? Credit cards are not used significantly in China or Germany for example. Can we find other methods, perhaps operator billing, cash-cards or similar services? Where we have a child audience this is particularly important as we need to ensure that players can't accidently make purchases and to engage with the parents who will act as gateway to any purchase.

The damage that can occur to your brand and just as importantly the trust between you and your players if this goes wrong can be considerable. To avoid this, it's worth going the extra mile to make sure that the process feels fair and deliberate. That might lose you a few sales in the short term, but this pays dividends in the longer term as long as your players feel they can trust you.

Location, Location, Location

The penultimate P is place. However, this isn't just about the physical place; in our digital age the nature of place has changed somewhat. Instead it's about understanding where your players' attention is rather than the traditional ideas of retail and logistical distribution.

For games we have an ever-increasing range of devices to target—and I don't mean the operating systems or OEM platforms. There are more important questions such as what form-factor of device you are targeting; is the game played on a phone, tablet, "phablet," console, smartTV, or all of the above? What about "smart" glasses or watches? Will there be a constant internet connection? How much local storage will there be and will the users be restricted in the volume of data traffic available to them? All these are practical considerations not just because they affect the product design, but because they present different delivery challenges.

As well as the practical limitations of the device come the situational issues that players might face and that are likely to affect their playing mood and mode as we discussed in Chapter 5. Place can affect the available choices, for example, playing a hardcore dedicated session requires us to settle into a defined space for a long duration. Alternatively, a casual "dip-in-and-out" collection of short bursts of play to pass the time. This behavior is often linked to the situation the player is in; such as on the commute, at school or work, waiting for a bus, or sat next to their family while they are enjoying their favorite TV program.

A Place to Talk

The more traditional way to look at place relates to where the potential player will seek out information about games and how you find the best opportunities to communicate with them. We have some amazing techniques in the games industry that give us greater access to customers than most industries. First, we know that players are often using their phone to play other games. This led to the rapid growth of cross-platform networks like Applifier on Facebook and Chartboost on mobile; these allow games to swap installs with each other. Most other industries don't have this kind of direct communication channel. It's no surprise that we saw the cost of acquisition on Facebook and mobile skyrocket in 2010–2011, with players like Zynga and GREE allegedly spending more than anyone else on in-game adverts.[10]

Acquisition will probably continue to get more expensive, especially as we have better mediation services targeted to support big brand media buyers as they start to take mobile seriously. Some games now command larger audiences than most TV shows and this will in time lead to greater demand. My guess is that we might just look back to this time and think that these record-breaking prices were in fact quite cheap.

Any Other Place

Other games are not the only place we can communicate. They just happen to be particularly direct and useful forms of access, which also means that there is lots of competition for them. We can't ignore other places where players congregate when they are not playing. We can look for correlations between playing behavior and other measurable (or at least researchable) factors and find correlations between, for example, whether they shop at a particular brand of supermarket or what specialist magazines they might subscribe to, or even which TV services they use.

Clear Communication

This takes us neatly to the last of the Ps, promotion. We know what our product/service is, whose needs it is designed to satisfy, what price it will command, and where we can communicate with that audience. Now we have to make sure we get across the right messages. As we discussed above, advertising is the thing most people think they understand. It seems pretty simple, we put out an advert of our game and we see a percentage of players click through. Better yet we can know which advert link triggered the download and use that to track value from that source. Added to that we can buy on a cost per acquisition basis so surely we have no risk, paying only for the number of installs. We can even AB test[11] different marketing approaches down to a very fine level knowing whether a green or red call-to-action button works best. This kind of precision marketing helps us to make better campaigns but it can't make a bad game any better. It can also fool us into thinking that we are being efficient.

The very fact that advertising is measurable means that we become biased to its influence. After all, we can't measure the benefits of PR or other indirect communications. These activities don't change behavior in a measurable way, but does that mean that they are a waste of time? There are influential industry leaders who claim that marketing, in particular PR,[12] doesn't work. However, we should consider those games that have become runaway successes without "any marketing activity." These games usually have a number of things in common, including an intrinsically compelling experience and that they cause some kind of "trouble." This particular combination has the effect that those people who play them want to show off the game to others or to write about them in the press. They might even, if they are lucky, catch the eye of the app stores and get the hallowed feature slot.

Create a Context

Remember our earlier survey of influences; 37.2 percent were highly influenced by word of mouth or social media; with 15.3 percent influenced by other media including web, print, and YouTube; slightly greater than the 12.4 percent from advertising. Importantly, as most of the respondents quoted multiple sources of influence, I suggest we can't afford to ignore any appropriate channels or forms of communication if we want the best chance to get the largest audience.

There is an old joke about marketing which says "I know that 50 percent of my budget is wasted . . . I just don't know which 50 percent." This kind of thinking is simply wrong. Marketing is not sales. Sales is about creating a funnel of potential clients, focusing on those that you can close and then closing them. Marketing is about creating the widest possible reach as well as a positive context where players become more likely to choose to get our game.

Immediate, Relevant and Gorgeous

Communicating with your players throughout their lifecycle is critical and the more we do this in person the better. We have already talked a little about the kinds of things that are important at the early stages of discovery, the first pattern we talked about in Chapter 5, which starts with the name of the game and the icon. When thinking about communication however, we can go further and look for the intrinsic qualities of our game and use that as the foundation for how we communicate with the player. During my time at 3UK we used a system to gauge the potential of any game based on three parameters. Was the experience (art & game) "immediate," "relevant" or "gorgeous?" "Immediate" asks us to consider how quickly the game concept will be understood from the combination of its name, icon, and—if necessary—a screen grab and description. "Relevant" is more about the internal consistency of the game but also how this consistency is applicable not only to the player, but also of any associated brand. The classic example where this went wrong was the RiotE game *Lord of the Rings Bowling*. Not only a terrible idea, but completely irrelevant to the brand's fan base. Finally, we should consider "gorgeous." This is a trickier thing to describe. It's not just about artistic beauty. Simplicity, cuteness and irreverence can all be gorgeous in their way. However, I've often been struck that, while it's often nearly impossible to say why something is gorgeous, deciding which of two ideas is most gorgeous seems pretty straightforward and surprisingly consistent among audiences.

Getting and Keeping Attention

Once we get past the intrinsic qualities of the game we should start to consider how we communicate to players within the game and how they interact with each other. As we have said, social elements and sharing are important factors. Think about what tools are available to both us and them to communicate with each other. How will this be administered and moderated, and how do you avoid damaging misuse? How often do you make updates? A regular, even predictable frequency of message or update can be extremely useful, but make sure it's relevant to their needs and don't be too predictable as important information might become overlooked.

Who Are We Talking To?

We also should consider a wider audience than our players themselves. Who are the "publics" we want to talk to and what messages are we trying to communicate? This is more than just to create awareness among potential players, it's also about making sure that we understand the shadow our game casts on those others who may never play. What impact will their opinion have on the people we hope to convert? If we send out blanket Facebook spam, is there any wonder that the non-player audience might start to get angry about this? Isn't it obvious that this will put many potential players off from converting to play? That doesn't mean we shouldn't use Facebook to communicate. Instead it means we have to ensure that these messages are valued even by the never-playing audience, or that what scorn we create does so in a way which motivates players to more deeply engage with the game. That's not an easy trick to pull off deliberately but I would suggest that the more negative behavior possible inside games such the Grand Theft Auto series created a response that built the game's reputation.

Magical Moments

The key for me is to find messages that ring true about the nature of the game concept and are fully realized inside the game-playing moments. These we need to create magical moments of delight that feel personal and unique to our players and that they actively want to share and give them the mechanisms to do so. Gameplay recording services like Everyplay from Applifier do exactly that by sharing video created by the players who want to show off what they are passionate about. This is a perfect way to encourages potential players to become excited about what the game represents and allows non-players to accept those messages as genuine expressions of delight.

Don't Hold the Press

Another key public is of course the press and other media. Bloggers and journalists need to feel valued and have the chance to say something unique about your game, something that will give their readership a reason to choose their articles. Managing your relationship with professional journalists is a very different thing to working with bloggers. There is an expectation of more thorough analysis of the content, although that is not always the case. Nurture the journalists who care about their work and who don't just push out the latest press release. They almost always carry more weight with their audience and will usually hang around in the industry longer. But be wary. They are always looking for a good story and may take a particular spin that wrongly represents your position. This can be negative, even damaging to your brand, game or company. You have to accept that their job is to write interesting articles for their audience, not to sell your game. And you have to accept that not all journalists are to be trusted. However, the best of them will respond if you correct them, perhaps by covering some new story or angle. The adage that there is no such thing as bad press isn't quite true, but Oscar Wilde was right that there is only one thing worse than being talked about and that's not being talked about. With bloggers, the motivation is more personal and often unique to each individual. It takes a lot of unpaid effort to build and then maintain a popular blog and that dedication requires a special type of person. Getting these people on side means we have to think about what their position or attitudes to the industry are about and how we respond to those interests. Bloggers usually respond very well to you giving them attention and especially if you take an interest in their motivations. If you look after them you can create a fanatical voice working for you, but it's hard to sustain that kind of relationship with large numbers of bloggers; just like journalists they want a scoop.

Getting Featured

If we want to gain a feature position on the app store we have to pay attention to the platform holder. I don't just mean Apple or Google Play here, think about PlayStation Network, Xbox Live, Steam, etc., even Facebook! In some territories such as South America or South Korea, the mobile operator still has a major influence. We need to give them a reason to give us the time of day. Already having an audience helps, but even when we are building that up we should try to pay attention to what that platform is currently focused on. Are there new hardware or OS changes that we support in our game that helps them in their needs? Choosing to exclusively release an update on a single platform can help get attention; perhaps even an advance, provided the opportunity is significant enough to get on the platform management's radar. As with all promotion we have to understand why they should care and communicate that to them.

Interestingly, the extent to which your game is localized into different languages, perhaps even culturalized,[13] the more scope you will have not only with the potential audience but also with the platform holders.

Thinking Professional

There may be many other "publics" you should pay attention to including investors, publishers or trade bodies. There may be other channels to consider—from outdoor posters to a promotion in a chain of cosmetic stores that happens to be the most popular with your players. If you want to deliver discovery you need to find an efficient way to use these routes to market and make sure that the "publics" have not only a reason to care but a method by which they can take action, ideally one where you can measure the success as readily as precision advertising.

What's the Point?

Delivering discovery starts within the game itself. It comes from understanding the values you want to communicate and the various different audiences you need to communicate to. You can't expect to be successful if you don't find the right balance of budget, effort and brand values that attract an audience.

Designers need to spend time thinking about the core marketing concepts presented here if they want a fighting chance to find other players who are willing to part with their hard-earned cash. Building a game for yourself is a hobby; building a game as a service requires that we consider our wider audience and how we can satisfy their needs.

Notes

1   OK, this isn't a real quote but does reasonably sum up a lot of the reactions I have witnessed by developers or producers about marketing people. They were rarely flattering. To be frank, a lot of marketing people had similarly unflattering opinions about the business sense of the development teams, and not always without reason. I've always sat somewhere between the two camps and tried to stay out of it as much as possible.

2   In the first six months of 2011 according to the *Flurry Blog*, the mobile games market went from 39 percent Free2Play to 65 percent. I think that counts as a pretty seismic shift in business model, http://blog.flurry.com/?month=7&year=2011.

3   I would generally argue that marketing has always been dependant on those magical moments of play, but in the era of box retail products it was possible to hide a number of sins with a good advertising campaign. However, there is a limit to how much you can put shine on a terrible game or even one that just misses the mark regarding the audience needs.

4   Technically the original 4 Ps have now been increased to seven; although there are contenders for 12 Ps, which are essentially providing more detail on each of the original four. For our discussion here we will stick to the classics.

5   In 1979 Michael E. Porter wrote *How Competitive Forces Shape Strategy* about how suppliers, customers, new entrants, substitutes, and competition affect any business.

6   We will talk a lot more about AB testing in Chapter 11.

7   I understand the term "dolphin" was coined by Nicholas Lovell on his blog, www.games brief.com.

8   We will talk about collecting data in Chapter 11.

9   This may sound a little strong, however, I'm serious. You need to pay a kind of loving attention to your product and its consumers; if you have no love for either then this will show through in the end.

10 I once got into trouble for saying this on a panel. I suggested that mobile advertising was becoming too expensive for many developers because Zynga and GREE were outspending everyone else. I honestly don't know how much they spent, however there was good anecdotal evidence that it was considerable.

11 In case you don't know, AB testing is a form of analysis where you present different
    options (game/advert/etc.) to a user and can see how subtle changes can increase usage.
    We will talk about it in Chapter 11.
12 Torsten Reil of Natural Motion said this at Games Horizon in 2012, a sentiment he
    repeated in an article on GamesIndustry.Biz, www.gamesindustry.biz/articles/2012-06-27-
    mobile-games-marketing-doesnt-work-at-all-reil.
13 It's important to consider cultural influences as well as language changes. For example,
    you can't default to underwear for female avatars in the Middle East and a game with
    skeletons in China can be poorly received. For more on this, check out my article on
    the topic on *PocketGamer*, www.pocketgamer.biz/r/PG.Biz/Applifier+news/feature.
    asp?c=53647.

Exercise 10: What Makes Your Game Social?

In this exercise we are going to look at the social aspects of your game. Not every game need have a social factor; however, there are some correlations between social factors and the proportion of users who spend money in the game. We need to consider what we discussed in Chapter 10 and how the different social levels impact our game design and the interactions between our players.

The objective here is to avoid simply jumping to a decision to blindly add social tools without considering the social meaning of each element. There is no point putting items in just because we have seen them in other games. We have to consider each in terms of their impact and effort to sustain, potential versus realistic return and the opportunity cost of other things we might be doing in our lives.

Key to your thinking through this exercise is the recognition of the need to set positive expectations that exceed the effort required to sustain the social interaction. There will always be external social pulls, however, you should think about how to sustain positive associations for connecting with others within this game. Thinking this way allows us to realize that social features require effort and can create stress among some players who can be fearful of a degree of humiliation, while others will see games as an opportunity to display their prowess.

Think about how you will introduce social elements in the context of trust, where players see the value of opening up their friendship profiles to the game, as opposed to the risk of exposing those friends to impersonal and unwanted spam. How you use this data should be trustworthy and honest and there is no better way than to use the tools as they were intended, i.e., to allow the player to express themselves. If this happens to be about their experience of your game then great; if the way they express this is unique to their performance or creativity while playing, all the better.

Once we have established the social context, will you expand on that with other social concepts? Will there be asynchronous or real-time play and how does this fit with the superfan game?

How will the game support the six degrees of socialization?	
How will you introduce social features safely?	
How can the player express themselves through play and share that with others?	
How can we positively compare short- and long-term measures of success?	
How can we create meaningful collaboration between users?	
What type of deliberately competitive play is there in the game?	
What are the longer term social tools for the game?	

WORKED EXAMPLE:

How will the game support the six degrees of socialization?	*Finding Anthony* uses a "family" system to allow players to collaborate on ownership of each district in the cityscape of the game. This is done asynchronously but with an opportunity to get multiple "family" members to coordinate their appearance in a space when trying to find the "girlfriend." However, access to each of the degrees of socializations is managed gradually and intended to expand the playful opportunity only for the most committed players; but turning that into a recruitment process for helping deepen the engagement of the other (less committed) players.
How will you introduce social features safely?	Players are only shown the social extensions after they complete the first few play sessions and only after they have completed the game in a particular location. This initially concentrated on the comparison of scores. Also only when they complete their first district there will be hints of the full "family" social model.
How can the player express themselves through play and share that with others?	The chosen paths used during play as well as the tactical use of power-ups will be stored in the recording for sharing so players can compare strategies for each separate location.

(Continued)

How can we positively compare short- and long-term measures of success?	Players have two core measures. Happiness associated with Anthonys family and status associated with the "family."
How can we create meaningful collaboration between users?	The family metagame will include opportunities to share resources between team-mates. The girlfriend metagame will provide a timing-collaboration mechanism.
What type of deliberately competitive play is there in the game?	Competition comes in the player's performance with each location/district. It will be possible to attempt to beat our friends under the same conditions as well as the ongoing play where the ever-diminishing number of brain slots and ever-increasing difficulty of the memory matching games will combine to provide a level playing field where experienced players have to take on ever more difficult handicaps in order to be able to beat new players' most recent scores.
What are the longer term social tools for the game?	The "family" you belong to will attempt to take control of the city (which, given this is a science fiction genre, can be any size megacity complex) by outperforming other families in a combination of top score and number of attempts in each location. Scores to hold any given location last only seven days, but transfer of ownership requires a player from an opposing family actively takes that space; they can't just be the last player to have made a score. Bonus scores come by completing the "girlfriend" hunt and is based on the number of family members that are present at that time and place. This will of course affect the specific location meaning that even a small family can take over a district held by a larger family if they are better coordinated. Players will be able to spend their happiness or status to obtain positions of authority within their clan (like a club within a given family) or within the family faction. These positions are always handled as auctions, meaning they can cost minimal amounts if they are agreed in advance but you have to trust the other players not to bid against you. The metagame will include tools to support communication, moderation, "spy" behavior, bidding for roles, advantages only available through roles, etc.

Chapter 11
Counting on Data

Coming out of the Dark

Once upon a time in the dark ages when we relied on physical distribution, games had to be completed and ready to go before they could be flashed onto a ROM or pressed onto a CD. In that era we were lucky if the game even connected to the internet for an occasional patch, let alone being able to be continually linked back to our own game servers.

Since the advent of reliable connections, even (largely) on our mobile phones and tablets we have been able to make really intelligent use of this stream of information, not only to create synchronous experiences, but also to capture data on the real behavior of our players and adjust the game experience in targeted ways for specific groups of players.

Connected servers can receive metadata from our various devices containing named variables associated with a specific player session and we can then use that captured information to see exactly how real people actually play the game we lovingly created. The more we do this, the more we discover how wrong we can be in our assumptions and we can then find ways to make fine detailed iterative improvements.

Knowing What to Measure

Data can tell us all sorts of things. How much money we are making? How many players do we have? How many we have ever had? Different terminology and acronyms are thrown about to describe metrics we can use to assess the health of our game.

Some of the most used terms include:

ARPU—average revenue per user (usually monthly).

DAU—daily active users.

ARPPU—average revenue per paying user (usually monthly).

ARPDAU—average revenue per daily active user.

MAU—monthly active users.

MAU/DAU—a percentage that helps assess the engagement level of your game.

D2[1]/D7/D30/D90—a percentage of registered users still playing after the specified number of days.

Churn rate[1]—the opposite of retention and usually measured by the total customers you had at the beginning of the month divided by the number you had at the end of the month, excluding the new customers gained that month. This number is closely related to the lifetime of a customer and if you have a 25 percent churn rate each

month this implies that the average lifetime of your customers will
be four months.

K-Factor—the virality of your game; how many people an average
player recommends multiplied by the percentage that downloads
the game.

Conversion—the percentage of players who have ever paid; often
further broken down into whales (highest spenders) and minnows
(lowest spenders).

CPA/CPI—cost of acquisition or cost per install describes how much
you have to spend in order to gain one player on average.

LTV—lifetime value, or how much revenue on average each player
generates before they churn.

Beware of Vanity

All of this stuff is good for your business and as a designer these metrics
also help you understand how well your game is doing. However, what's
most interesting is how these numbers change in response to your
ongoing adjustments and upgrades to the game. I'm not suggesting that
the numbers don't matter of course, these are the variables that tell you
whether you have a viable game or not. However, there is no absolute
right number, as long as you are making more money than it costs to
build and operate the game.

These metrics allow us a way to track how much effect our incremen-
tal improvements over time are having and the direction (positive or
negative) they take each time, which is what matters. From a design perspective we need to avoid falling into a vanity trap. It might be great for
your marketing team to be able to talk about your total registered users,
but unless you keep track of your D30 retention you could find yourself
in real trouble. All-time statistics, like total registrations, only ever go up
and we can confuse that with success. Talking these things up might distract people such as data-confused journalists and investors, but beware,
as most of the credible ones will see that for what it is. Instead we need
to use data to help us improve our designs, so let's look at a number of
techniques that everyone should use.

What Game Are You Playing?

The first technique we will look at will consider how we find the data we
are missing, that we can't collect. That might sound odd, but think about
this. We can only capture things that a player actually does. With Apps we
generally can't capture when they log out of the system, unless we are really

lucky and they choose to press the quit button. Most people don't. They switch between apps and turn off their devices, which means that our game almost never has the opportunity to upload the data of the closure of a session. This becomes particularly relevant when a player doesn't ever return and we never get the last post of data, i.e., when they have churned.

It's actually not that easy to know with certainty whether someone has actually churned or not. But it is likely that if they don't return within a month that the habit of playing has broken and usually we won't see them again. There are exceptions. With PlayStation Home we found that a large percentage of users came back to see what new content we had several months later, which is probably a factor of its role as a part of the console experience.

Looking for Trends

We can't know for certain if players will be coming back, but we can look at trends. For example, where was the last data point the game did best and does that seem to be a significant dropping off point for other players? Better yet, if we can map the first-time user experience against specific stages of the game we could post relevant data points to measure what stages those players got through and where they dropped out. If we are systematic about mapping this flow then we will be able to identify where the player failed to reach the next stage of the game and this gives us a very clear idea of where we might have a problem.

Comparing the progress of all of our players allows us to plot the behavior of thousands of players across the user journey and will tell us how significant an issue the problems we identify might be. This makes it easy to prioritize what we do next.

Filling the Funnel

This kind of report is called a funnel analysis[2] because when drawn vertically it always ends up looking like one. More people go in at the top than trickle out of the bottom section, which will progressively reduce in size as players drop out at each stage.[3]

There is a problem with this, however. As we make changes to the platform we will inevitably impact the flow of the players through the game and we need a method to test the effectiveness of such changes. The best thing to do is to break down players into sections or cohorts of players with similar characteristics or who experience the same essential service over a specific time span and then compare the behavior between different groups. For example, we define one cohort of players as those who started playing after we released version 2.3 of our software and measure them separately from the cohort of players who started with version 2.4.

Tracking Players by "Days Since Download"

This ability to filter out comparative groups of players can be extremely powerful and allows developers and designers to get really useful analytical information based on actual behavior rather than just asking for feedback. Personally, I like to use a slight variation on cohort analysis. Rather than collating groups based on an actual dates—e.g., all users who started playing after build version 3.12.1—I like to compare all players using that version based on the number of days since each one started playing. In other words, I want to see how long each member of the cohort compares from the same baseline of behavior rather than the release data of the version. Why? It's all about asking the right question. Focusing on the version of the build players are using is useful to allow us to compare that release and its performance against other releases. However, it assumes that players of that release are somehow identical. They won't be. Their commitment to playing our game will vary. That doesn't matter if you are only interested in the release performance. However, if you want to illuminate players' attitudes it helps to compare their individual duration of play. Of course you could do a separate cohort based on each day, but that not only risks data overload but also makes it harder to compare like with like. Taking players of the same build and then looking at how quickly they drop out based on their personal duration of play helps us illuminate more detail of what may have gone wrong, and the funnel analysis will tell us where. Asking the right questions in this way makes it much easier to identify how the lifecycle process actually works in our game.

What's Relevant?

Making the right choices about what data is relevant to capture or not is essential if you want to be able to make the right decisions about how to continually improve your game. We could just capture everything, as we don't know what will be relevant in time. But that can become costly to store and can also can lead to you becoming blinded by the volume of data, unable to isolate the relevant information. However, at the same time you don't want to capture too little because often we don't know what we don't know. So we have to ensure that we store as many potentially relevant data points as we can, the last thing we want is to discover a correlation to performance based on an attribute we don't already capture. This creates a dilemma that most designers have no experience in solving, especially if you come from the console world. However, there are models out there that can help us to get our heads around this conundrum.

Food For Thought

For me I like to use a model from the food industry, which was first developed in combination between the Pillsbury Company, NASA, and the US Army Labs to provide safe food for manned space expeditions. It's called hazard analysis and critical control points (HACCP)[4] and is widely used in the food industry to this day. There are seven principles:

1. Hazard Analysis

Identify the potential safety hazards and the potential preventative measures. In the case of a game, this is generally to identify the experiences in a game that can lead to players churning from confusion, frustration and boredom. We then need to know what we can do to identify when those moments happen and how we can improve those when they occur.

2. Identify Critical Control Points

These are the critical steps or procedures in the manufacturing process where making a change will have a significant impact. For me one of the best examples in the food industry is when to test for metal content accidently dropped in the packaging or food. There is no point testing for this early in the manufacturing process as the machinery itself may subsequently introduce metal into the food (i.e., things drop off). So you leave metal detection until very late in the process. For our industry we need to consider the game as a flow and identify what level of detail becomes valuable to signal a decision made by the player, not least as we have to balance data-posting against the processes of the game. It's unlikely that uploading every footstep made by a player in a game will be useful. However, this will vary for every type of game. For instance a first-person shooter noting the location of the player every ten seconds as well as, perhaps, every shot they make or when they take damage.

This information could be used to create a heat-map to see how they interact inside each level. For an MMO this would probably be overkill and it might instead be more sensible to simply capture the players' location every 30 seconds as well as the location of every combat encounter and its outcome.

3. Establish Critical Limits For Each Control Point

In the food industry there might be some tests where it's not as simple as pass/fail for any given hazard so the process will consider whether the degree of a hazard is considered significant or not. Similarly in the games industry we want to identify how significant each of our data points are and establish limits that allow us to know if we are meeting our objectives or not. It's hard to establish what we think this might be until we go live, however it's often worth looking at data captured during free testing to establish a baseline of expectations. This will quickly be replaced by the real data of your first cohort of course, but having a baseline allows you to at least have considered your expectations.

4. Establish Control Point Monitoring Requirements

This is the stage the food industry looks at the tools they have to measure the problems and then will define how these are to be implemented. In the games industry we will have to build into the game the ability to post and capture the data points we have identified as critical control points and to establish how we will report on these issues in a format that the designer can use.

5. Establish Corrective Procedures

In food this is all about working out a systematic method to respond when one of these hazards occurs and how they then go about fixing the problems before the issue leaves the factory. In games we need to establish how we manage and interpret the data we have captured and feed that back into future updates of the game or perhaps use existing service management tools to communicate the problem to players so they can avoid the issues.

6. Review the HACCP Process

Finally it's important to review that the process you have set up is working properly for its intended purpose. There is no point following a procedure that doesn't actually achieve its goals.

7. Establish a Record-Keeping Process

Documenting what you have done is essential, especially in the food industry where this process is regulated. We also want to have appropriate records in games, not least as it's important that we learn from our own history or be doomed to repeat it.

Thinking like this means that we have to take a holistic view of our game and look for the process flows that each player will go through. It's an enormous area and to do it full justice we need both a good handle of statistical mathematics and to take time to understand what each data point means from a player perspective. However, what I hope to do in this short chapter is to get you started thinking about what data can do and how you can get started.

Data Protection or Too Much Information?

Once we have established the data points we want to collect we then need to take some time to work out the data model that will allow us to most efficiently collect, store and retrieve that information.

Using the HACCP model we can work out the information we want to capture but we need to work with the development team to turn this into a conceptual data model. That means looking at the data elements and defining them in terms of what type of information they are and how that information relates to other data points. So if we have a player entering a scene we need to know the player's ID, the session ID for that game, and potentially the level or location they are interacting in. We don't need to know that player's real name for the purpose of improving the performance of the game, although there are places where we do need to identify them in some way—for example to confirm their purchases, to display their high-scores, or in relation to moderation purposes. Outside these areas we have to be very careful about real names, even alias names. There is a legal obligation in most countries to avoid creating any identifiable information, especially if they might be children, as part of our data protection responsibilities. This is an area where it's always worth getting legal advice and making sure that your terms and conditions of play cover your use of data. Collecting data against a PlayerID is a good start, but you will still have to be careful about how this is made available and indeed largely you should prevent its use in reports at all, except where absolutely necessary for the functioning of the business. We usually don't need the details of the individuals to get useful information on performance so this isn't really any loss from the point of view of managing the game. We are more interested in the relationships between each data point and we need consistency in how they are captured, for example each player will only have one PlayerID, but they will play many sessions that might include multiple levels, which may also include interactions with other players and multiple plays each with different results for each player.

Infer What You Like

We also don't need to capture every piece of information, just the variables that might change. We can infer other information from the combination of these variables and the known reference data. For instance we don't need to know where in a level we find a specific corridor, that location is static, contained in the level map. We just need to know the XYZ coordinates. This kind of unchanging information we call reference data and we can use this to infer more detail about the events we are capturing. It's not that these data points never change but any changes to them happen at predictable moments, such as updates, so are outside the frequency of play.

Draw Yourself a Map

Drawing these out into boxes with lines connecting them[5] can be very useful as it also helps us not only map out the flow of our game but also helps to rationalize what data points we actually need to capture and what we can infer through the report. For example, we might want to capture how many locations a player visits in a game session. We can capture the date/time of entry into a given SpaceID by a specific named PlaycrID and using the same SessionID. This string of data tells us everything we need to know on the database in order to work out a specific player's path through the locations in the game over any given playing session. We can use our reference data to identify the map used in the SpaceID and cross-reference other players who were also in that location (identified by the SpaceID) during the same session (i.e., SessionID). Of course, the report we create from this data doesn't show the actual PlayerID, instead we show the total number of players who pass that point in the game and we can even compare this process across different cohorts.

It's hard to stress how useful it can be to take the time to map out this data. Not only does it make it much easier for your coding team to translate your data requirements into a database structure, it also allows you to make sure that you really understand the flow of the game, which feeds back into your game design. Part of this analysis should be to work out how frequently this data will be uploaded and how much structure and flexibility you will need to create reports. All of these factors affect the costs, complexity and reliability of the solution you will need to get useful results.

Losing My Connection

You also have to consider what happens when players are not connected. Are they still able to play? Will the game store the data in cache? How long will it do that for? What happens if that gets corrupted? Too many developers assume that players will find themselves in the best possible connection all the time, but we all know the reality is that there are always black spots and being unable to connect at times is something we cannot avoid. However, how can we be running a service if we allow the player to continue playing while they aren't connected? Are there ways to allow the game to continue, even at an impaired level? We don't want the lack of connectivity to break our carefully created, regularly repeated playing habits. This creates lots of questions about how the client-side of the software (the part run on the device) works and how it interacts with the server side (the part that runs on the network). How much data can we keep in storage in the cache, how long can players continue playing without a network connection? How do we encourage them to reconnect when there is data coverage? How do we avoid players manipulating the locally held data? What happens if players change the time/date on the device?

Connected Experiences

Similarly, we have to think about the server; what happens if too many players update information at the same time? How do we separate live operational data from historic data? How do we ensure that the reference data for a game is updated alongside other updates to the platform? What about malicious hacker behavior? How do we avoid a "denial of service" attack where we get thousands of spurious connections every second? How do we avoid a "man-in-the-middle" attack where someone intercepts the output from a game to our server? There are lots of potential problems. Many of which are resolved (or at least minimized) by using HTTPS[6] posting (which uses SSL validates that the source and recipient are accurate and encryption to protect against eavesdropping and tampering) but that comes at a cost in terms of performance.

Designers often underestimate the complexity and overestimate the usefulness of using specific data points. Developers on the other hand often over specify the robustness of data platforms, but we do need to consider the security, flexibility and costs involved in such solutions.[7]

Expanding Possibilities

Once you have captured your data, the possibilities explode. We can interpret historic data using techniques using prepared reporting tools or even directly using SQL (Standard Query Language) to "slice and dice" the available information into nuggets of insight, such as the funnel analysis we have already mentioned, but in addition we can look at real-time data. This requires a very different reporting system but can provide brilliant information and an instant view of what players are actually doing at that moment in time. This type of analysis is really useful for live operations teams rather than designers specifically, however.

To Be or Not To Be

There is one technique that has radically changed the landscape, however. AB testing. In this approach we offer up to different cohorts of users different versions of our game. The differences can be very simple, perhaps different colored buttons on the "buy" options. Indeed it's important that these changes are discrete and isolated from each other, although there is no specific limit on the number of alternatives we can test for each discrete change. The idea is we see the responses of the players in the cohorts we have selected and determine which alternative has the best effect in terms of the use of that feature. It's an extremely powerful technique as it allows us to adapt extremely quickly to the needs of our audience based on what they actually do rather than what they say they do. However, it's not without its limits. We have to be keenly aware of two things. First, that although the majority might prefer one version of the change, other users might actually prefer one of the alternatives. You may well be segregating your audience based on the behavior of the larger number of users rather than opening up the game to a wider audience. This process will, if you are not careful, become more pronounced over time as each movement towards the "majority" may further alienate the minority audience, reducing their numbers further. The second issue is that AB testing doesn't tell you why the change worked and quite often will have unexpected consequences. The most telling of these is the longevity or lifetime value of the customer. Take a game where the player is presented with a choice of buying a small amount of in-game currency at one price or a much larger amount at a heavily discounted price. We may well see a massive increase in revenue in the short term if we emphasize the highest price option; e.g., £69 for 10,000,000 gems. However, what this might hide is that, although this price point works for our most engaged players, it may alienate or even scare off other players who are still in the learning stage. Putting reminders to buy things, and at higher costs, will inevitably drive new sales but it may well do so at the cost of the lifetime value of the players. Worse still, it may cause more delicate players to churn early. It's possible that these guys would never have spent as much, but it's more likely that you will have capped your potential long-term revenue.

I'm not telling you that AB testing is a bad idea—quite the opposite. I'm just saying that the use of data is complex and easy to get wrong without great care. We need to appreciate exactly what our data means and its consequences. That is like a form of shadow that each change to our game design will cast. The only way to understand this shadow is to talk to our users and get some insight, something raw data alone won't give us.

Testing is a Process

Player surveys, focus groups and formal play-testing sessions have gone out of favor recently given that we can capture such a huge amount of information about what players do. They are unreliable and messy and can't help you predict future actions. However, this kind of qualitative research can provide you with a good understanding of "why" players behaved in a particular way. Understanding motivations is key to making the right choices about what we see coming out of the raw behavioral data we capture, and without talking to players, how can we get that right? This shouldn't be considered as a one-time thing. Good testing is a process that allows us to compare behavior over time, not just in a single snapshot. It also doesn't have to be too expensive and, done well, can help your validate major feature changes in a way that opens the game out to new possibilities and new audiences rather than just relying on the feedback of the audiences you have.

This is important as your design process shouldn't ignore opinions of other users, especially those who don't currently play our games.

Balancing data and insight together means you can adapt and expand your audience appeal in both the short term and the long term.

On the other hand, we must also be careful to understand the difference between opinion and data. When we show our games to other people, we inevitably influence their responses to us. They may want to please us or to show off how clever they are. I'm not suggesting people will be deliberately awkward but they will inevitably be influenced by your presence. This is one of the reasons it's so important to create the right repeatable conditions for play testing; not just going down to the local bar and showing random people. Similarly when you make a release to a beta community, compare what they say with what they actually do—especially, after you make significant updates to the flow or difficulty of the game[8]. Compare the reactions and behavior, but more than that, isolate the differences between new participants to the beta after that release was made to the established players. Something that used to be easy but is made harder might get a bad reaction from established players, but may at the same time enhance the retention level of the new players. We have to be careful with our interpretations as they might not be as obvious as they first appear.

Summing Up

Capturing data about how players play your game is now as much a part of the design process as creating game mechanics or the monetization model. This may seem to be adding more work and effort, but in fact will pay dividends to you. The more data you have, the more insight you will gain and the easier it will be for you to test and improve your player's experience. This has become a critical tool for the designer and we should embrace it.

However, to make this work for you it's really important to ask the right questions. Knowing what you need to know is critical and often we can be confused by a wrong interpretation of what our data means. This often leads well-meaning developers who want to make better games to fail and simply produce games that are better at making money but are in the end unsatisfying and alienate their own core audience.

Getting this right is about capturing enough information so you can isolate the unknown variables without risking the data blindness that comes with capturing everything. The only way to do that is to look at what actions correspond to genuine choices by the player and even just documenting that will help you have a better insight on how your game will perform That's a worthwhile exercise in its own right.

Notes

1 There is a debate over whether we should use the term D1 or D2 to measure the first days retention. Personally I prefer to use D2, but some prefer to think that the first day of play is day 0 and use D1. Churn is an oddly useful measurement. It's negative focus (i.e., looking at the number of people who leave your game) but this allows you to think about what you need to fix and how imperative it is to do that. It's psychologically different from how you might respond to increasing retention and also makes it easier to argue for resources in your team, http://en.wikipedia.org/wiki/Churn_rate.

2 Funnel analysis is a tool commonly used in sales analysis as it helps understand where in the cycle we have to focus our attention to increase the rate of conversion, http://en.wiki pedia.org/wiki/Funnel_chart.

3 As well as looking at which players leave your game at particular points is also useful to compare that with how many act in positive ways, for example, sharing their successes and failures through the games social channels. We don't necessarily want to entirely throw away a moment in the game many players love if a few players leave at that point—there might be other reasons they are leaving.

4 I first became aware of HACCP in my first full-time job (before I started in games) where I was involved producing software for food technicians, mostly in chocolate manufacture. It came up again when I worked in the pensions industry looking at online security and electronic document storage and now seems to follow me into data capture for games, https://en.wikipedia.org/wiki/Hazard_analysis_and_critical_control_points.

5 The brave among you will want to check out a systematic approach for documenting entity relationships called UML (Unified Modelling Language). This is used in software engineering, object-orientated programming and, of course, data modelling, but don't let that put you off—it's pretty a useful approach to learn, http://en.wikipedia.org/wiki/Unified_Modeling_Language.

6 While it's not a universal panacea for all things in online security, the HTTPS protocol is a vital component of what makes the internet function for businesses. Essentially this is the combination of the normal HTTP (Hyper Text Transfer Protocol) and the encryption protocols provided SSL (Secure Sockets Layer)—more recently updated to TLS (Transport Layer Security), http://en.wikipedia.org/wiki/HTTP_Secure.

7 On the plus side there are a number of services out on the market that can help, some like Flurry are free (at the time of publication at least), as long as you don't mind the limited options and the fact that your data will anonymously go into the pool of market data that Flurry reports on its blog. Personally, I think this is a good idea as it gives you a real benchmark of your relative success.

8 Before we launched the 3G carrier Three in the UK we conducted countless focus group tests to understand what users would want most from the new service. Video calling kept coming up as the most important innovation, but it flopped. Why? Because making a call in test conditions was nothing like the real-world where you didn't know if you had coverage, your friends had a compatible phone, etc. Add to that the risk of being found in your underpants or having to stare at your boss when on a video call, even if they aren't telling you off. Reality and expectation are rarely the same.

Exercise 11: How Does Your Design Encourage Discovery?

In this exercise we need to work out how our game design itself contributes to the discovery process and what elements in the design make it more likely to take advantage of any opportunity for either in-person or online social discovery. Additionally, we will look at some of the basic elements you need to consider to make sure that players have the best possible chance to understand what your game is about and why they will select that game not only from the app store but also why they will remember the icon on the device and select it again a second and many subsequent times.

In working through this exercise we need to consider the way in which our game design works for our objectives to be found. The art style and gameplay can be extremely important in this as they have to convey the relevance of the game to that player in an immediate and gorgeous manner. We often only have the name and the icon to explain why players should care and this means we need to capture their imagination as simply as possible. In the real world we should AB test both of

How does your design affect the opportunity for discovery?	
What is the game's name and icon that instantly communicate what the game is about?	
How does the art-style, gameplay and story concept feel relevant?	
What about the art-style, audio, gameplay and story concept feels gorgeous?	
Where is the opportunity for players to share personally unique magical moments?	
Why will the recipients of social messages from players care about this game?	
Why will journalists or advocate players talk about this game?	
What features allows the platform holder to feature this game?	

these in detail, but for the purposes of this exercise just write down your initial thoughts, we can improve on them later.

We should also think about how the game creates magical moments of delight that players actively want to share with others and why their friends will care about those moments. Will they be able to create unique expressions of their gameplay ability or creativity through your game? Further than this we need to consider not just the players and their friends but also the other audiences. Why will journalists and app store managers care about your game?

WORKED EXAMPLE:

How does your design affect the opportunity for discovery?	Finding Anthony is a game that will attempt to not only be entertaining, but to explore the difficult human theme of dementia. However, we don't want this to be at all patronizing or uncomfortable to play, hence the setting in a science fiction context. Throughout the design are opportunities for meaningful sharing; however, to pull this off, the interactions with mobile enemies (near miss, collisions, and easy escapes) should each have large number of alternative and comical effects.
What is the game's name and icon that instantly communicate what the game is about ?	Finding Anthony should use Sopranos-style gangster imagery but with a robotic twist. It should be bold and simple and memorable, e.g., the face of the gangster but with the forehead not quite fitting properly.
How does the art-style, gameplay and story concept feel relevant?	The Blade Runner art-style, repetitive, yet constantly more difficult gameplay, and issues with both family and "family" should resonate with the increasing confusion of the character and the use of repetition and routine to overcome problems with the memory system.
What about the art-style, audio, gameplay and story concept feels gorgeous?	The illusions to Blade Runner and The Sopranos should feel familiar, yet different. The design should feel comfortable and yet contained in them is the principle of an untidy and decaying mind that is struggling against all odds to keep control of its environment.

(Continued)

Where is the opportunity for players to share personally unique magical moments?	Each gameplay session will be recorded and shared as video through services like Everyplay. The interactions with the mobile enemies as well as the successful matching of memory tiles will have a visually satisfying moment and the completion of a level will display a momentary sense of normality (which will decay over time if the location is left unattended).
Why will the recipients of social messages from players care about this game?	The gameplay relies on the player selecting the right path and timing to avoid mobile enemies as well gratifying animations when you successfully combine memory tiles. Watching your friends' solutions and timing should be intrinsically joyful, especially where the timing is very close. Failure should also be as funny as possible.
Why will journalists or advocate players talk about this game?	The twist about the game allowing us to think about dementia is interesting, but we don't want to labor that point in order to avoid it becoming a cynical exercise. Instead the concept and story of "finding the girlfriend" should include sufficient ambiguity as the real story will be revealed over a story arc of several months— communicated through each successful discovery of her location.
What features allows the platform holder to feature this game?	The game should always be created with the latest iteration of the platform tools and will seek to use new features wherever possible. We want to avoid exclusives, but we will look to create platform-specific exclusive moments. Additionally, we will seek to provide widespread localization into multiple languages.

Chapter 12
Service Strategies

Thinking Like a Service

The majority of the focus of this book has been the player experience and the way that building games as a service adapts and adjusts to the evolving engagement of the player over their lifecycle. However, as a designer we can't ignore the changes we have to consider from the delivery side of the experience, including the necessary changes to the development process itself.

This manifests itself most obviously in one term that is thrown about by consultants and panelists at conferences all the time: the minimum viable product (MVP). It's a pretty simple principle but one I believe is often misunderstood. This just isn't about making the smallest thing possible or the cheapest thing possible before launching it. This principle is about building something you can test and learn from. If we are going to test something, we have to be able to measure it and we have to create something from which we can build further. Of course we will have to decide to constrain what we are going to build to something we can release in a sensible timeframe, but more than that, we are building a foundation for our eventual service. This doesn't mean we have to compromise on the vision we have for our game, it just means we have to focus on the core values first and be willing to pivot as we discover the players' reactions.

Success Is Not a Straight Line

Pivoting is an often used phrase in business strategy and many designers might find it uncomfortable to take on board. Yes, it means changing what you are doing. Yes, it can be hard. However, successful pivoting for creative content still has to stick to what was valuable in the original creative vision, it shouldn't ignore the original core objectives, even if the changes have to be radical. If the core vision is wrong there is no point trying to pivot, instead we need to rethink from scratch using the information we have learnt. Usually, it's not the core vision that is at fault but the implementation approach we took. This might be about the playing mechanics, the longevity of play, even the art-style, but essentially any failure means that our hypothesis about our players' reactions was wrong. But rather than seeing this as just failure on our part we can use it as an opportunity to learn. I have no problem with failure, which is a good thing as I've been involved in many more "near misses" than outright success stories, and usually it's been because the concept was way too early. Each one has provided me with a way to review the way I think and many of the lessons in this book come from those "failures." You rarely learn as much when you are truly successful, but you can only learn from failures where you are honest about the process. I know how easy it is to blame yourself or others, rather than looking objectively at the circumstances.

The Lean Startup

One of the most important lessons of *The Lean Startup*[1] and other such guides is that we shouldn't fear failing,[2] but rather make sure we fail fast, and before we have spent all our money. Better yet, we should make sure that we take special effort to ensure we can measure our results in a way that will yield the best insight allowing us to learn as much as possible for the next release.

This probably sounds like it's just iteration. All game developers and designers understand the importance of iterating in order to perfect gameplay. However, this is profoundly different. We are looking to minimize the development impact and release something to our audience before it is complete. We can't spend months or years perfecting every aspect of the game. Instead we have to pick our battles and focus on something we can deliver efficiently and quickly. That also means we should try to avoid making the same mistakes we have made before and learn from other developers' failures to avoid their mistakes too, or at least the most obvious ones.[3]

Simply Focus

Development is always about compromise and there is the classic conundrum described in the Triangle of Development, where we can choose any two of the best quality, time to market, or cost; but never all three. However, we can always choose to reduce our scope, to reduce the number of features down to a level where it is possible to deliver good quality, in good time, and at a reasonable cost.

The curious thing is that this kind of focus is that we often get the best results by simplifying the game complexity down to a level that also happens to be much more accessible to a wider audience. I believe this is one (of many) reasons why some of the successful mobile and tablet games are based on relatively basic gameplay concepts. If we use the data capture principles outlined in Chapter 11, we can then measure the meaningful control points in the game allowing us to work out where improvements are likely to have the biggest effect.

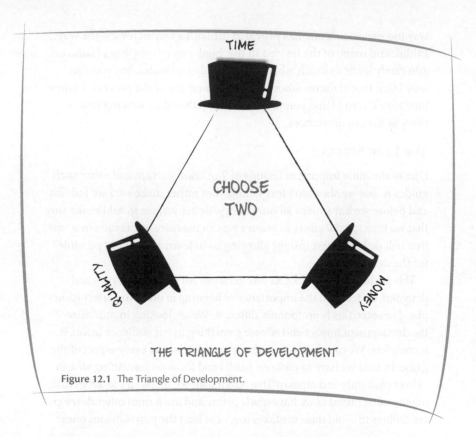

Figure 12.1 The Triangle of Development.

This kind of simplification is precisely why we spent time talking about the game anatomy. If we can start with a repeatable core mechanic, build that into a narrative context, set within a wider metagame, then this allows us to better structure a game experience that can be tested and developed further, iteration by iteration. Simplification for our game becomes easy to achieve by focusing our attention on that very repeatable core mechanic.

Getting Things in Order

Choosing the right features to concentrate on is incredibly emotional. I have spent most of my career having to do this and it's always painful. The only way I have found to do this successfully is to make a simple list of all the features and put them in order, the most important first. Each feature needs to be defined as a distinct, single piece of work that takes no more than a sprint (usually 1–2 weeks) to complete and test.

Anything larger than that needs to be broken down further into its component parts. For example, implementing a commerce platform needs authentication, inventory management, purchase flow design, UI design, UI implementation, merchant process, etc.

Once we have our list then we put the list in absolute priority order. This has to be entirely honest and you have to find ways to avoid emotional decisions as far as possible. Where there is a decision to make, try to consider the perspectives of our target players—at the end of the day, it's their needs we have to satisfy to be successful. Importantly we are not deciding which features we want to deliver, simply the order in which we will work on them. This is good news because that we never need lose our most favorite feature,[4] we only have to defer it to a later release. That takes some of the emotional sting out of the decision-making process. That one thing that you hold most precious in the design concept might not fit into the initial release, but we can bring it into a later update and use that to help make a big deal out of that later release. Of course if a feature never makes it into a release then we will come to realize that perhaps it wasn't that important in the first place. At times like this we have to "kill our darlings" (or perhaps use them to inspire our next game).

Creating an absolute list is just the start of the planning process. This information feeds into the development process and is used to create schedules of work, but let's come back to that when we talk about agile development. Suffice it to say that we will find that we need to find an advantage to staggering our precious features between different releases, not least in order to sustain engagement. This allows us to "tell" our players our vision for the game, step by step, building a progressive anticipation of what is to come and, hopefully, trust that we deliver on our promises.

What is Minimum? What is Viable?

As we work with the development team to allocate our priority tasks to the available resources, we will find out quickly that it will take a number of different sprints to build a product that is suitable for the initial release. We have already worked out the priority so the question will come down to which sprint delivers a product with sufficient functionality to release. This will rarely be a level of quality of product that you are happy with. Indeed if you are not at least slightly embarrassed by the experience, then you have probably waited too long.

What's important is that the initial release needs to convey the intention of the vision of your game (at least at its core) and be sufficiently self-contained to function . . . i.e., it won't crash and has just enough playable material to make sure players won't immediately give you a terrible rating. Deciding if your game is viable is incredibly challenging and it depends on the specific market segment you are targeting. Always start with a friendly alpha or closed beta audience.[5] If you can't manage that then perhaps consider external test teams or an audience in a limited location, such as New Zealand. The important thing is to find an audience who are not emotionally involved and who can not only provide honest feedback, but who you make feel special enough that they trust you to respond to that feedback. This way you will be more easily forgiven for versions of the game that fail to satisfy completely, therefore you can get their feedback earlier without causing them to churn.

If for some reason you can't do this kind of early release, then the demands on quality of the initial release will be much higher. Indeed we have seen that the minimum viable quality bar rising all the time. That means that, although you should continue to keep your initial proposition small, you have to ensure that the level of polish of that initial section is as high as possible to avoid losing your audience at the most critical time (i.e., full launch). That being said, get the game in front of people who aren't emotionally involved just as soon as it is possible; what matters is that you test realistic user behavior.

Testing Times

Getting information for users about your game ideas is vital, and not just when you release your MVP. Testing should be incorporated throughout the development process including old-school focus-group testing where possible. Have a group of people you trust to give regular feedback on the ideas and the progress of the implementation, but make sure you regularly test these assumptions with new people who are not emotionally engaged with the project. This doesn't have to be expensive, but should be done as formerly as you can afford. Ideally using a series of open questions that involve interaction with the game and that can be recorded without the players being obviously observed.

This type of testing can only give you opinions. Focus testers notoriously can only tell you what they understand and, like all data research, should only inform your decisions, not determine them.

Having a product in front of an audience with the ability to capture real-user data is much more powerful than focus testing. The game is no longer a theoretical concept; instead it is a living thing providing telemetry that allows you to understand how each twist, turn, and opportunity for play are explored by real players. You can compare their behavior with your findings of how people played the game during your internal usability tests and use all of these sources to inform your own design insight. The military have a saying that no plan survives contact with the enemy. The same could be said of your game design.

Life After Launch

The kind of information we can get from a live product is precisely why it remains vital that we get a MVP to market as soon as practically possible. The faster we can start to get useful, unbiased data, the faster we can adjust our prioritization process. I'm not suggesting that you change what your team is working on in mid-sprint, that would clearly be counterproductive. We should already have to plan for ongoing releases. However, make sure your next sprint is able to take into account information you have learnt from the one you previously released. As far as possible, treat each subsequent release as its own MVP, delivered predictably with each aspect measured in a systematic way, meaning we can learn what works best for our game and build a deeper engagement with the player base. It means our service is not static, but continues to grow organically. However, in order to take advantage of this we have to make sure we build into our development approach the resources and processes that allow us to continue building the service after launch. If you are used to building box-retail games you know that by the time the game hits the shelves the team has usually been all but disbanded and the collective expertise has now been lost to other projects (or worse yet, made redundant). What little remains of the team may not have enough detailed knowledge to make more than minor adjustments to the experience beyond the most essential bug-fix patches.

This way of working is extremely inefficient and expensive. By keeping our requirements focused and limited with many releases over time, we don't need as many developers to get to launch and we have a longer period of time post-release to continue to invest in that experience while we have an income coming into the organization. Don't get me wrong, you will find the balance of staff needed for a service changes over the lifecycle of the product, however this will be a much easier transition than we see with large games product releases.

Of course that means that much of the development will happen after the initial release. There are many estimations as to what proportion of development happens after the release of a MVP, but I would suggest that it's around 80 percent of the total development effort, perhaps more for products with the best life-time value. I appreciate that this sounds like a lot (and it is) but this effort is about building on the original implementation and creating a long-lasting full experience over many years. Most importantly, this has to be sustainable with the revenue from the game. That's the difference here. We are not taking years before we release a product, we are releasing something fast and using that revenue to sustain our ongoing development in order to build an audience and a revenue stream.

Small Teams, Fewer Specialists?

There are risks of course because it will be much harder to employ rare specialist skills to create the ultimate experience if we can only have smaller teams. We also lose out on the broader experience presented by the larger team structures. However, the gains are huge. The efficiency of running a smaller team more removes layers of bureaucracy overheads and makes it so much easier to collaborate between different disciplines of art, code and design. The more specialized tools and expertise we can buy in through third-party services such as middleware platforms, payment systems, cloud server infrastructure, and game engines such as Unity, Unreal Engine, Cocos, etc.

Staying Alive

However, even with smaller development teams using high quality third-party tools, we can't be sure of success. If the audience has to wait for months for each update they will think the game had died and will quickly lose interest. We need to be able to update changes to the game regularly, at least weekly but better yet daily. Indeed from my time at 3UK we found that the more regularly you changed what players saw, the better. In our case this was the front page of the games product. We went from changing this from once per week to once every four hours—3Italy went even further and changed theirs every ten minutes. The more regular the change the more frequently players returned to the service.[6] Obviously it's not possible to adjust the underlying game code at this kind of pace, but it is possible to create a pipeline of new content, configurable events, and automated promotions, as well as functional releases over time. By planning a process of releases each week in advance you can make it look to the audience that you are producing material each day even though in reality it might take months to deliver any one feature through code, test, and publishing cycles. You don't have to make everything available just because the features have been completed. Staggering the release of content and experiences over time really pays dividends.

Falling Down the Waterfall

This takes organizational change and may well be resisted by the development team. There are techniques out there that are well worth investigating but I will focus on "agile" and in particular "scrum." But first let's talk about the traditional method of project managing software development is known as "waterfall." In this model, development is seen as a sequential process, flowing inevitably downward. It comes from the manufacturing tradition where making design changes later in the flow are prohibitively expensive and have knock-on consequences that are unpredictable. It all starts with requirements analysis.[7] This would be more systematic than just thinking up whatever features we want. This is about documenting our designs in detail and expressing them from the perspective of what our consumers will need to enjoy the game.

Writing our ideas out and breaking them into specific sprint-sized requirements has the added advantage that it forces us to consider all of the specific necessary steps to play the game, which, usually, in turn means we know all the things our developers need to build. Sometimes the document is called a "project initiation document" or sometimes a "marketing requirements document," but I prefer to call that the "game design document." This document shows our requirements in a form we can communicate with the technical team to convert the design into a specification, which should then tested against the requirements before coding starts.

Getting the Team Onboard

The design document also serves as a great tool to help the designer to get the rest of the team on board with the project. Hopefully, they will have spent time talking to all the members of the team in order to ensure that they not only understand the game idea, but are committed to it. There is nothing worse than a development team that is apathetic about your game concept. The development team's role then is to translate the designs into technical specification documents that outline the planned development approach, then these specifications need to be agreed back with the design team to check they satisfy their requirements. Once the tech specs have been agreed, the development team can proceed and, assuming you got everything in the design right when it comes to testing, we simply test the results against the original specification, which of course should match the original requirements. Finally, once that testing is complete, we release the product and everything works with only occasional maintenance. At least, that's the theory.

Getting Agile

The trouble with the waterfall approach is that games aren't easy to pin down into absolute conditions or test cases. We don't always know whether players will find our game entertaining or not. We can't know how different mechanics will work in combination, even if we try to time-box things. In short this process fails because it doesn't support iteration.

The agile system[8] is based on the acceptance that project requirements and solutions evolve and proposes that the best way to deal with these changes is through collaboration and time-boxed iteration steps, rather than fixed deliverables. It works well by starting with the underlying vision for the project, agreeing a short and regular release cycle, and focusing on prioritized deliverables that can be completed in that timeframe. This approach has its problems too and is not as efficient for larger projects as well as making it difficult to deliver large and complex features that don't fit into the agreed release cycle timeframes. However, as a way to direct the development team within the context of a wider strategy it can be hugely beneficial.

The most common version of agile development seems to be scrum, which has a number of "rules" that the development team needs to adopt. These can seem a bit odd to veteran developers, but many have become fanatical converts to this approach.

The Product Owner

There are three core roles in the process. The product owner[9] is the person who owns the strategy. They have to be the representative of all the stakeholders, most importantly to champion the customer (in our case the player). It's their role to translate the vision into a strategy for the project as a whole. Each requirement needs to be defined using self-contained customer focused user journeys, each of which are broken down into functionally simple user cases. These are simple phrases that describe the user (the player) and what they want to be able to do using everyday language such as:

As a player, I want to be able to quickly locate the next available level suitable for my playing ability. In the event that I am an experienced player, I want the option to be able to select my own choice of level, overriding the choice I am presented with automatically.

These requirements often benefit from discussion with the development team or the scrum master to assess their suitability in terms of size and structure; however, the validity in terms of customer experience should be outside their remit. Personally, as a person who has often been in the product owner role, I like to have a good idea of what their impact will be in the overall experience and especially in terms of acquisition, retention and monetization. We use these factors to determine their priority and we use that to position them in the product backlog. As we have said before, avoid using vague priority settings such as P1 or VeryHigh; use an absolute order for each and every line item from most important down to least with only one item at each priority number, even if that causes you hours, even days of anguish—it's worth it.

Each sprint is expected to deliver each requirement as "ready to go," but that doesn't mean the product owner will want to release the code at the end of every sprint. They need to have an idea of where the MVP line is on their backlog—in other words to know what is the true bottom line as to what you can release—but despite that, they still have to put all the requirements in a single order.

The Development Team

The second role is the development team, whose collective role is to take all the requirements according to their separate specializations and skills and try to turn them into deliverable tasks that can ideally be completed and tested in isolation within the sprint. The duration of a sprint is typically 1–4 weeks within which the development team will concentrate on the deliverables they have committed to focus on, based on the product backlog prioritization. The progress of each sprint is generally displayed publicly with a "burn-down" chart showing the remaining work to be complete for that sprint each day. They need not be particular hierarchies within a team, although in larger groups there will often be a mentoring role for some of the most experienced members. Agile development is more about making better products together and quicker rather than reinforcing artificial labels.

The Scrum Master

The third role is that of the scrum master. These are the people who keep track of the progress and who attempt to maintain the momentum. Interestingly the scrum master need not always be a producer or project manager, sometimes having a lead coder take on this role can also be highly effective, as long as they are able to commit to the process. They host a daily meeting (same time and location each day) where everyone can attend, but only the developers can speak. They are asked what they have done since the previous day, what they are planning to do that day and what blocks they have encountered. These are documented and the scrum master will help work through a resolution of that problem outside of the meeting with only the relevant people. These meeting should always end after 15 minutes—a tricky task at best, but with everyone knowing the time this creates a sense of urgency that avoids wasting time unnecessarily. In the end if something needs further discussion, that should happen outside the daily scrum anyway.

If you are dealing with bigger teams, then rather than expanding the time available it's better to separate out the different scrums into separate teams. Then after the daily scrum, there will be a scrum of scrums, allowing each team to present its activity and blocks to the wider business. This "cell" structure is particularly powerful for scale, provided that each scrum (cell) can focus on the solution of its own problem, rather than splitting large problems across multiple cells, which usually breaks down.

The objective is to limit the management overhead and productivity impact on the development team while still giving the wider business a clear idea of what the real progress is and what might be causing problems for individual team-members. The scrum master is critical to this progress and their working relationship with the product owner is critical to the success of the project. They are each other's check and balance and both need to be committed to the team's vision for the project.

In my experience as product owner I am aware that the reality of this is that you and whoever is responsible for production delivery will fall out at times, even on the best of projects. However, you both need to appreciate the other's perspective and be able to separate the project from the personal. Successful teams can argue passionately and still happily go for a beer or play *Call of Duty* with each other afterwards.

Time to Review

At the end of each sprint there are two further (also time-boxed) meetings to review the progress. In the first, the "sprint review meeting," the purpose is to present the results to the product owner and other stakeholders as well. This usually includes demo of the features currently complete and "ready to ship," as well as an assessment of the progress against the sprint backlog (that section of the product backlog committed to by the development team for the sprint). This meeting should also be time-boxed, typically for between two and four hours depending on the project. At the end of this, the deliverables should be signed off by the product owner who will determine if the current deliverables are sufficient to justify a release (either the MVP or a new update). If that happens then this should be passed off to a team to complete end-to-end QA testing and commence the submission process.

The second meeting is a "sprint retrospective" where the team-members will review the process, progress, and ability to resolve blockages. The purpose is to first understand what worked and what didn't, then to identify opportunities to improve the process for the next time. This isn't a witch-hunt, it's about empowering the team to continually improve their capabilities and should be a chance to people to air their concerns, frustrations, and, importantly, congratulate themselves on their ongoing effort.

Have a Break

After the sprint it's useful to give the developers time to recuperate and have a change of pace. This is a great opportunity to have the team spend time experimenting with ideas, to learn new things, or to prototype complex elements for the project. This has to be a time limited period—for example 2–5 days depending on the normal size of your sprints—and should usually be driven by the development team themselves, although that doesn't mean it can't involve the product owner. Indeed its often a good idea to switch around the roles and to get some of the team to try something outside their normal skill set, if only to get a perspective of those roles. There is no expectation that any of this work will be used in future projects, but this should be used as an opportunity to identify new creative possibilities and reward team members who exhibit the most innovative contributions. This is not wasted time; at best it can transform a project, perhaps even scope out the seed of a completely new game. At worst your team will have had a chance to stretch their skills in areas that they normally don't get to. Just as importantly, it's an opportunity for them to feel appreciated for making their own choices as well as helping to re-energize them for the next sprint.

Publishing is Not Development

The publishing should be treated separately from the development process, although many small developers don't have the resources to run more than one team. This requires us to first validate the quality of the deliverables from the development team, which is hard to do if you are evaluating your own work or that of your team. There are many agile developers who swear by the test-driven development approach[10] alongside scrum, where each technical specification includes a test that confirms the feature has been delivered correctly. This implies that there will be no need to do separate QA testing at all. I'm a little more dubious about this as I feel that you should always do end-to-end testing to ensure all the pieces map together. That being said, the scrum process requires that a developer takes responsibility for the quality of their code before they check it into the project, including taking into account not only the functions of the section they have built but also its compatibility with other systems.

Despite this, as a product owner we also have a responsibility to ensure that the end product is in a suitable state for release on behalf of the consumer. With that in mind, here is a breakdown of the different stages of QA testing.

Unit Testing

We usually start with unit testing, taking the specific class or module relating to a single feature and check this against the test script written by the developer themselves to match the original requirement. The aim is to test that the function performs to the specification within its own context. At this point we are not considering any interactions with other systems and if those are important to the ability to test this specific unit, the interaction would use a "test stub" or simulation of the dependent modules.

Once we know that the feature works according to the specification, we need to test it in context with the other modules of the platform, which means we need to complete and test the integration,[11] while along the way demonstrating the performance and reliability of the combinations. We have already demonstrated that both modules work correctly according to their specification, so we can usually narrow down any issues to the way they interact.

End-to-End Testing

Once all the modules have been tested against each of the other modules they are directly integrated with, we should be able to raise our sights higher. Here we need to confirm that the end-to-end experience is performing correctly against the original specification. If it is we can proceed to launch. Doing this, however, requires us to consider a number of different testing approaches. User acceptance testing allows us to confirm that the overall experience is working against the objectives originally set out by the product manager, while stress testing allows us to prove that the platform will be reliable under extreme conditions, and in particular it's worth considering hacking issues such as packet-sniffing, distributed denial of service (DDOS) attacks, and man-in-the-middle attacks, as well as just simply how the platform would function should you get 10–100 times the volume of users you currently expect all turning up at the same time.

Release Candidates

It will take a number of sprints to get a polished, functional release that you have the confidence can deliver the minimum viable experience, including all the data capture you need to be able to learn for the next release. It will involve compromise and won't be exactly what you had originally envisioned, but it does have to be a self-contained "complete" experience in its own right. You are now ready to release it through your publishing process. This might be as simple as following the submission guidelines for the platform you are working on, whether that is a publisher, Steam, iOS or Android. This will take some time and may often involve rejection. There may be changes to policy, or even regulation, in specific territories that, as a developer, you won't necessarily have been aware of. This will require someone to make the fix and to do that in a rapid manner—throwing out your otherwise perfect sprint planning. How do you deal with that if you don't have multiple teams? I'd recommend that you always allocate time in the sprint to bug-fixing and use that time when necessary. If you don't need that time in the end there will always be bugs the developer can look at or perhaps we just get started on the next highest priority feature on the backlog that didn't originally make it into the sprint. The joy of scrum is that we aren't worrying about how many features make it into the sprint, instead we are focused on how much time to dedicate to that development phase. There should be no need to do crunch again, ever!

Preparing For the Next Sprint

If we are careful and line up the process there should be tasks that run in parallel during the development and publishing processes. We might have a week window to review our backlog, fleshing out the specifications and write our requirement specifications. This could be followed by a week where the development team write their technical specifications and unit test scripts that would be reviewed by the product owner and their peers. We get 2–3 weeks of intense development, with unit and integration testing happening in parallel. Finally 1–2 weeks of end-to-end testing, including user acceptance testing before it's submitted to the platform holder. Over the next week the development team gets to experiment and learn new things while we await the results of the publishing process, and the product owner works with the team leaders on the details of the next sprint, including time to resolve any bug fixes with the second week before going live being used on the technical specification process. The whole pipeline might take 7–9 weeks to complete. If we have the resources to support multiple teams there is no reason why they can't push forward a release twice as fast, handing the baton of the "current" version to each other, but you should absolutely remember that your team-members might have a life or family and you will have to accommodate for little things like sickness or holiday.

Releases Without Releases

Features aren't the only thing we release over time. We also have to look at the goods we offer and consider how we can deliver these more frequently than each software upgrade release. There are two key strategies here. The first is to have some time or procedural unlocking process for "new" items that happen to have been embedded in the application all along (and therefore have to be created prior to the release being submitted). Or alternatively (and my preference) we should have a method that allows the game to user the server-side to deliver updated content.

Server-based distribution of in-game content is a really powerful design strategy that can really unlock your revenue potential as well as your ability to deliver rapid improvements to your games experiences. However, you have to be careful that you comply with the requirements of the platform you are using and you must realize that servers have an associated ongoing cost linked to the level of usage, although cloud-based systems such as EC2 servers from Amazon or Azure from Microsoft can help you mitigate problems with reliability and scaling. There are even complete service providers such as Game Sparks and other specialist server infrastructure providers, such as Exit Games for multiplayer platforms.

You then need to create (or find a provider with) a platform that allows the game to identify what assets are available to each player and make these available to them alongside the unlocking of achievements or specific purchases made in the game, and usually this has to be done working with the platform provider.

Thick and Thin Clients

Thinking about servers means we have to think about whether the client can function when the user is unable to access the internet. We can make the decision that the game can only be played when the player can access the internet, but that comes at the cost of the overall experience. Whatever our decision (and sometimes its unavoidable depending on our game design) we have to ensure that we take care to separately consider the design of the client software and how that operates when there is no connection to the server. Can we cache the activity of the player and upload that in the background when the connection returns? Do we enforce a reconnection within a specific timeframe, or do we simply throw away the data of their behavior while not connected? There is a tension between a "thin client" approach, which treats the server as the main source of functionality and a "thick client" approach, which delivers the minimum reliance on the server infrastructure. Both approaches are a compromise and need careful planning. Regardless of the approach, only the server can be trusted in terms of data integrity, any client can be hacked.

Server Deployment and Roll-Back

Getting back to the server whatever solution we implement needs us to have a mechanism that allows you to test and check content going live can't accidentally bring the game down or other less critical problems such as "missing textures." Even then you should ensure that there is a method to roll-back any release if you later find there is a problem.

Build for Flexibility

Think carefully about the flexibility and range of goods and assets you want this process to support. That will affect how the client functions and how it needs to function to be able update each element. In particular how will you deal with the fact that you can't take away or significantly change assets that people have already paid for—even if you update the quality of your graphics engine? Think in particular how you can skin or otherwise customize the playing experience driven by the player and by the platform. I'm not just talking about selling customization goods (although that can have value), I'm talking about how we can manipulate the player experience from the server in order to create events that at least visually (perhaps also adding some specific minigame) update the experience without necessarily updating the app itself—provided you don't break the rules of the platform holder. Apple in particular has some quite restrictive rules designed to avoid misuse of server process that you should be aware of.

It's not a trivial process to set this up. It needs careful planning and generally the platform support is something that needs to be managed in parallel. If you have a small team this might even be out of the question without third-party support. But its potential if you want to be able to deliver regularly changing experiences including daily challenges, monthly events, and quarterly "seasons" in your game can be phenomenal for retention and monetization.

Delivering Ongoing Service

Service doesn't end there. Service also means having the tools to support moderation, community interaction and, of course, to engage with players as directly as possible whether that's through Facebook, Twitter, YouTube, or other more specialist platforms like Everyplay. Focus on how you will deliver that experience and how you can maintain its support (and costs) over time. Choosing the right service tools is vital but we don't have space in this book to be able to discuss that in any detail and, as with every area of this book, I strongly recommend you research the key areas for yourself.

Summing Up Service

The point of this chapter is that delivering a service requires a fundamental change in the way we approach development. It's about smaller focused teams delivering ongoing sections of our game offering over time so we can test each section in isolation as well as demonstrate to the users that the experience has life and ongoing investment that they can choose to reciprocate. We are not trying to create everything in advance of their engagement and instead will respond to their needs from a functional point of view, just as we will respond to their community, moderation, and social needs. I didn't go into detail about how these latter essential components of service can be delivered, as that probably deserves its own book. The key in my mind is that we approach each step in the delivery chain one at a time, break down each problem into its components, and work out the priority. If you can understand that approach you will be able to resolve every problem as you will have understood the fundamental point of creating a service . . . we only have to do each step at a time, but there will always be more steps to take.

Notes

1   Eric Ries' book *The Lean Startup* has quickly become the bible of many small indie studios. Personally I wasn't all that interested in the book as I rarely see much value in business strategy gurus, until I read that one of the quotes in the book came from Geoffrey Moore, author of *Crossing the Chasm*, http://theleanstartup.com.

2   One of the key differences between UK-based investment and that of the USA (particularly in San Francisco) is that the UK investors seem to find failure in previous ventures as an entirely bad thing, whereas US investors see failure as an opportunity to learn— provided you demonstrate that you have! I suspect this is partially because the larger funds in the US mean that they can afford to be less risk-averse, but this attitude also clearly pays dividends.

3   Avoiding making the same mistakes as other people have already made is what makes it difficult for me to decide how I feel about Peter Molyneux's *Curiosity* from 22 Cans. Molyneux has often said that this project was an experiment, but I find it hard to identify what lessons they may have learnt from the project that weren't already obvious from researching other projects. Don't get me wrong, they certainly will have learnt a lot as a team, but was that project the best way to learn them? The game presented a significant networking challenge, and they unsurprisingly had a significant server outage in the early days—a problem that was both predictable and avoidable. It might have been expensive, but cloud server infrastructure was created specifically for managing unpredictable

scaling problems and there were plenty of precedents out there on how to avoid such problems. There were other obvious things, such as the behavior of some users creating crude imagery and offensive comments, while others tried their best to "clean up" those messages—so far so obvious. Of course the real answer is that *Curiosity* wasn't a minimum viable product at all. It was a marketing tool where the team had to learn the hard way how to pull all these techniques together, allowing their mistakes to be public, showing their commitment to learn, and building trust with 3 million players. In the end the reveal we had all been waiting for was about their next title *Godus*. Now that's brilliant marketing. www.telegraph.co.uk/technology/10084700/The-end-of-Curiosity-teenager-crowned-God-after-winning-game.html.

4   To extend William Faulkner's quote in games, like "in writing, you must kill all your darlings," http://en.wikipedia.org/wiki/William_Faulkner. This remains true even with service-based delivery; however, prioritizing features to a later release is much less painful to do that the actual slaying of your favorite ideas.

5   Traditional software development defines the alpha as the first release and usually to friendly or internal audiences. A closed beta is a release to a select invited audience where as an open beta is open to all comers who pass specific criteria (e.g., signing an non-disclosure agreement). Some services spend years in open beta, while others, like PlayStation Home, never leave the beta stage, largely to communicate to the public users that the platform will constantly be in development.

6   There is a level of diminishing returns to the frequency of change, but the average return rate of the active user generally matched the rate of change.

7   There are some formal processes that help developers use waterfall development approaches for software development, most notably PRINCE2.0. Apparently this is an acronym for PRojects IN Controlled Environments and derived from a UK government standard for IT system project management, http://en.wikipedia.org/wiki/PRINCE2.

8   Agile has many forms but essentially focuses on the collaboration of cross-functional teams, which fits neatly with the games as a service model, http://en.wikipedia.org/wiki/Agile_software_development.

9   I know some people don't like the term "product owner" as it denies the shared nature of the creative process. You could use terms like "champion," "requirements manager," or "producer," but in the end someone has to represent the consumer and "own" the product in some way. It doesn't have to diminish the role of the rest of the team.

10 It's often a good idea that the developer writes a technical specification and test script for each section of code they are to develop and then have that signed off by the product owner. This ensures that both sides have a clear understanding of what is needed and how to demonstrate that it functions correctly. It is also worthwhile having a senior developer—often the scrum master or a person responsible for other modules with which this code has to integrate—to review to tests and consider potential integration problems.

11 There are several approaches to integration testing, including smoke-testing, big-bang, top-down, layer integration, etc. However, this is more detail than we need to go into in this book, http://en.wikipedia.org/wiki/Integration_test.

Exercise 12: How Will You Capture Data?

One of the most powerful tools that comes from using a connection with a server is the wide-scale capture of data. However, while there is a temptation to capture everything, we should take time to work out what data points will allow us to understand what things, as it can be as bad to have too much information to sort through as having too little. Worse still is to have the right information but to have collected it out of context, making that information irrelevant. This is a tricky balance to reach as its often only after launching your game that you can identify the oddments of data that prove to be the most insightful. However, that doesn't mean we should collect meaningless confusing data.

In this exercise we will consider how you can collect as much mean-ingful information as possible by understanding the data that actually matters to the commercial and design performance of the game. We will use the HACCP model described in Chapter 11 as a way to help us understand the flow of the game and use this to identify data points in the game that are most likely to help us understand the performance in our game.

This starts by looking at what kinds of hazards we are trying to mea-sure as well as where in the game we can find the control points that are

How will you capture data?	
What are the hazards we are trying to identify in terms of access to play, behavior, churn, etc.?	
What are the control points that allow us to identify patterns in use of our game?	
What about the critical limits or KPIs that we will us to measure success objectively?	
What monitoring strategies will we use?	
How will we review the monitoring process to confirm it is accurate?	
How will we store and use historic data separately from live operational data?	

most meaningful in terms of their value in interpretation. We should also try to have an idea of the expected range of the data points for each of these tests so we have some kind of benchmark to know what success looks like. Finally we need to consider how we monitor and review the whole process, including the separate storage (and comparison) of historic and operation data.

WORKED EXAMPLE:

How will you capture data?	We plan to collect data on each meaningful interaction within the game and to use reference data as far as possible to extrapolate the specific interactions where possible.
What are the hazards we are trying to identify in terms of access to play, behavior, churn, etc.?	We want to know where in the overall experience players stop playing so we can fix them. We want to identify the triggers that successfully lead to the use of purchasable items. We want to know how to improve each level and understand what make them enjoyable to play or cause players to churn. We want to identify the most valuable players in terms of acquisition, retention and monetization.
What are the control points that allow us to identify patterns in use of our game?	App is started. Player personalization is selected. Player set-up is competed. Game location is selected. gameplay commences. Player selects a path (spawn point and target location are needed). Player is intercepted by a mobile enemy (location, time and effect). Player completes a successful "memory match" (including type). Player received a reward (including type). Player uses a power-up (including type). Player achieves target objectives.

(Continued)

	Player achieves secondary objectives. Player connects game account to their social network (including reference to player's historical performance at that time). Player joins a "family." Player participates in a "family" dialogue/action.
What about the critical limits or KPIs that we will us to measure success objectively?	We are looking to obtain at least 40 percent day two retention, 20 percent day seven and 15 percent day 30 (ideally significantly higher). We are looking for at least 80 percent successful completion of the target objectives first level for all players who initiate that game level. We are looking for at least 60 percent successful completion of the target objectives first level for all players who initiate those game levels. We expect 10 percent of players to connect their account to a social network. We expect 4 percent of players to engage with the "family" metagame.
What monitoring strategies will we use?	Data will initially come through a load-bearing queue, stamped with its arrival time (allowing a comparison with time sent). Data collated while the game was offline and sent via the cache will be marked as such. All data will pass through an operational database, which will keep track of the current status of play; however, the information will also be passed through two additional systems. The first is live monitoring, which will show the rate of incoming packets and comparing the sent and received timestamps broken down by each measured activity. This will allow alerts in the system to identify inappropriate behavior as well as early warning of potential technical issues in the game. The second is the historic database, which is used for offline reporting by

(Continued)

	the commercial and design teams for their analysis of the performance of the game as a whole.
How will we review the monitoring process to confirm it is accurate?	The live monitoring system will show the rate of data into the platform as well as the deviation from the historic data in terms of last week, last month, last year, etc. Additionally, every sprint will include a task to review the data requirements of that sprint and its impact on the data capture as well as reference information used on the platform.
How will we store and use historic data separately from live operational data?	The platform includes separate long-term storage database as well as a live monitoring tool. The accuracy of the historic data will take precedence over that of the live monitoring.

Chapter 13
The Psychology[1] of Pricing

The Karate Kid

Throughout this book we have talked about design, rhythm of play, socialization, and even agile development in the context of the lifecycle of the player. But none of these chapters have really, except perhaps superficially, addressed the one burning issue of all developers engaging in Free2Play design—how do we make any money?

My objective in the writing structure of this book has been to prepare the groundwork so that in this, the later stages of the book, your game design is already ripe for effective monetization. I'm trying to pull off a *Karate Kid* moment where Mr. Miyagi[2] gets you to clean his car (wax on . . . wax off), which happened to create a kind of muscle memory that supports good martial arts techniques.

If you have been working through the exercises you should have a game concept in mind for which you will have isolated what elements contain the essential "fun" as well as those elements that create the context, allowing the player to repeat play time and time again. All this has then been applied across the lifecycle of the player and we have used several lenses to review our game from such as the Bond moments or *Columbo* twists we introduced in Chapter 9, or the ideas of levels of player interaction we introduced in Chapter 8.

Why Should I Buy? (AIDA)

Now we can get down to the meat of making money without fear of compromising the playing experience, but first we need to try to understand what happens when people make a purchase.

The way we buy things has been analyzed in detail for decades and in particular one model remains a core part of sales and marketing theory. AIDA[3] (awareness, interest, desire, action) makes us think of the transitional nature of a purchase decision and has been intricately linked with the idea of doing funnel analysis since the 1960s; arguably this is where our use of funnel analysis to help us analyze player behavior from game data came from.

Assuming that we have already considered how to get our game discovered, the important take-away here is that it's not enough for potential players to be aware of our product, or even interested. We have to create a sense of desire and create a reason for them to act; to get them to take the step to install, play . . . and then pay.

The AIDA model is important for designer to understand because it provides us with our first understanding of the levers we can use to increase our revenue. We all know that discovery is a problem and that we can only generate money if we first have people finding our game. That leads us to identify strategies that can increase the proportion of target players becoming aware of our game. Taking this as the only criteria would be a mistake of course, because it becomes increasingly expensive and inefficient if we don't also take into account the audience who are likely to be interested. We can't take this interest for granted, as we have already said, and we need to stimulate that interest as part of our marketing effort but more than that, if we are to create action we have to provide a sense of urgency. Making any purchase is risky and the dynamic of the uncertainty of the outcome of a purchase against the consequences of not making that purchase contribute to buying anxiety. These are further complicated by the social consequence of such a decision (what will others think?) and other more practical needs we might have at that time.

Games are essentially luxury products, which means we have to go further than just demonstrate that the player needs our product. We have to create the conditions that allow them to give themselves permission to play and purchase. We shouldn't be afraid to admit our products are valuable to their players. We can confidently offset players' natural uncertainty by creating an expectation of delight. We can build in social value, even make clear to users what they might be missing out on, and this will help them make that step to invest in our game. However, to do this we have to acknowledge that games have a self-indulgent quality, an impractical but delightful value that is different than for more functional goods. It requires the player to be able to set aside their other needs for a period of time, something some call the "abnegation of responsibility."

Let Me Off the Rollercoaster

It's something people do all the time. We know we should do the washing up but we would rather watch our favorite TV program, so we set aside the things we should do in favor of things we want to do; we want someone to let us off the rollercoaster of our mundane lives if only for a minute or so. Doing this and choosing to play a game is easy enough if you are already a committed games player, but for a mass-market audience the option of playing a game used to be considered alien. The Facebook revolution for games was to introduce simple, easy to access games content in a social context, which made it a simple way to communicate with people you care about as well as others who just had a shared interest. Now this revolution has spread across multiple devices and has broken down almost every barrier.

We are All Marketers Now

But there have been consequences and one of them is that as designers we can no longer expect the marketing team to build that excitement. We have to take part of the responsibility and create conditions within the game that help them to engage with our game. We can't take that step for them. We can remove blocking events, such as poor UI or relying on prior "gamer" knowledge and we can use narrative, art and social context to create anticipation for our game. However, our audience still has to make the decision to play on their own.

Part of understanding what motivates players is to understand the nature of need states. This way of looking at buyers comes from the model proposed by A.H. Maslow, which suggests different levels of need start that determine the motivation of people. He postulated that until the lower-level needs states were fulfilled, people couldn't aspire to complete the higher levels. It's a model that has been debated and questioned endlessly and there is no scientific evidence that the model is valid. And yet it has been one of the single most useful tools I have found in my career. Obviously, games are different from food, water, etc. They are an entertainment product. Therefore, I made a variation on Maslow's model, arrogantly called "Oscar's Hierarchy of Games."

Thinking about this model allows us to make sense of the player lifecycle in a different way. If we don't entertain our players, there is no game. If we don't create trust, there is no revenue. If there is no one else playing, why I should continue playing? If I can't show off, why should I keep buying? Only when all of these levels are satisfied and I still see value in playing and paying, can I really make the most of my game and therefore only then will I spend as much as I want on the game.

Playing is a Delicate Thing

We have to appreciate that the decision to play is a delicate and fragile thing. It requires a level of confidence on the part of the player and willingness to engage. That willingness—like the suspension of disbelief we talked about in Chapter 2—fluctuates differently at different stages of the player lifecycle.

"Discovering" life-stage players will have taken the first step to play your game, but other than time and the bytes of storage needed to install the game they have no investment (or utility) in your game. "Learning" life-stage players are already investing their time and trying

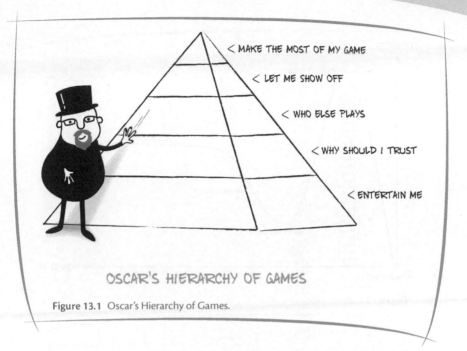

< MAKE THE MOST OF MY GAME

< LET ME SHOW OFF

< WHO ELSE PLAYS

< WHY SHOULD I TRUST

< ENTERTAIN ME

OSCAR'S HIERARCHY OF GAMES

Figure 13.1 Oscar's Hierarchy of Games.

to gauge how the game fits into their lifestyle, which makes them particularly vulnerable, but at the same time they are closer to reaching the point where they become, at least in principle, willing to make a first purchase—if they can see that this will make their gameplay even better.

Buyer Remorse

Getting to the first purchase, indeed even getting the player to download at all follows a conversion process. We have to generate enough anticipation of value that exceeds the barriers to install/purchase such as fear of the unknown, cost, fear of looking stupid to others, willingness to invest the effort, etc., of the potential players/payer. Immediately after taking the action to download or buy we find that the player/payer experiences what psychologists would call "post-purchase evaluation" or what I (as a marketer) prefer to call "buyer remorse."[4] This is a sense of regret that comes after making a purchase, especially luxuries, that stems from a number of influences including the guilt of extravagance or suspicion of being overly influenced by the seller. In the case of games, it can be thought of as a form of post-cognitive dissonance

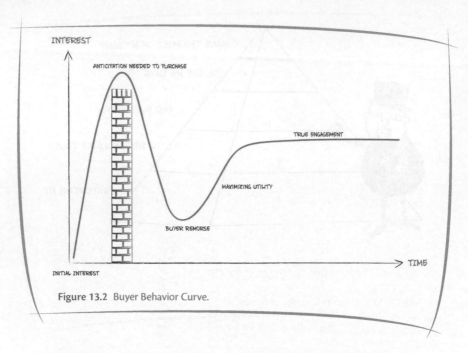

Figure 13.2 Buyer Behavior Curve.

brought about by the gap between the anticipation required to buy or download the game in the first place, the reality of their initial experience of play and the awareness of other games they might have selected instead.

The graph above is an adaptation of the Gartner Hype Curve,[5] which is normally used to look at the reactions to the adoption of new technology from the initial trigger, through the peak of inflated expectations and into the trough of disillusionment. From my observations, buyer behavior for technology adoption as well as games follows this same path.[6]

A player's initial expectations prior to accessing a game, whether purchased or not, have to exceed their expectations of the difficulties and opportunity costs associated with that action or users won't download or purchase. Players have imperfect knowledge about your game and the value of your game to them, and they will automatically fill in those gaps with something idealistic and personal that you can't possibly supply. This remorse can be a temporary state as long as we continue to deliver value as a service and as long as they believe they can gain value or utility. The greater the gap between their expectations of the game and the reality of the experience, the more likely they will just churn.

Setting and Beating Expectations

If we want players to survive this buyer remorse, we need to get them through this stage quickly. We should do our best to set their expectations as accurately as possible before they make their decision and, where possible, deliver more than we promised. Think back to Chapter 5 where we talked about six seconds to get them playing. This was specifically to help us deal with manage the initial "remorse" following the download of the game. This chapter also talked about giving players a sense of achievement within one minute. This stage is about taking the player further into the game, to provide deeper engagement, and to encourage them to see the value in the game, reinforcing their confidence. Similar principles apply with purchasing. We need to deliver on the value we are promising again and again, if we want to encourage repeat purchases, and we want to find ways to remind them why that decision to buy was worthwhile. If our users feel we used underhanded techniques to "sell" them goods they didn't want, they will resent us and churn anyway, probably complaining to most of their friends about our game along the way.

Showing Friends What You Have Bought

Having social elements in games can really help create a positive atmosphere around the purchase of goods. Players tend to feel more willing to try making a purchase in the first place when they see others doing so, but they will also have the opportunity for positive feedback in their choices to buy. This creates a significant reduction in the risk that buyer remorse will damage your player's commitment to your game. However, we should consider the principles outlined in Chapter 8 in order to get the best effect from such social elements.

Building Utility

If you look again at the Buyer Behavior Curve you will see that after "buyer remorse" comes maximizing "utility." This is an economics term to describe the invested value of an asset. For the purposes of this book it isn't about money, time invested, or even entertainment, it's more about the remaining value a player attributes to the asset. Maximizing utility is about players wanting to get the most of playing the games they have already invested in.

The motivation to continue and work back up this curve is driven by the player's need to maximize whatever utility remains in the game and the ability of the game to provide ongoing expectations of future value.

Buyer Remorse Business Models

It is usually easier for a premium game to sustain the interest of the player after the initial purchase because the level of investment is tangible. A premium game has to be pretty terrible if I'm going to quit before I've given it a good try.

Freemium games can't assume that there is any utility to exploit and therefore have to put much more emphasis on the ongoing experience of the player. We need to try to build utility through positive experiences before the player feels they have to start spending money. For example, we should try to expose the player to some of our paid-for virtual goods through the free play of the game. Imagine we offered limited access to consumable goods or new aspects of gameplay that would otherwise be exclusive to paying players as a reward for successful play, either directly or through some kind of in-game currency. Players would see these as benefits, valued by the effort required to obtain them. This way we not only align their expectations with the reality (thus minimizing the buyer remorse), but we can use this to create that sense of anticipation encouraging them to make a real money purchase and, importantly, feel good about the value they receive. This approach is about communication the value of our virtual goods, not exploitation.

Tease or Try?

I would also say that this model helps explain one of the conundrums about the limited success of trials and level-based sales. For decades we have seen games offering a "lite" or demo version, perhaps as a cover disk on a magazine. The trouble is that as easily as they increase value, the demo can just as easily diminish the potential sales. The reason is that although a demo will communicate things about our game, they also tend to satisfy our curiosity about that game. It allows us to play for real without having to part with our hard earned cash, dropping us straight into buyer remorse based on the gap between our expectations and the reality, even if the cost/effort to access this was relatively small. Our imperfect knowledge of the game is now cleared away and there is little opportunity to build excitement. If the demo doesn't lead the player up and out of this trough to re-engage with us then the likelihood is that the player will churn. However, because demos generally cap the experience in some way, the player is left unable to gauge the potential value of the full game as they never get to experience it. Demos suffer, like freemium games, from the lack of invested utility, but (usually) without ongoing scope to retain and tantalize the user for what's coming next. Trailers don't have this effect because they simply contribute to the anticipation of the game, the player never gets actually experience the game.

Level-based games suffer from exactly the same problem and are usually a terrible way to monetize a game. Countless otherwise great games have been broken from a commercial perspective because they ignored the need to tantalize players about what was coming next; the same lessons we learn through Chapter 9 with the *Flash Gordon* cliffhanger.

Engaging Players

I'm taking a long time to talk about this Buyer Behavior Curve for another reason. It matches directly with the player lifecycle we have been discussing throughout this book. The "discovery" life-stage is all about building up anticipation to get users to the point where they download our game. The "learning" stage is about retaining the delicate, tentative engagement as the player learns about how the game fits into their playing habits and builds their confidence until they are able to reach "true engagement." If we look at player lifecycles in this way it reminds us of what's happening for the player at each stage, and asks us to consider every play and purchase as part of their journey as they immerse themselves within our game. That's what it takes be build lifetime value.

Premium Problems

As we have talked about in Chapter 5, the different business models affect buyer behavior differently. The premium (upfront payment) purchase casts a shadow on the behavior of the user. First the upfront price creates a pay-wall, which adds to the other barriers and blocks the player has to overcome before they access the game. We have to create sufficient anticipation in order to get them to decide to download the game *and* part with their cash. The effect is that a significant number of people will abort the download as a direct result of the upfront cost. It's hard to estimate how many people would have downloaded, but looking at the number of downloads in the Paid and Free Chart gives us an idea of the scale. In May 2012 *Distimo*[7] showed that to get in the top 25 Free

App Charts in the US store required 38,400 downloads per day, while to get in the top 25 Paid App Charts took only 3,530 downloads per day. Similarly, just for the games category this needed 25,300 downloads for the free chart, but only 2,280 daily downloads for the paid. If we assume this ratio is typical, and that the aggregate quality of the top paid and free games is equivalent, then it's a reasonable hypothesis that having a pay-wall at all inhibits up to 90 percent of potential downloads daily. That's an exponential number of potential users we will never play our game. We don't have the chance to entertain them, to try to convince them to play, to generate revenue from them. Of course there are counterarguments.

Premium Positives

Setting a price above the minimum ($0.99 on mobile) is also a way to communicate positive values about a game and, when combined with a known, trusted brand, you may find that you can get a sizable audience past the pay-wall. A price tells the player something about the product's quality, at least in the mind of the developer, and increasingly includes a promise that we will limit the financial exposure of the player. For those players understandably concerned about the never-ending costs of "free" games it makes some sense, but it won't sustain a service model in the long run.

There are games where this is really the only choice as they won't have been designed to sustain a service approach. I don't believe that there is any game genre that can't work as a service, but that doesn't mean every design will incorporate that thinking. If you design a one-off product, premium may be appropriate but never go with the lowest possible platform price. That way lays financial ruin.

In addition, a premium price ensures that the player has utility invested in the game, which provides them with an internal incentive to play through the game past their buyer remorse. It's much easier to keep them playing and, ironically, it makes them more willing to spend money with you again.

Paying Every Way

No wonder the idea of a "paymium" game with both upfront price and also in-app revenue models has a lot of appeal for developers. The trouble is that by charging upfront and inside the game we are breaking the promise implicit in the premium price, that this is all the player will be required to spend. There are some great examples like Rodeo's *War-hammer Quest* where the quality of the app both satisfies my desire to play and creates anticipation for future levels, but their failure to deliver regular map updates has meant that I have fallen out of that habit of playing that game, leaving my desire to spend unsated[8].

From a buyer behavior perspective, paymium is the worst possible of models. It creates both a pay-wall before purchase as well as a sense of distrust among players who feel there is no end to the demands of the game on their wallet. However, commercially, especially if you have a strong gaming brand, it can deliver a reliable upfront as well as ongoing income stream. This in turn can make it easier for the developer to focus on improving the playing experience. My sense is that in the end paymium is a fudge, a way for designers who are too timid to adapt to the freemium model to find a compromise at least in the short term. My suspicion is that this approach can work, but it will damage the potential size of the audience, caps the spend of players, and damages the lifetime value of the players. Of course you can drop the upfront price later, but you will still have lost huge number of potential players and there will only be a few games where this is worth the risk.

Finally Free

This leaves us with the freemium model, games that monetize through some combination of in-game goods and advertising. There is no pay-wall to cross, but of course there remains the opportunity cost presented by the huge range of alternative games available. Getting players to download your game is no trivial matter as we have already discussed. But once we have the download we have to face a real problem. Players still have the equivalent of buyer remorse but have no invested utility in our game to help them get through that and up to the engagement stage. We have discussed in detail strategies to overcome this problem throughout the book, but particularly in Chapter 5 and Chapter 9. These focus on leveraging what we are best at to sustain the audience's attention, by making a better game. It is my assertion that this process is so necessary for the survival of a freemium game that it will drive game design forward in a Darwinian way; survival of the fittest game design. Freemium designers in the end have to make better games. But if we can do this, and build confidence and trust along the way, it will be easier for some of those players to be open to spending money with us. Not just once, but if those purchases are themselves satisfying, perhaps they will purchase time and time again.

One important difference between premium games and the freemium model is that we are the retailer inside the game, we are not reliant on the app store to do our retailing for us. There is no competition for where we get energy crystals inside our game, only us. Equally, we can't blame someone else if we have picked the wrong price, wrong bundle, etc., and no one buys our goods.

I Can't Get No Satisfaction

Assuming we manage to get our players past their initial buyer (or download) remorse and up into the stage where they are truly engaged we will find it increasingly easier to repeat the process, time and again. But, there are limits to this. Regular spenders often will have a personal threshold[8] or budget that they are prepared to spend (or at least a price point below which they won't think about how much they have spent). They may temporarily go past this limit, but each time they do the risk is that the subsequent buyer remorse will cause them to reconsider their engagement with the game at all. Bill shock—in other words the discovery that you have spent considerably more than you expected on a service at the end of the month—is a genuine cause for concern and will not only lose you a customer, but they will also tell their friends.

However, even if we keep our player satisfied, enjoying our game, that is not enough for them to continue spending money.[9] There needs to be a motivation and incentive to help them decide to take the action to make the next purchase. We need to consider every stage, every play, every purchase to be a new start on the lifecycle; with discovery, learning, engaging and churning stages for each element. This is tremendously challenging to perfect, but in the end it is a game design exercise as much as it is a marketing one.

Don't Nag, Give Reasons to Act

We should of course be careful to ensure that our legitimate attempts to maximize revenue don't become counterproductive. We can't afford to be seen as nagging and if we are this will detrimentally impact the longevity of our players, causing them to churn.

On the other hand it's worth considering the impact of a decision by J.C. Penney[10] in the US to remove misleading sales, such as 20 percent off for a shirt that had never been sold in that store at a different price. They also removed misleading pricing, such as $4.99, which of course is essentially $5, but feels like it's closer to $4. This failed spectacularly and they lost customers and lots of money. Was this because treating your user-base as intelligent is a bad thing? No, even though these policies were actually better for the consumer, they didn't feel better for the consumer. Seeing a cheaper price for the same item is not the same as being told that the price is cheaper, buying a $60 pair of jeans for $20 feels awesome, even when we know we are being kidded. There is no excitement in finding a "bargain" when you are just told the straight-forward price. The way the experience feels really matters. For example, when I am presented with a special offer of 25 percent off a new car in *CSR Racing*, that feels awesome, even if its impact in the gameplay isn't all that significant.

Spending Your Subway Fare

Of course how a purchase feels changes according to the circumstances and we should consider the different mindset of the player prior to playing a new level as compared to when they are just about to die because they are running out of health. The psychological principles can be explored by looking at the ideas of Hot Cold Empathy[11] where we see people's decision-making process being affected by their emotional state. The more visceral a physical or emotional affect (hunger, desire, fear) the greater effect this has on our short-term decision-making process. Games are masterful at building engaged emotional experiences. Imagine that you were playing *Space Invaders* in Tokyo in 1978, you fail to beat your high score for the nth time and you are so mad you want to smash the machine in a rage. If instead of going home and trying another day, you are presented with an option to "continue" by putting in another 100 yen coin[12] then you will almost certainly do so. When we are hot with emotions like this we feel compelled to rummage through our pockets and spend our subway fare home. This principle means that we are open to manipulation by cynical companies—it's a disturbing thing to realize. On the other hand, the lack of emotional engagement can also be problematic. Although this means we can make more rational decisions, we are also likely to underestimate the value of opportunities when we approach a subject matter coldly.

A Warning

You might think that me talking about Hot Cold Empathy means I think we should exploit the phenomena; in fact I believe it's a warning. If players succumb to a decision to buy only because we "trick" them into it while they are in the throes of some visceral emotion, we will exacerbate the buyer remorse they feel later. Any short-term gain will be irrelevant compared to the ongoing revenue formed from a habitual and rewarding engagement with our players. Service-led experiences need to provide a balance between emotional engagement and delight; we have to care about our users making their second, third, fourth, etc., purchase and still loving our game. That isn't to say we ignore the value of emotions to help trigger a call to action. If we don't deliver goods at the point where players engage emotionally we not only lose a sale, but we fail to satisfy what they expect from game—I'm just saying we mustn't do it cynically.

Can I Afford To Lose?

Another emotion-led factor involved with purchase is the idea of loss aversion.[13] This is an economics principle that explains that people will feel a much greater impact from the loss of $100 than the impact they feel from a windfall of $100. Similarly we tend to place a higher value on something we don't own than something of the same financial price that we do. It has a particular effect when there is some element of social competition at play, making this particularly relevant to game design. There are a number of ways we can use this. The first is called the "puppy-dog sale," where we imagine that we are a pet shop salesman. A family comes in and the child and one parent are interested in having a puppy, but the other parent isn't fully convinced. So you offer to allow them to take the puppy home, to see how things go for a week; they can always return the animal after that week. Once the dog is settled into the home, it's going to be pretty hard for the reluctant parent to convince the rest of the family to return the animal after that first week because they will have to take this away from them. I like this analogy as it also allows us to talk about the biggest problem with relying on fear of loss. What if the new puppy is a nightmare? They might bite cables, eat slippers or leave "presents" on the carpet. It doesn't take much to go wrong to outweigh any level of loss aversion when the buyer remorse is this palpable and the dog may end up back at the shop before the week is up.

Examining loss aversion lead us to consider the idea of what it is we might be losing. If we use the virtual goods in our game to build utility into the player's gaming experience then we are deepening the engagement over the longer term, rather than diminishing the lifetime value of the player.

If You Can't Stand the Heat . . .

Let's not forget the influence competition has on loss aversion. If others can see and then admire or disapprove of the goods we can buy/don't have in a game this will multiply the impact of any loss aversion. This means that if what we offer is obviously "cool," there might be considerable pressure to spend money on that asset. Of course the opposite is also true, once it has gone out of fashion, the fact that we own the item can suddenly become quite negative in terms of popular perception. Different people have different reactions to social pressure. Some lead, some follow, and others carve their own path; what is consistent is that they need to be seen to act in that way. Part of how we define ourselves is in comparison with others, even in games. We should not underestimate the benefits from finding a way to ensure that players can see others purchased goods, partly as discovery and partly in terms of social capital.

The Price is Right . . .

There is one core economic principle at the heart of the success of the freemium model and this is the reason why in the end services will continue to be so dominant in for games. Price elasticity of demand is a

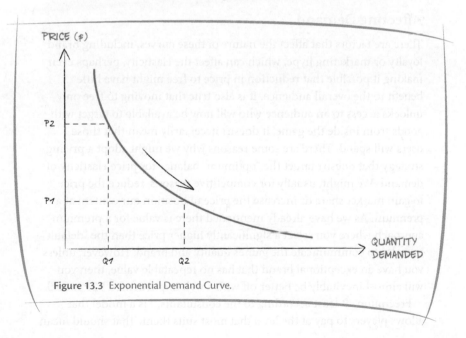

Figure 13.3 Exponential Demand Curve.

way to show how demand responds to changes in price, assuming that supply remains constant. There are many factors to take into account, but we typically expect the changes in price to have a relatively constant, say that most games will conform to the classic Exponential Demand Curve, which means that the rate of change in demand itself changes in proportion to the reduction in price. At the highest price, we see the smallest number of purchasers and similarly at the lowest price we see the largest proportion of users taking up the game. In this case each time we reduce the price, the proportion of new players we can acquire will increase by a larger proportion. The biggest difference will be between free and any minimum price. When we are selling goods upfront, our objective is usually to find the optimum price in order to obtain the largest number of users. However, by removing the initial price we move the spending decision into the game, where there are no other competitive suppliers. The same mathematics shows the effect on price of an increase in supply for the same level of demand causes the price to drop in the same way. Given that we already have an almost infinite supply of good games content on the Apple and Android app stores there is no doubt in my mind that this would have naturally driven the price down to free anyway.

Affecting Demand

There are factors that affect the nature of these curves, including brand loyalty or marketing hype, which can affect the elasticity, perhaps even making it possible that reduction in price to free might have little benefit to the overall audience. It is also true that moving to free only unlocks access to an audience who will now be available to target with goods from inside the game, it doesn't necessarily mean that those users will spend. There are some reasons why we might adopt a pricing strategy that doesn't target the "optimum" balance for price elasticity of demand. We might, usually for competitive reasons, reduce the price to gain market share or increase the price to position our content at a premium. As we have already mentioned there is value for a premium approach where you select a significantly higher price than the "default" in order to communicate the game's quality and brand. However, unless you have an exceptional brand that has no repeatable value, then you will almost inevitably be better off with a well implemented F2P model.

Freemium, at least according to the consultants,[14] is a model that allows players to pay at the level that most suits them. That should mean that we get every possible combination of price and users. The trouble is that's not quite true. As we have already noted, the second and subsequent purchases are affected by the context of the previous experiences and the changing nature of risk.

Pricing and Risk

Different types of goods have different risk profiles and this affects the how much involvement[15] a user will take in their decision-making process. Complex goods tend to require a greater level of investigation, even when the cost isn't all that significant. A simple consumable good, such as an energy crystal that gives me a temporary boost to performance, is a low risk in the short term. It's usually cheap, cheerful, and has no long-term complications as it disappears after use. This isn't a complex decision, but the context of an almost infinite supply of games, players need to be fully immersed[16] in your game for this to be a simple decision.

The complexity level increases when we are looking to make our tenth or 100th purchase; longer term questions affect our decision. While consumable items have an immediate value, they don't (generally) generate any added utility in the game. In fact the paradox is that because they get used and then are gone, in the long term they represent a significant risk to the player. On the other hand, a durable good, for example a well of energy crystals that gives you ten crystals every day (as long as you return) has a sustained benefit in the game, something that I enjoy most only if I come back every day. This type of good generates ongoing value and additional utility for the game. It's usually at a more significant price than a single crystal and represents a longer-term commitment than perhaps recently converted users might be willing to make, which conversely means it represents a greater short-term risk.

Rent and Buy

The effect of time-based risk and pricing is something that became highly important to the success we had at 3UK with the games service. We initially launched with rental games at 50p for three days. Seemed like a great idea at the time, but with the added complexity of a billing API we found it hard to get enough games ready prior to launch. It was a disaster. We failed to get any significant number of sales and had to react sharply, offering full-price games to buy outright at £5 each. The really interesting part came when we analyzed the results of our sales.

We saw that the majority of sales were from "buy" games, but we found that there was a significant anomaly. Games with rent and buy versions sold more than three times the others, and rent reflected only 20 percent of the total revenue.

Part of the reason for this success was that presenting two prices with different levels of value proposition makes it easier for buyers to choose the more expensive option, but it also allowed them to choose the longer term, more stable, more expensive option.

Opening the Gateway

Hopefully with all this you can see the importance of the psychology of buying behavior. In practice we can't identify the influence of what drives a player to buy, but these key aspects can help inform our thinking and increase the chances that we have to convert more players to payers at the same time as building lifetime value; increasing the perceived utility in the game.

The best examples of how we can apply these techniques come during the transitional moments of the player's engagement with our game. These are also the points that require the most attention in terms of game and monetization design, particularly the first purchase.

As we have said before, after the initial download we find the important lesson of the learning stages is to help deepen our engagement with our players. We want them to stay with us, to become engaged. We need to ensure that we demonstrate that spending money is going to be worthwhile, even an aspirational goal. But it's not something we expect from the player. Indeed we understand that doing so when their level of interest in the game is at its lowest point is going to backfire on us. It is later, once we have shown them the value of their investments in terms of time and effort and shown them the value of truly engaging that we can start to consider how we convert them to actually buying something for real money. When we do it needs to be what I call a "gateway good,"[17] an in-game item that is designed to be so obviously of value that it shows new players that spending money isn't a big deal.

It needs to be a simple, obvious benefit for the players and at the same time create a level of delight that will charm the player as a reward for investing in the game. This idea of charming and generous delight is important when designing all of our goods as it's just as important to build retention after the purchase as it is to gain the money for each individual item. More than that, however, a gateway good needs to be a promise, not only of the value of the item itself, but something that sets the expectations for all future purchases in the game. We will look into this more in Chapter 14.

Setting Price

It will probably be quite clear that nowhere in this chapter do I give any specific advice on setting price. I appreciate that might be frustrating, but it's deliberate as (of course) I want to limit how quickly this book goes out of date. The other reason is that every game is different. We usually have a minimum price we can sell any items for, based on the platform; for iOS this is $0.99. This is useful for low-pain threshold items, but as we have already stated elsewhere charging higher than the minimum payment allows you to communicate something about the value of the game or in-game virtual good. More interesting is the dynamic of changing price. The price elasticity concept should apply to goods inside your game as much as it does to whether players buy upfront or not. However, there is no competition for virtual good suppliers for your game, and the decision to purchase is specific to their playing experience. As a result, although there will always be an associated opportunity cost for other purchases, it seems that in-game goods are essentially inelastic.[18] This means that reducing the price won't dramatically affect an increase in sales; that's not a license to charge a ridiculous amount for those items of course. The only way you can really know what the right price is for the goods you sell is to test it. Use common sense and competitive comparison to avoid obvious mistakes and always start with slightly higher prices that you can easily reduce later. You will get a lot more negative feedback if you put prices up. Then again even this can be mitigated if you introduce new items as "introductory price" as this warns players upfront that the price might change later and at the same time makes purchasers feel special as they were clearly smart early adopters.

Beware Shadows

Whenever we introduce revenue items into the game we have to remember the shadow they place on the experience and in particular how they impact the flow from the game. Interruptions for advertising interstitials can be as damaging to the overall experience as a poorly designed payment process.

Making the decision to make the first payment is a huge psychological barrier for anyone; regardless of the price. If there is anything that gets in the way of them fulfilling that process they will blame you and your game—even if it's an unrelated, unavoidable problem. Make sure you test this process repeatedly, even after launch as you will have to rely on third-party services at some point in the flow. One of the reasons Apple's AppStore has been so successful is that the vast majority of its users have already entered their credit card details into the service. That means those users don't have to do anything new to pay for their items in your game. They will have already experienced the familiar flow and will feel it is safe to do that. However, this isn't always the case with other platforms like Android and especially when you are using other third-party payment systems like Boku or WorldPay. Using external systems is a very good idea, but your responsibility as a developer is to make sure that the set-up process to spend money with you is done as simply and easily as possible. Trust is the most valuable currency; without it no one will spend real money.

Making Your Mind Up

The more I research the psychological triggers to making a purchase the more it seems to come back to the question of trust. There is a natural aversion to being "sold to" and yet we find ourselves buying goods all the time and sharing our best purchases with our friends. There is a "hunter-gatherer" aspect to the act of shopping, which itself is a source of gratification.

The question of how we support players through the inevitable buyer remorse that comes from the act of downloading or buying items in our game is I believe key to success, but more simply it defines the difference between a product and a service. Do our players "buy" our experience or do they "belong" to that experience? How we respond to the question changes the way we create content—hopefully for the better.

There are some basic ethical principles that all business should all adhere to:

- Disclose any risks associated with your product or service.
- Identify the added features that will increase the cost.
- Avoid false or misleading communications.
- Don't use high-pressure sales tactics.
- Don't mask selling as another activity (e.g., market research).

There is good evidence[19] that shows that being upfront with users about what is free and what costs money can actually build trust and confidence in the game. That kind of clarity means that there are no bad surprises; no shocks to the bank account. Services have to build trust, it's the most valuable currency.

Freemium games at their best inspire players to become more deeply engaged; at their worst make them feel used and exploited—and inevitably churning.

Notes

1   Using the term "psychology" as a chapter heading calls for a little more due diligence and scientific research than other chapters and my fast and loose "marketing mindset" couldn't do this justice without some external advice. So I want to thank Berni Good of http://cyberpsychologist.co.uk for her kind feedback and support in this chapter. Of course any mistakes are my own and, to be clear, I'm not a trained psychologist. The other flaw is that I'm mixing psychological principles and economic principles and, to be further clear, I'm not a trained economist. However, the good news is that I am a trained marketer, and we are used to blurring such boundaries.

2   In the classic 1980s film *The Karate Kid* where Mr. Miyagi was the caretaker at the school who just happened to be an amazing karate instructor. I'm not referring to the more recent update, which is a fine movie but not the one I loved when I was also being taught karate by my own father.

3   The term AIDA is attributed to E. St Elmo Lewis, an American advertising and sales pioneer, http://en.wikipedia.org/wiki/AIDA_(marketing)#Purchase_Funnel.

4   Buyer remorse is also thought to be linked to the "paradox of choice," a theory by American psychologist Barry Schwartz in which, as the range of choices increases, the level of distress associated with making a decision also increases. More than that, as the range increases, customers start to expect that one choice will be "perfect" with no drawbacks, and this leads to circumstances where it's almost impossible to be satisfied with any purchase, http://en.wikipedia.org/wiki/Buyer's_remorse.

5   The Gartner Hype Curve is a tool used by technology companies to understand the potential consumer response to new technology triggers from the initial excessive expectations and how they build up based on the limited information available prior to the release of the concept. This is followed by a dramatic negative realization of the realistic limitations of that technology, at least in the initial practical delivery. However, this disappointment can be recovered as the approach becomes normal and gradually we return to a positive acknowledgement of the technology's contribution.

6   The buyer remorse curve is based on observation of the sale of games content. However, this is an assumption, a hypothesis, yet to be rigorously tested. However, don't take my word on buyer behaviors. There are some great books on the subject including Michael R. Solomon's *Consumer Behavior; Buying, Having, Being*, www.amazon.com/Consumer-Behavior-Edition-Michael-Solomon/dp/0132671840.

7   *Distimo*'s article on the number of downloads to be able to get in the top 25 chart can be found at www.distimo.com/blog/2012_05_quora-answering-series-download-volume-needed-to-hit-top-25-per-category.

8   In October 2013 Rodeo released a new Region and playable characters which I immediately purchased and playing this has delayed proof-reading this book. I've not found

any academic sources to support this principle, but I have found in several different businesses that players allocate for themselves a "personal threshold" in their spending. This might be a number of games or goods per month or a subconscious budget. This might appear to be suspended when we offer a retail sale offering cut-price deals across the whole platform, but I often find that the player take their spending into account by lowering their purchase behavior in subsequent months. At 3UK in particular, we discovered that classic retail sales were actually counterproductive; players would spending three times their threshold in the month of the sale but those who didn't churn through "bill-shock" would subsequently reduce their ongoing spend down to a third of normal over the next two months. In the end we would have slightly less revenue. This might be anecdotal, but I believe it's something that warrants further study.

9   Bong-Won Park and Kun Chang Lee, in an article in *Computers in Human Behavior* uncovered that game satisfaction with the gameplay was not enough to ensure the gamer has perception of "value" when confronted with the decision to purchase. See "Exploring the Value of Purchasing Online Game Items," *Computers in Human Behavior* 27(6): 2178–2185 (2011).

10 J.C. Penney's change of strategy may not have been a bad idea, but it was at least poorly implemented and the consequences for the business was dramatic. The following article talks outlines the issues and questions the execution problems, www.forbes.com/sites/stevedenning/2013/04/09/j-c-penney-was-ron-johnsons-strategy-wrong. Additionally, there is a great video on *Penny Arcade* that compares the J.C. Penney situation with the use of in-game loot drops in *Firefall*, www.penny-arcade.com/patv/episode/the-jc-pennys-effect.

11 American psychologist George Loewenstein looked at how human behavior was affected by intense, visceral emotions, causing us to act against our best interest when agitated and to potentially underestimate effects when we are not, http://en.wikipedia.org/wiki/Empathy_gap.

12 In 1978 the classic *Space Invaders* game was cited as the reason why the Japanese Treasury had to dramatically increase the production of 100 yen coins, used not just for playing games but also widely in order to use the Tokyo subway system, http://en.wikipedia.org/wiki/Space_Invaders.

13 Interestingly there have been some studies that question whether the idea of loss aversion even exists; however, I believe that it is useful at least as a lens when thinking about virtual goods design, http://en.wikipedia.org/wiki/Loss_aversion.

14 Again I have to admit to doing this myself. It's a useful shorthand, but the reality as I explain is more complex.

15 It is useful to learn about the buyer decision-making process and the differences between high and low involvement purchases and the following link has a good short summary, www.tutor2u.net/business/marketing/buying_decision_process.asp.

16 Building immersion is one of the key strengths of games, although there is some debate over what exactly immersion is from a psychological perspective. J. Kirakowski and N. Curran did some interesting research looking at RPG games and immersion which provides a useful framework to think about this, see their chapter "Immersion in Computer Games," in *Computational Informatics, Social Factors and New Information Technologies*.

17 The "gateway" term comes from theories about drug-taking and hypothesises that the use of less deleterious drugs such as tobacco, alcohol, and cannabis lead to a movement onto stronger substances. There are many criticism of this idea in particular that it commits the logical fallacy of "*post hoc ergo propter hoc*," however it does provide a shorthand that makes it easy to explain some of the attributes we want for our first purchase. I should also stress that this isn't intended to equate virtual goods with selling drugs.

18 On September 5, 2013, at COL 3.0 in Bogata, Colombia, Jamie Gotch of Subatomic
    Studios talked about how their data confirmed in-game virtual goods were essentially
    inelastic within their tower defense game *Fieldrunners*.
19 In press.

Exercise 13: Writing Use Cases

Now the exercises get a little more serious. So far we have just been exploring our ideas and, hopefully, you have been testing them with paper-prototypes or perhaps even exploratory coding during voluntary downtime.

Before we start investing real valuable time and coding in earnest we need to make sure we really understand the details of what it is we are going to make. We need to have confidence that we have communicated each element for the development, art and audio teams so that there is no ambiguity over our objectives. We will then ask them to respond to us with their proposed solution to our use cases for us as product owners to sign-off. This way of working vastly reduces the risk of building something different than we intended, although until we go live that is still no guarantee that the result will work as we envisaged.

Start by looking at the core mechanic of your game and break that down into specific separate elements. For each of these elements we will consider who the "actor" is (i.e., the person initiating the use of that element) and the circumstances of that action. You also have to consider what the function is expected to do and the relationship of that use case with other functions. If you are familiar with UML (Unified Modeling Language)[1] that can make it easier to communicate in a more formal way; however, it's not always necessary.

You will want to repeat this process for each of the features of your core game mechanic as well as each feature in the context loop and metagames.

Priority	Feature	Actor	Use case	Function	Related
1					
2					
3					
4					
5					

Finally you need to determine the priority of these use cases in absolute order. This means marking the most important feature as number one and then working down from that priority with only one feature occupying each priority number.

N.B. if you want to do this online, the system will allow you to list lots of different use cases and then prioritize them as needed.

WORKED EXAMPLE:

Priority	Feature	Actor	Use case	Function	Related
1	1.0 District map	Player	. . . sees a map of a section of the city district with locations where I can play.	Map used to select levels and show playing progress.	
5	1.1 Mission pop-ups	Player	. . . sees a UI popup with a hint about the game type at that location and the duration that the mission remains available.	Popup is used by player to prioritize missions to play.	1.0 District map
2	2.0 Location map	Player	. . . sees a 2D flat plane layout with a 3D perspective. Map contains a range of 20-40 objects as well as obstacles.	Map is used as playing area for the game.	
3	3.0 Anthony	Player	. . . uses Anthony as an avatar by drawing a path form the spawn position to one of the objects.	Player draws a path on the location map which Anthony will follow at a set pace.	2.0 Location map
4	4.0 Mobile enemy	Player	. . . sees a mobile enemy who moves across the map of the location. Collision causes Anthony to have to restart that specific move.	The game includes a series of mobile enemies which act as mobile obstacles to play. The more sophisticated the pattern the more difficult the mobile.	3.0 Anthony

Note

1 Personally I'm not as familiar with UML as I would like to be. It is a useful standard and helps with the communication with developers and data analysts. To find out more about UML check out www.uml.org.

Chapter 14
Tools of the Trade

Making Money

You should now have your head around some of the key theories and principles about how players buy content and how as designers we need to think in order to engage users and keep them paying. In this penultimate chapter we are going to take a look the practical reality of what we will actually do to make money. To do this we will take a look at the various potential sources of revenue and how we can present those elements to give us the best chance to build the widest possible paying audience as well as maintaining high lifetime values.

Brought To You by Our Sponsors

Let's start with advertising. This is often one of the first revenue mechanisms considered by developers when they think about a "free" game. It's a formula that has been used to deliver content "free at the point of consumption" and has historically been synonymous with radio and television[1] programming. It's also something that has been widely used to generate revenue for web and mobile developers; but with games this has sometime caused problems in terms of the reaction of the user, usually when the adverts unduly interrupt the player experience. Despite that, the advantage of being able to gain some revenue without having players themselves make the purchase decision is significant. This is an approach that really rewards scale and where players contribute simply by coming back and playing.

Paid, Cross-Promotion and Incentivized

There already exists a healthy ecosystem for advertising in apps, particularly games with several companies specializing with different approaches and tools. Indeed, I would argue that games are one of the most effective markets for advertising. Where else can you advertise within your competitors' product (where your target audience will be) without negatively impacting their performance? The most obvious approach in advertising is the classic "paid" adverts, which are pretty straightforward, with costs charged off a rate card or auctioned off using a calculation based on either useful views (effective CPM[2]) or response (CPA[3]). As well as classical paid ads there are cross-promotion networks such as Chartboost, Appflood and Applifier's Facebook service, which introduced the concept. These often combine the traditional paid approaches, often using some form of bidding system, allowing the developer to buy installs at a better price, but perhaps from less effective games (from a conversion perspective). What makes a cross-promotion network different from paid ads is the opportunity to offer an "install swap" mechanism, creating an exchangeable currency from each install your game delivers for other games in the network. Importantly, this means you can bank the value of your installs helping the discovery process for your later releases, even your new products.

Then there are incentivized download services, such as TapJoy. While these have been barred from iOS apps, there can be good value gained on other platforms by using some form of incentive to encourage the player to act, often using in-game currency. This becomes particularly clear if both games share the same virtual currency. However, adding any incentive will change the dynamics with the potential for unintended consequences; for example, if you pay only on install this can create a wave of players only interested in getting the virtual cash and never playing the game.

Getting On With It

Choosing the right partners requires you consider a wide combination of factors. First there is the relationship with that partner, not always an overriding factor but if there is a level of trust then this can help with problems as they arise. Next we have to consider the simplicity of the integration process. There is always an API involved and you never know when this will conflict with another API you are already using; testing and implementing always have a cost implication. You need to know what revenue you can expect from each impression or install and what their fill-rate will be; in other words how effectively they use your inventory (that's the number of places in the games where you can place an ad). There are mediation services out there that can help you access multiple ad networks with just one integration, but you do need to be careful how much they impact your end revenue for the game. It's especially important to understand how the ad revenue for your game is calculated by those networks. It's often done on a different basis than the way it is sold—for example, you might buy on a cost per install and sell on eCPM—this approach gives the ad platform some wiggle-room for their profit.

Implementing the API is usually the easy part, apart from the regression testing. The complication comes in how you decide where in the game you are going to place the adverts and whether these will be links, banners, interstitials, still images, animations, or even full videos. The placement and timing of adverts is crucial. Despite the temptation, try to avoid putting adverts in the way of the flow of play for the freeload ing players. Advertising might seem to be the only revenue we get from them but without them we don't get the 'Network' value that encourages other players to discover and spend money. We can't afford to lose them so we can't just shove an advert in their way at every possible point. This wears away at their willingness to continue to return to the game. We want non-paying users to think that our game is valuable enough to justify the advertising and that without it they wouldn't have the free experience they enjoy.

Keeping the Flow

When placing the ads, look for points in the game that naturally work alongside the state of the player—such as loading screens or just before returning to the menu screen—and make the ads easily skipped. Measurement of the player response here is really important. Test and confirm that your placement of an ad supports the longevity of a player as well as working out whether it helps gain an increase of revenue. Also consider the use of "opt-in" advertising, such as GameAds from Applifer [4], where the player accepts the "burden" of watching an advert in order to obtain some in-game currency. This makes the "free" currency more valued as the player understand that it helped generate some income for the game and at the same time it required some effort on their part to obtain, even if that was just to watch a fun clip of another game. At worst this will help extend that player's engagement with the game and may just show them the value of spending money directly helping convert them to become paying users.

Is Advertising Up To Standard?

Advertising has its place but, at least at the time of writing, the vast majority of advertisers were either other games or they related to gam- bling services. This means that there is a lot of recycled cash passing through the system, i.e., where I spend the advertising revenue I earned in my game on advertising that game in other games. I suspect this will change rapidly as mainstream consumer brands start to see the poten- tial audience size within games, which already has overtaken anything offered within the TV industry. Brands like Red Bull and Audi have a reputation for being willing to experiment, but for other brands to embrace the opportunity within games we have to demonstrate reach, frequency, and repeatability. Reach[4] means the size of addressable audience among the target demographic the brand is interested in. Importantly this is about the potential audience size offered by the medium, not the actual numbers of people who will be exposed to the commercial messages in reality. Frequency refers to the number of occasions the user will be exposed to that advert. This is a key factor that influences the effectiveness of the advert, alongside the message, format, and creative quality. Repeatability, on the other hand, refers to the advertiser's needs to be able to take the same promotional material and use that unchanged across lots of different providers; it's about packaging the advertising material so that it can be leveraged across as wide a range of channels as possible. Outdoor billboard posters all conform to a set of standard sizes ranging from the Adshel (1800×1200cm) to the 96 Sheets (12000×3000cm).[5] It's this last part that we have yet to really work out, from the perspective of the bigger brands. They expect to some predictability of where their advert will appear, how frequently, and to know that the experience will be suitable for their art style. If we are going to reach out to brands on a more consistent basis, we have to find easier ways to ensure they can create consistently repeatable experiences across multiple applications.

What Measure Success

It's hard to find good data, to judge success in advertising for games; anecdotally the cost of acquisition can be up to $6, but the best reliable source I can find is *Fiksu*'s cost per loyal user[6] which in July 2013 reached $1.80. This is a milestone in that mobile acquisition costs now have reached the same heights as Facebook games did prior to the downturn in social games.

From personal experience, largely taken from data based on social games from Papaya Mobile, is that I would expect 24 percent of total revenue to come from the contribution from advertising. However, this seems to vary widely. Some developers, notably Rovio and Kiloo, once their audience reaches a daily critical mass advertising of multiple million daily active users, can achieve the necessary reach to generate very significant revenues. Without this critical mass, ad revenues can be disappointing. Rovio went further than this by creating their own media channel with their own weekly *Angry Birds* animated series embedded into the games. They are now working with Disney and, if successful, they are likely to change the way many people consume this kind of content.

Virtual Goods

The sale of in-game items is critical to the success of a game as a service; to be able to make this work we have to be able to separate which part of the game is central to the experience and which generates a sustainable audience from aspects of the game that are added-value propositions that can be sold to that audience. The term "added-value" is essential. We are not trying to remove the reasons to keep playing, but we do need to create value that encourages players to get ever more deeply engaged.

We also want to find ways to be make our game scalable in term of efficient production. That means we need to find things that are easy to duplicate or encourage repeated use of the rest of the game, rather than having to incur large costs to sustain the experience.

For example, if we take the time to hand-make something beautiful in the game, we want to make sure that it is going to be used by as many people as possible. Similarly, we want to sell things as efficiently as possible, the posting of a new database entry that counts how many health potions you have is incredibly cost-effective and has a clear value-add to the player.

But What Do We Sell?

In order to work out the right products to monetize we need to go back to what we talked about in Chapter 3 and start with the mechanic. In that chapter we talked about the importance of challenge, which is essential to the fun of any game, and the conditions that can improve the flow of the play. The challenge might come in the form of how much damage you have do, how fast or accurately you have to drive, or even the ability to think enough steps ahead to place an item correctly. Using this knowledge we need to isolate items where we can adjust those elements, ideally through the soft variables that change the strategy rather that the "win/lose" conditions as we discussed when we talked about uncertainty in Chapter 7.

To put this in more practical terms, let's take the example of a first-person shooter where we might consider of alternative weapons or upgrades that deliver the same damage (leaving the difficulty unchanged) but with different combinations of accuracy, power, or frequency of shot; playing into the preferences of the user. In a driving game we might adjust the components of the vehicle from tires to suspension, even the exhaust, and adjust the car's performance within a range of ability. This kind of thinking applies to any game and helps you identify any number of different potential virtual goods. Anything might make a suitable candidate for goods to sell— from in-game currency, energy crystals, ammo, different weapon choices, different vehicles, power-ups that clear matched lines of gems, new levels, etc. We then have to think about how selling those items will affect the overall experience and what value they will add to the player from their perspective. To do this requires us to apply the concepts of the buyer behavior we talked about in Chapter 13 to these goods. Will creating alternative weapons (and their associated strategy) add to the joy of playing the game or simply create a mechanism to guarantee winning by spending? Will adding a new level be an efficient way to increase revenue or might it be more effective to increase retention? If we use a fuel mechanic, will the "friction" we add to the game to make this work increase players' engagement due to the impact of notifications to return back to the game later? At the same time we have to ask ourselves that most important question, "so what?" Why should the player care about this new virtual good, in what way does it solve a need for them, and how does it make the game better?

Sometimes We Have To Say No

Not every game has mechanics that easily support monetization without causing too some kind of a negative reaction among the players. However, it is always a useful exercise to think about the role of each variable in the game and how we might be able to convert them to a revenue model, even if it's uncomfortable. The deliberate choice to not use a potential monetization method, to preserve the integrity of the playing experience, is as important as the need to avoid missing new ways we might trigger a purchase, generating added value to the player.

Monetizing Context

Once we have assessed the mechanics, we need to look at the context of the game and, once again, isolate potential elements that can sustain the experience longer. This will consider elements that help define out progression within the game, whether that's about the journey a player goes through or the narrative of the story. Often this means looking at those items that multiply the rewards we obtain for our efforts, so that we can buy a bigger, better-looking car or farm.

Sometimes this will include the ability to purchase unique vanity or narrative elements, provided they contribute to the telling of our own story or provide a means of comparison with others, e.g., I completed the "Kobayashi Maru."[7] Once again we have to consider the consequences of charging for these items and determine if doing so will increase the enjoyment and retention of the game. Selling a larger storage area for your player to put their collectable items is a classic example that affects the state between gameplay sessions. However, the idea of restricted use doesn't have to be limited to storage, it could be a slot for a weapon you use in combat, a maximum capacity for your in-game currency or the area you have available to farm your crops. We can go further and apply emotional values to these goods, even use them to help customize our experience. This about the effect of an option to spend money to access my own Constellation Class starship in *Star Trek Online*; for me, as a moderate Trekkie, this was irresistible. Finding the ideal retail items within our game, whether at the mechanic level or at the context level, is fundamentally a question of game design. The only difference is that we have to again ask the question "so what?" from a user perspective if we want to know that this will be a viable product to sell.

Given Three Options—Pick Two

There are some general principles that help us ask the right questions about the implications of specific virtual goods. Tadhg Kelly[8] in his blog, *What Games Are*, talks about the Freemium Triangle as an attempt to resolve the dangers of accidently creating a "pay to win" scenario where players could in effect buy away any challenge. The idea is that if you assume that monetization comes down to boosters (temporary enhancements such as a special weapon with limited shots or a token that turn the red gems blue), unlocks (permanent access to a feature like a new car or larger farm) or skips (such as fuel to unlock an energy restriction, healing potions, and the ability to skip a cooldown period), then you decide that you can offer any combination of two of these elements, but not all three. This way you can isolate at least one of the core dimensions of game design from being beaten simply by spending cash. This leaves the designer a safety net and means that their game will continue to follow the principle that the shared rules of play should be fair.

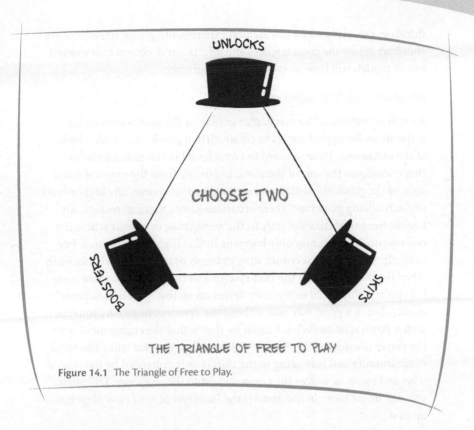

UNLOCKS

CHOOSE TWO

BOOSTERS

SKINS

THE TRIANGLE OF FREE TO PLAY

Figure 14.1 The Triangle of Free to Play.

Does Fairness Matter?

There are other designers who don't believe this is necessary. At one of the GDC 2012 Roundtables there was a discussion on F2P design where the consensus was that "the only people worried about Fairness in Free2Play games have never done it." It's hard to take a comment like that out of the context (as I have just done) and still do it justice. What I think they are saying is that much of the concern over game balance that is expressed when it comes to F2P is a distraction, a straw man argument made out of fear. On the other hand in late 2013 there was a counter reaction against the idea of 'Pay to Win' suggesting goods should have no effect on play. For me the trouble is that Designers (and Players) aren't experienced enough with F2P design to know the right strategy. Whatever design strategy we take with monetization we should do this thoughtfully and with that in mind I believe that Tadhg's Triangle remains a useful way of thinking, especially when you are first experimenting with freemium. We shouldn't ignore the consequences and affects our decisions over monetization models will have on our playing experience.

Monetizing Metagames

As well as looking at the mechanics of play or the game's context for inspiration, for opportunities to create virtual goods we can also look at the metagame. Here we need to consider all of the characteristics that encompass the role of the game in our life from the physical space around the game, the social interactions, and, of course, any higher-level self-actualizing gameplay. There are some games that can realistically benefit from monetization only in the metagame, or at least where the real revenue opportunity only happens in this higher perspective. For example, *Clash of Clans* comes alive in terms of monetization only really when the player unlocks the clan system and the group collective combat system. This social experience drives an almost "pyramid-scheme" quality, but in a good way and without the criminal negativity implicit with a Ponzi scheme. What I mean by that is that the engagement with the player is extended by the other players they interact with. The sense of community and belonging to the clan is only enhanced by the shared wins and losses as well as the commitment to the challenge. Of course you will invest more in the game if the "survival of your clan" depends upon it.

Review Your Candidates

Once this review process is completed and we have worked out the best candidate goods for our game and how they impact the flow of play we need to consider exactly how they are going to be bought.

Consumables

Many of these items will be consumable, limited-use items that grant a temporary bonus or ability, such as higher power ammo. They should also tend to either have a measurable but still limited effect on performance or, better yet, influence the softer variables; how we play rather than whether we win or not. Other goods might focus on increasing the results of our actions, such as a coin doubler or experience point boost, which are only valuable once the specific play session has concluded. Some of the items might even be specifically to protect against negative things happening, such as an insurance policy against your plants withering. All of these contribute to play in some way and should be easy things to appreciate and value. However, once they are used they are gone (until you buy more of course).

When looking at a consumable good we have to think of them in one of three conditions. First, what is their role as a "gateway good," is their value obvious and immediate? Second, why would you continue to spend money on them over time, particularly later in the playing experience? In other words, will players find the ongoing need for an endless supply of these items still appealing at the later life stages, or will these become a "nagging" influence? Finally, we need to consider how players will respond to purchasing them at "hot" moments. For example if we offer a health potion at the point of the player dying (allowing them to continue), will that enhance the playing experience or simply feel like we are being manipulative? The reality is of course that it depends. Offering goods at the point of need is a good thing provided that the design of the user flow is focused on the player's entertainment. For example, as well as offering that last minute top-up, we can also reward players for thinking ahead, storing potions they discover through play as well as offering a bundle or discount if they buy health potions in advance. Paying close attention to these kinds of details will pay dividends. Better yet we should think how the game-play can be enhanced through the choice we offer the players through of the goods available.

Balance In All Things

Consumable goods are not the only way to sell items in the game, but they can be effective provided they deliver delight and some opportunity advantage to the player when using them. We should also be fairly generous about how we make them available to players free of charge, not just at the beginning of play; perhaps not as much as a player might want to use but enough that they don't resent the game for withholding access to them. We want to build a level of comfort and familiarity among our players for the goods we have on offer, while still giving the player a reason to want more of them. If they really add value to play, rather than just being a tax on poor playing, then there is good reason that players will actively want to purchase more. It's a very fine line between being generous and removing the need for buying them at all or the whole idea becoming seen as a source of nagging for money.

BOGOF Retailing

As we have already said, we are the retailers now, and as such we can use the techniques any local shop might employ to encourage players to spend more with us. Why not sell a bundle of our consumable goods? Buy one get one free (BOGOF), a pack of 12 for the price of six, and other volume discounts all become useful ways to increase the perceived value and which in reality have no practical costs for us to deliver the extra items, except regarding the opportunity costs of that player making a subsequent purchase. These items are consumable of course and the whole point of them is that the player will want to use them up in order to gain the benefit. There are risks of course including the need to avoid misbalancing the game if we give away too many consumables. However, the biggest issue with consumables is that they generally don't increase the players' investment in the game. Once they are used, that gameplay benefit is realized and I have to buy another to get the benefit again. There is no ongoing utility being built up inside the game.

One of the things that has surprised me with games like *Candy Crush Saga* from King is why they only offer you one "save me" power-up for 69p when you get to the end of a level without meeting the success criteria. If they offered a bundle of five, perhaps even ten, at that point then the player would not just get better value, they would be helped through their current level and still have a number of additional power-ups that can only be spent by playing the game more. Perhaps they tested this and it didn't return the same revenue potential, who knows? However, these are the kinds of things that are worth testing for your game.

Something More Durable

That takes us onto the durable goods where players make a (generally larger) payment into our game to get access to an item that generates an ongoing aspect of the game. That's different from permanent goods such as special weapons or one-time upgrades of the player's tools, equipment, or other abilities to play the game. These one-off purchases do have an ongoing consequence, but I would argue that these rarely add ongoing utility into the game. They don't create deeper reasons to return to the game. Permanents can be great sellers and some game genres, including tower defense games such as *Fieldrunners*, reportedly get the majority of their virtual goods revenues from them. They can also provide a touch of glamour to a game. The appeal of buying a +5 Vorpal Blade is much greater than buying five +1 Damage Crystals. Permanent items are aspirational, but once obtained become part of the default setting of your game.

A Well of Crystals

Instead I want you to consider durables goods that you buy once, but that expand the choices of play or stimulate the player to return to the game in order to maximize their benefit. My favorite example is the Well of Energy Crystals.[9] This is a one-time purchase that generates the usually purchased energy crystals that grant me fuel to do more in the game and I will probably have already been buying them as a consumable. The Well might cost of about the same as buying ten individual energy crystals, but delivers ten crystals over 24 hours if you come in to collect them. This kind of virtual good delivers real utility into the game for the player and doesn't inhibit the player buying another extra energy crystal should they feel excited enough to do just that one extra task that day. Indeed, it gives players permission to feel more relaxed about buying the odd energy crystal because the knowledge that they are going to get more tomorrow anyway makes it their choice to spend money, rather than having the game overtly influence them to do so.

New Vehicles

Another example would be the purchase of a new vehicle in a driving game or a new spaceship in space exploration game. Designed well, these durable goods introduce new strategies and options that are only possible if the player returns to the game. In *Real Racing 3* the player can access specific races based on the cars they have in their inventory and they can race each car separately while their other cars are being repaired. This means that the available time players can intensely engage with the game expands as the player invests further into the game.

The Slot Machine

Durable goods can influence game progression in other ways to reflect the progress of the player in the game's context as well. Imagine that you have a hover vehicle with three power-up slots. The player gets to choose what items to put in those slots—perhaps a weapon or a shield system, an extra life or rocket engine. All of which contribute to their strategy of play. But as a durable good you might be able to purchase a fourth slot. Unlocking a fourth slot doesn't guarantee that the player will beat the others, although it will influence the outcome.

Collectable Card Games

The use of durable goods to influence strategy choices has long been employed in collectable card games and these in turn are becoming a heavy influence on the monetization design of freemium games. They come in "booster" packs with a random selection of cards. Some of these will have a temporary effect (e.g., mana or land) to be spend to release other more durable cards (e.g., creatures or spells). However, the strategy of their use and influence on the gameplay becomes ambiguous as they are combined. Many mobile games that use this approach allow cards to "improve" by discarding duplicate or unwanted cards, creating a more significant card. Importantly players don't have to have large decks of cards to play, even to win. However, they will usually have an easier and more interesting time if they collect additional cards. We don't have to take the metaphor of the cards literally. We could take a racing game and have different brands of engine components that combine together differently to improve the car in unique ways, right down to the details like the number of teeth in the gear ratios, if the audience will respond to that.

Sacrifice

An interesting side effect of the collectable mechanic emerges when you introduce the ability to sacrifice duplicate or unwanted cards in order to enhance other cards we prefer. This creates a way to significantly scale the number of cards any player might need if they wanted to invest to guarantee access to the most exclusive cards. Imagine a basic level 1 Fire Creature Card. We find a duplicate of this specific card and decide to discard that in order to evolve our card into a level 2 Fire Creature Card. In order to obtain a level 3 Fire Creature Card, we have to evolve another pair of specific cards and then discard that resulting level 2 card. As we keep going on this pattern, we start to exponentially increase the number of cards a player needs to guarantee access to the highest level creatures. Combine that with the concept of rarity often used in these games and this becomes very interesting. Cards might come in different levels of rarity—common, uncommon, rare, and super-rare for example. Of course that value will only increase if you have a strong social element allowing players to see each other's "cards" and to exchange them. The use of the collectable card game model probably deserves its own book because it has subtle depths, yet is infinitely flexible. However, be wary in your use that you don't try to use it too literally or you risk turning the mechanics of your revenue model into a game in itself. That could easily distract from the game you intended to make. The objectives and mechanics of a collectable card game are as much tied up with the artwork and revelation of the next card as they are with the game itself. That playing model is very much targeted to the collector reward behavior described by Richard Bartle that we referenced in Chapter 2, and unless that was your original intention it can introduce a lucre-ludo-narrative dissonance as we discussed in Chapter 6.

Converting Currency

One of the most powerful tools available for monetization is the in-game currency. These are usually a value generated through the action of play that can then be used to exchange for items within the experience. We talked about this in Chapter 7 when talking about the role of uncertainty generated through imbalanced economies. The term "currency" is largely interchangeable with "resource," except that a currency is usually available for exchange with any item, where as a resource will have a specific use and, by inference, restricts progression for items within its type. For example, gold might be used commonly in a game to purchase buildings, crops, and equipment, but buildings might also need clay, crops might also need fertilizer, etc. The role of currency in gameplay is also multifaceted. It's a reward for progress, indeed in some games it is the only relevant measure of our progress. Such games can often devolve late in the player life cycle into an attempt for the player to earn as much currency as possible. Currency can also act as a useful gatekeeper for later stages within a game—you can't defeat the werewolf unless you can afford the silver-plate armor and sword as well having all the necessary skills. The widespread use of in-game grind currency also gives the freeloading player the sense that they can indeed explore every aspect of the game, they just have to be willing to extend the level of grinding they are willing to do.

Buying currency is possibly the most natural form of consumable purchase. Players already understand what that currency can buy if they have been playing the game and earning money through play. However, if we sell that money then we need to seek other mechanisms, typically other types of resource, in order to sustain the gatekeeping mechanic. It's vital, as we have already said, that buying currency doesn't defeat the purpose of playing late in the lifecycle. Resources have similar risks associated with them especially if you allow some level of "exchange" or "conversion" between resource types—something that is usually a good idea from a player's perspective. However, if you allow this, consider introducing some counterbalance mechanism to prevent another kind of "pay to win" arising by mistake. For example I want to exchange clay for fertilizer. I can do that if I have bought the market building, and then I only get one fertilizer for every two clay and 100 gold I sacrifice. Alternatively allow players to exchange material between them at an exchange rate the players agree, perhaps even take a commission from those transactions using the same resources or the in-game currency. This is often at least as valuable for the social bonds that it helps build between players as it is in terms of stimulating the desire for buying more in-game currency. Another option might be to have a maximum wallet size; the purchase of larger items needing a larger wallet.

Many games introduce a second or third currency, usually specifically a premium currency, such as gems. These can provide a second rhythm of play, in terms of the generation of value through play. Premium currencies can often still be generated through play, but at a significantly slower rate than the standard currency. They are also needed to purchase the higher quality items within the game, the best examples will be for all practical purposes out of the reach of freeloading players. We can also clearly separate items purchased using a premium currency from those available using in-game currency, both offer different aspirational values. This makes sense as long as their value instills a sense of increased value for that item and an increased desire. However, it can just as be discounted if it seems impossible for a freeloading player to access any of those items.

I believe the premium currency approach can usually be better employed if it requires players to make a dilemma choice about how they play. If this slow-burn currency can be used to either sustain the player in their current game or saved for later to exchange for a valuable upgrade, which then matters more to the freeloading player? Of course that means that paying players who spend money don't have to face that dilemma. This can create a reason to spend, but risks backfiring should this become "pay to win." To get around this problem we might be tempted to increase the number of different currencies in the game; rarely a good idea as this reduces the value of having a currency at all, so it becomes just another resource. Another alternative is to make it so that players can't actually buy the premium currency directly.

Experience points are an example of premium currency that should never be sold. Instead we can offer goods, consumable or durable, that increase the rate at which we can earn those currencies. The idea of a coin doubler is commonly used, or perhaps an experience point potion (granting a 10 percent XP bonus for the next hour) although to be honest I've never liked them myself.

Thinking Differently

Goods need not always be based on positive actions. Often it's useful to turn existing models "on their head" and consider them from the opposite position. For example, is there a way you could create factors in a game that impair the performance of the player in specific circumstances? For example, introduce wear and tear into a game when the player is using their equipment; imagine I have a sword that is reduced in sharpness—and hence the damage it can do—after 100 combats, perhaps it might even break. I can invest my time and my grind money in repairing this sword, indeed that would make a great minigame, and in doing so I might happen to use up some resources. Perhaps I could pay some NPC in the game (or even another player) to repair it for me?

Infinity Blade on iOS had an amazing model along these lines, which I am surprised I've not seen again since. Each item of equipment provided the player with a bonus to their experience, but there was a cap over time on how much extra experience in total they would gain. This forced the player to change to the next weapon that they could afford, etc. This stimulated change, broadened the experience with a range of different weapons, increased the engagement with the game, and stimulated the collecting instinct around those items as well as requiring the player to spend some of their in-game currency. Wow! Just by having swords give you experience boosts!

Turning Off Ads

There is a temptation with developers to offer a way to switch off adverts by paying. This makes sense especially if we feel that the adverts are driving players to leave the game, or if their presence is inhibiting their propensity to spend money. However, I wonder if this option is sometimes used inappropriately. Often the negative reaction to adverts can be attributed to a highly vocal minority and their removal has little positive benefit in practice. I'm not saying we ignore this minority entirely, but instead we should focus on what it is that they find problematic. This might be possible to correct by considering the placement and flow of the advertising you use in the game. Another reason why this concerns me is that only the paying players are likely to purchase the "no-ads" option. These are the very people who potential advertisers want to be able to communicate with, and who make advertising in your game particularly valuable. Giving these users the option to opt-out may well so badly affect the value of the audience to advertisers that the revenue you gain from the "turn-off ads" purchase might not come close to off-setting the advertising income you would otherwise have gained. Don't give in to an emotional decision, work out whether advertising revenue is important for your game and, if so, make sure its implemented to minimize any negativity from the audience. Getting the best implementation needs to consider the location and timing of display for each ad, the player lifecycle, and the use of "opt-in" methods.

Levels and Episodes

There is another traditionally popular method of revenue generation that I find problematic. The sale of levels is commonly used by platform and puzzle games, as well as in the form of DLC for console games. There is much similarity between level sales and "try before you buy." They rely on the player being exposed to the game first, getting a familiarity with the experience and then making the decision to purchase the next installment. The trouble is that players are often satisfied with the experience they have just had and don't have enough anticipation of value from the next installment to make that purchase. The range of players who access each subsequent level will diminish and with it the critical mass of the audience. Further than that, the freeloading players can't access that material and this further diminishes the perceived value of that content. As we discussed in Chapter 13, selling levels and trials rarely delivers good value as it creates barriers and buyer remorse. It's also a very inefficient approach, as the levels are usually the part that takes the most effort and skill to create; wouldn't we rather players get to experience all of the beautiful, expensive to produce, game material we have spent months creating rather than sticking it behind a pay-wall and have no one seeing it? That doesn't mean that level-based games have no place in a freemium world, but it does mean we need to think very carefully about the best way to monetize them; perhaps using grind currency to unlock each subsequent level. Ian Masters of Plant Pot Games came up a superb metaphor that can help us when we look at making a level-based puzzle game work as F2P. Think of each level as a spinning plate. We have to return to them regularly in order to keep them spinning, so we can set off the next spinning plate/level. The idea of having to regularly return to previous levels in order to gain the points/coins needed to unlock the next game is a powerful one and gives value to ongoing repeat play.

A Mixed Model of Monetization

Every example of different virtual goods or advertising models we have discussed in this chapter will have a role as part of a mixed approach to monetization. Indeed the greater the range of choices and payment methods available to players, the more you will convert to paying at all, just as we discovered with the rent game discussed in Chapter 13.

We have a story to tell our players, not just in terms of the game, but also in terms of the ways they can engage with the game that they love and what works for them will change as their engagement with the game changes. We need to offer predictable opportunities and calls to actions, such as the bundles or last chance "save me" power-ups alongside apparently "random" offers that seem personalized to that players' needs and likes.

The way goods combine is important and we need to continue to think as retailers and consider opportunities to sell more items to the converted player through the use of "bundles" or collections of related items. This can include: BOGOF deals; a "booster pack" with a selection of random power-ups; special offers on the next vehicle or weapon we would love to get our hands on in the game. Even randomized mystery boxes that grant the player a random item, as used so successfully by Kiloo.

Be Careful with Randomness

We have to be a little careful about how convoluted some of these promotional experiences become, especially where there are random factors. Randomness in terms of what you gain for your money can take us a little too close to gambling for comfort. This became an issue in Japan because of the concept of the "complete gatcha" (*kompugacha*) mechanism, where sets of random cards/goods are purchased in order to discover rare or ultra rare collectables. Complete sets of these collectables are then used to obtain yet more rare items. The Japanese government announced in August 2012 that they were going to investigate this issue and that caused a drop in the share price for DeNA and GREE.[10]

A Question of Ethics

It seems almost inevitable that we end this chapter talking about the questions of appropriate use of monetization models. This "complete gatcha" question and others like it continues to ask us to face up to questions of ethical approaches to the monetization of games. Similarly, in the UK, the Office of Fair Trading announced in April 2013 that they would investigate the in-game marketing techniques being used in games aimed at children. Their initial findings, which were announced in September 2013,[11] included eight key guidelines. The principles seem relatively straightforward, but there is still concern over how some of them might actually operate in practice, so we expect these will change. They inform developers that they have an obligation to prominently and clearly communicate all material information about the game including the associated costs before it is downloaded. Developers need to be contactable and able to respond to consumer complaints and refunds. Developers should not imply that payment is necessary to continue to play when that isn't the case, should give equal weight to the non-payment option, and in particular should not attempt to exploit a child's inexperience or credulity or directly coerce them. Finally, payments should only be taken when there is informed consent and with the agreement of the account holder. Of course it's recommended that you consult the documents themselves and perhaps a legal professional to ensure that your games comply.

These findings don't present an objection to the principle of selling in-game items in particular, they are about ensuring ethical practice in terms of retailing in-app purchases to children to and making sure that there isn't a reasonable likelihood of "accidently" triggering a purchase on their parent's card.

Other legal changes have also already come into force in the USA with COPPA (Children's Online Privacy Protection Act)[12] where developers now have a responsibility to identify if the majority of their audience for a game or service are children (under 13) and then manage the capture of data and use of adverting material accordingly. This won't be the last such law on the subject developers will have to comply with.

There is no excuse for using excessive or aggressive practices in game design. We are making entertainment products and these should focus on the art of engagement, not how much money we generate. To my mind this isn't a question of ethics; the ethical arguments are often hypothetical, even hysterical, rather than real.[13] It's a practical question about what kind of business we want to create. If we go fishing with dynamite we kill all the fish, if we go fishing with line we only get the fish that are attracted to our line but the lake remains sustainable and we can continue fishing forever. The problem with us constantly arguing over the ethics is that the more we have that debate the more likely it is that someone will come along and ban fishing (not dynamite).

Notes

1   The soap opera format of advertising-funded serial dramas is widely credited to Irna Phillips, an American writer and actor, with *Painted Dreams* in 1930 on Chicago's WGN, www.otrcat.com/soap-opera-radio-shows.html.

2   CPM is cost per mille (thousand) views rather than cost per impression; eCPM is a hybrid of cost of impressions and the click through rate (CTR). It allows buyers to gauge the effectiveness of a campaign.

3   CPA is cost per action or acquisition, which usually for games usually refers to the number of installs obtained.

4   Again I need to own up that (at the time of writing) I am working for Applifier and there are other suppliers of opt-in advertising. Reach is a key metric for advertising buyers as they are looking to maximize the potential opportunities for their brands at the lowest cost. The advertising industry has had to evolve with the rise of the internet, but it's been a long slow progress despite the decline of TV audiences.

5   There are a limited number of standard-sized and shaped-for-billboard advertising that significantly helps advertisers with reach and repeatability, www.clearchannel.co.uk/useful-stuff/billboard-poster-sizes.

6   *Fiksu* define a loyal user as one who returns at least three times to the app, www.fiksu.com/blog/cost-loyal-user.

7   In case you didn't already know the Kobayashi Maru is an infamous no-win scenario test at StarFleet Academy in *Star Trek*, where James T. Kirk was the first person to ever "beat" the scenario by reprogramming the computers (in short he cheated!).

8   Tadgh Kelly, author of *What Games Are* and at the time of writing Developer Relations for Ouya, www.whatgamesare.com/about.html.

9   Don't worry, I understand that the use of "energy" has become a little suspect of late, it's just a convenient example for explanation of the concept. That being said, there remains value in the ideas behind energy, if only because of its ability to create a reason to return when the energy has recovered. I believe this came up in Chapter 5.

10 The founder of GREE and at the time Japan's youngest billionaire, Yoshikazu Tanaka, lost an estimated $700 million off the value of his shareholding in GREE the day that was announced, www.forbes.com/sites/danielnyegriffiths/2012/05/08/gree-dena-social-gaming.

11 The OFT Report's initial findings on children's online games can be found at www.oft.gov.uk/shared_oft/consumer-enforcement/oft1506.pdf.

12 Details of COPPA compliance can be found at www.coppa.org.

13 I'm not saying that there aren't unethical designers out there. I'm not saying that there aren't apps that exploit people. I'm just saying that most cases of this argument are being discussed based on hypothetical cases. The real cases should, of course, be prosecuted and the perpetrators handled accordingly; they are damaging our industry beyond measure.

Exercise 14: How Will You Monetize?

In this the final exercise we come to the (potentially multiple) million dollar question: how will you make money from your game? We should now know the flow and structure of our game in detail and as a result of taking the design approach for games as a service it should be a relatively easy task to understand where and how we will use all of the available monetization processes. As we do this we have to be sensitive to the psychological influences on the player's purchasing decisions including in particular buyer remorse and price elasticity of demand.

We want also need to consider how the attitudes to spending match against the life stages of the player in order to maximize the potential and in particular how we build value or utility into their experience.

We want to know if you will charge an initial fee prior to the download of the game and if so how will you manage the impact on the number of installs this will impede. Then there is the counterargument, if you don't have an upfront cost then how will you offset the lack of any initial invested utility in the game? We want to understand what virtual goods you plan to incorporate and what combination of consumable (one-time short-term use), durable (ongoing value) or permanent (one-time upgrade) you plan to use.

How will you monetize your game?	
Will you charge an initial fee prior to the download of your game?	
If charging upfront, how will you offset reduced number of downloads? If not, how will you build initial utility?	
Will you include advertising? If so, what type and how frequently will it appear?	
Will you sell consumable virtual goods? If so, what types, prices, and frequency of purchase?	
Will you sell durable virtual goods? If so, what types, prices, and frequency of payoff?	
Will you sell permanent virtual goods? If so, what types, prices, and frequency of purchase?	

WORKED EXAMPLE:

How will you monetize your game?	Finding Anthony will be monetized through a combination of virtual goods and limited advertising.
Will you charge an initial fee prior to the download of your game?	No the game will be free to download.
If charging upfront, how will you offset reduced number of downloads? If not, how will you build initial utility?	We will get players into playing as quickly as possible and create a meaningful reward within a minute of play. This reward will be in the form of consumable power-ups earned through play as well as a mysterious narrative.
Will you include advertising? If so, what type and how frequently will it appear?	Opt-in video advertising will be used to motivate the players to obtain "free power-ups." The available power-up will vary throughout the day in order to make sure players get to try all of the items for free. Push advertising won't appear until the player has at least completed the first district of play. Where it does appear will be when the player has just been successful and about to move onto their next game.
Will you sell consumable virtual goods? If so, what types, prices, and frequency of purchase?	Yes—all the lowest level power-ups will be available for purchase in bundles of ten items for $0.99. However, higher level power-ups can be purchased or created by "burning" the lower level ones. These include speed-up, pause movement, rewind, slow-down, etc.
Will you sell durable virtual goods? If so, what types, prices, and frequency of payoff?	Yes—players can buy durable goods that are placed at appropriate locations in a district they own and that create the named power-up at the stated level at a rate of 12 per day. The costs range from $1.99 for level 1 power-ups; up to $9.99 for a level 5 power-ups.
Will you sell permanent virtual goods? If so, what types, prices, and frequency of purchase?	Yes—permanents include additional brain slots and customization for the avatar (all of which offer the effect of a "permanent" power-up depending on level).

Chapter 15
Conclusions

Reaching the End

So here we are at the end. Throughout the book we have take the time to look at the design principles and psychology involved with the creation of a service and to use that to generate revenue. But more that that, what I hope we have done is to make you reconsider what gameplay means and how we can expand the choices available to us by reimaging a game as an ongoing relationship with the player.

If I have succeeded in my objectives, the question of whether to go freemium or not will have become irrelevant. Instead we will be focusing on the delight of players and finding a more sustainable way to deliver entertainment to them.

However, this isn't a book that will tell you exactly what the formula is for success, I have only tried to get you to ask yourself the questions that matter. No one can teach you to be a better game designer through a book, but I hope to help you make that step for yourself by considering the values and factors at every stage of your design.

Being a successful commercial designer means taking the time to consider the art (in its widest sense) and the experience as well as the revenue potential for our games. To do that we have to consider the roles of the game mechanics we use as well as the context in which we use them. We cannot ignore the real-world impacts on that gameplay, whether that's the social experience or the external pressures on our players. If we want longevity we have to consider how the metagame empowers players to sustain their engagement, we can't assume that having a fun game is enough.

Understanding the rhythm of play, our use of pace, and schedules of reinforcement are essential to delivering our promise of a service, rather than just another game we play once. Building on that engagement by using familiarity, but still bringing a sense of uncertainty is essential if our players are going to find the fun in the game and better yet feel compelled to share that with other players.

It's not just about the player of course, although they are central to our thinking. We also have to consider how we function within the market place and engage with the other audiences including publishers, app stores and the wider press. Responding to those audiences will impact how we design our game and the way we empower players to share their experiences with others. That sharing process has become a critical success factor given the scale of the competitive environment, and understanding the effort needed to sustain those social connections is similarly important.

Then we have to consider how we assess our success and build into the experience mechanisms that allow us to fairly judge whether we are satisfying our players' needs without overly compromising the vision we have for our game. This leads us further into having to consider how we work with our colleagues in order to deliver the game and find ways to resolve the associated technical problems that arise because we have taken the decision to use the power of the internet, whether as a "thin" or "thick" client experience.

Finally we looked at the psychology of paying and how this affects our objectives as designers. It's the objective we started out with—make something entertaining people are willing to pay for. At the end we still have to put the players' fun first, otherwise we have no answer to our most important question, "so what?"

If there is one thing I want you to take away from this book, it's that question. "So what?"

Amazing Possibilities

This is an amazing time to be a game designer and the challenges will only increase. However, I hope that my experience as collated in this book has provided some small insight into how you can still change the gaming world. Even if you don't have the biggest, smartest team you can still create a work of art that is unique to you and that others will want to enjoy . . . even be inspired by. And if I'm right, then you can still make enough money to be able to do it again.

There will still be stand-alone premium AAA (marketing budget) console game products, although certainly fewer than in previous generations. There will be a similar number of freemium services that will hit the zeitgeist enough to make mind-blowing profits like Supercell and King did in this generation. But there will continue to be success for many more games companies outside the top ten lists.

I believe that the move to services will create a more stable, sustainable business climate supporting a larger ecosystem of games developers, making more than a modest living from clusters of loyal happy players.

That seems like a perfect environment to encourage more focus and attention to making better games, perhaps even to create experiences we want to tell our kids about. After all, if we just wanted to make huge amounts of cash, we could have gone and gotten a "proper job," couldn't we?

Index

T - #0067 - 071024 - C312 - 229/152/17 - PB - 9780415732505 - Matt Lamination